MARKET TRADING TACTICS

WILEY TRADING ADVANTAGE

The New Options Market, Fourth Edition / Max Ansbacher
Trading without Fear / Richard W. Arms, Jr.
Neural Network Time Series Forecasting of Financial Markets / E. Michael Azoff
Option Market Making / Alan J. Baird
Genetic Algorithms and Investment Strategies / Richard J. Bauer, Jr.
Technical Market Indicators / Richard J. Bauer, Jr. and Julie R. Dahlquist
Seasonality / Jake Bernstein
The Hedge Fund Edge / Mark Boucher
Encyclopedia of Chart Patterns / Thomas Bulkowski
Macro Trading and Investment Strategies / Gabriel Burstein
Beyond Technical Analysis / Tushar Chande
The New Technical Trader / Tushar Chande and Stanley S. Kroll
Integrated Technical Analysis / Ian Copsey
Trading the Plan / Robert Deel
New Market Timing Techniques / Thomas R. DeMark
The New Science of Technical Analysis / Thomas R. DeMark
Point and Figure Charting / Thomas J. Dorsey
Trading for a Living / Dr. Alexander Elder
Study Guide for Trading for a Living / Dr. Alexander Elder
The Day Trader's Manual / William F. Eng
The Options Course / George A. Fontanills
The Options Course Workbook / George A. Fontanills
Stock Index Futures & Options / Susan Abbott Gidel
Contrary Opinion / R. Earl Hadady
Technical Analysis of the Options Markets / Richard Hexton
Pattern, Price & Time / James A. Hyerczyk
Profits from Natural Resources / Roland A. Jansen
The Trading Game / Ryan Jones
Trading Systems & Methods, Third Edition / Perry Kaufman
Trading to Win / Ari Kiev, M.D.
The Intuitive Trader / Robert Koppel
Nonlinear Pricing / Christopher T. May
McMillan on Options / Lawrence G. McMillan
Trading on Expectations / Brendan Moynihan
Intermarket Technical Analysis / John J. Murphy
The Visual Investor /John J. Murphy
Beyond Candlesticks / Steve Nison
Cybernetic Trading Strategies / Murray A. Ruggiero, Jr.
The Option Advisor / Bernie G. Schaeffer
Fundamental Analysis / Jack Schwager
Study Guide to Accompany Fundamental Analysis / Jack Schwager
Managed Trading / Jack Schwager
The New Market Wizards / Jack Schwager
Technical Analysis / Jack Schwager
Study Guide to Accompany Technical Analysis / Jack Schwager
Schwager on Futures / Jack Schwager
Gaming the Market / Ronald B. Shelton
The Dynamic Option Selection System / Howard L. Simons
Option Strategies, 2nd Edition / Courtney Smith
Trader Vic II / Victor Sperandeo
Campaign Trading / John Sweeney
The Trader's Tax Survival Guide, Revised Edition / Ted Tesser
The Trader's Tax Solution / Ted Tesser
The Mathematics of Money Management / Ralph Vince
The New Money Management / Ralph Vince
Trading Applications of Japanese Candlestick Charting / Gary Wagner and Brad Matheny
Trading Chaos / Bill Williams
New Trading Dimensions / Bill Williams
Long-Term Secrets to Short-Term Trading / Larry Williams
Expert Trading Systems / John R. Wolberg
The Ultimate Trading Guide / John Hill, George Pruitt, Lundy Hill

Market Trading Tactics: Beating the Odds through Technical Analysis and Money Management

Daryl Guppy

John Wiley & Sons (Asia) Pte Ltd
Singapore • New York • Chichester • Weinheim • Brisbane • Toronto

Originally published by Wrightbooks Pty Ltd under the title, *Trading Tactics: An Introduction to Finding, Exploiting and Managing Profitable Share Trading Opportunities*

This revised and updated edition published in 2000 by
John Wiley & Sons (Asia) Pte Ltd
2 Clementi Loop, #02-01, Singapore 129809

For distribution throughout the world, except Australia and New Zealand

Acknowledgments: All charts created by Metastock using data supplied by Stock Data Corp, KeyQuotes, Winrow Marketing, Electronic Information Solutions and ODDS.

Daryl Guppy 2000
e-mail: 100035.406@compuserve.com
http://www.guppytraders.com

Other Wiley Editorial Offices
John Wiley & Sons, Inc., 605 Third Avenue, New York, NY 10158-0012, USA
John Wiley & Sons Ltd, Baffins Lane, Chichester, West Sussex PO19 1UD, England
John Wiley & Sons (Canada) Ltd, 22 Worcester Road, Rexdale, Ontario M9W 1L1, Canada
John Wiley & Sons Australia Ltd, 33 Park Road (PO Box 1226), Milton, Queensland 4064, Australia
Wiley-VCH, Pappelallee 3, 69469 Weinheim, Germany

Library of Congress Cataloging-in-Publication Data
Guppy, Daryl J., 1954 –
Market trading tactics: beating the odds through technical analysis and money management/ Daryl Guppy.
p. cm.
Includes index.
ISBN 0-471-84663-5 (alk. paper)
1. Investment analysis. 2. Investments. I. Title.

HG4529 .G87 2000
332..63'2042—dc21

Typeset in 11/13 pt Berling Roman by Linographic Services Pte Ltd
Printed in Singapore by Fabulous Printers Pte Ltd
10 9 8 7 6 5 4 3 2 1

Contents

PREFACE

TRACKING THE GHOST OF EL DORADO

As a child I was enthralled by the abandoned rusting hulk of the Eldorado gold dredge stranded on Reedy Creek near Yackandandah and captivated by small clear vials filled with gold dust laboriously panned by an old prospector from mountain creeks in Australia's north-eastern Victoria. Despite broken nails, aching muscles, erratic returns, the dirt, dust and heat, I have always found the lure of prospecting for metals and minerals irresistible. Now my prospecting tools are the computer, the Internet, the stock market database and charting software — and the lure is still irresistible. The dust is banished by air-conditioning and only fingers ache from keyboarding. Yet the exploration principles remain the same.

The El Dorado sought by the Spanish conquistadors and described by Diaz in *The Conquest of New Spain* did not exist. Ours does. Every day the market surrenders a rich line of lode to the best traders. We have a choice between a pot of gold and a working gold mine. In this book I explore some ways of finding the lode and bringing it on-stream to build a working gold mine. I am not a market wizard so the techniques in this book require no specialist skills. The bulk of my income comes from trading the market and like many traders who have moved from working for a wage to trading for a living, just duplicating my wages is enough to keep me happy. There are fortunes to be made — and lost — in the market. Better prospectors make, and keep, these fortunes.

This book is written for those who want to survive, and for those who, while not aspiring to market wizard status, would like to more aggressively manage market risk by finding, exploiting and managing trading opportunities. These are skills needed for survival as a position trader. They are the basic skills on which day trading success is built. If you are prepared to pit your prospecting skill against those who have traditionally held the keys to the market, then this book will help equip you for the expedition.

Bull market conditions encourage novice traders. In a bull market the market pays for your mistakes as the general rise in stock prices allows for quick recovery of losses. In a bear market you pay for them. Some of what is written in the following chapters may appear to be unnecessarily complex or detailed, but when the bear bites, these are the basic disciplines that separate the survivors from market victims.

The processes described in this book are easy in principle but some are very time-demanding if applied indiscriminately. We start with broad selection procedures and as the list of trading candidates narrows, apply more specialized trading tactics.

SERIOUS TRADING

Trading is frustrating because, despite all the groundwork required before clicking the mouse button or picking up the phone to enter, or exit a trade, the market may still slip between your fingers.

Understanding the analysis, being in tune with the market, initiating and completing scanning processes and fine-tuning the financial aspects does not mean a trading opportunity will be revealed. The market does not owe us a living. Despite the hours of research, there is no guarantee that the stock will be available at the price we think is appropriate. There is no guarantee of any real trading opportunities identified by our painstaking analysis. There may be none that match all our criteria.

This is annoying, but it is only fatal if we settle for second best. As a private trader we do not have to trade. We can afford to wait until the best opportunities arise. This protects us from a market indifferent to our existence and survival.

There are always some market situations where the tools of technical analysis appear useless. This does not diminish the effectiveness of the tools. In the same way that a carpenter does not use a screwdriver to build a house, so a trader does not attempt to use technical tools in trading situations where they offer little help.

As traders we look for those opportunities compatible with the tools we are most skilled in using. To pretend that our particular tool kit will expose the secrets of all markets, or of any market segments is foolish. As traders we want to identify our strengths and weaknesses. By trading on our strengths, matching our trading style, and using the appropriate array of tools, we become better traders.

Success does count. Virtuosity is a theoretical skill if it does not wring financial rewards from trading. Trading approaches that mimic the apparent complexity of the markets are not always the best at understanding the markets. More difficult does not mean more accurate. Simple trading strategies score direct profits in complex systems so we aim in this book to dismember complexity into its simplest components. Here is the foundation for trading tactics.

A ROAD MAP FOR DISMEMBERING COMPLEXITY

Systems and systematic behavior are at the core of complexity. Complexity is a dynamical system positioned on the edge of chaos where a single event — the butterfly effect — could tip it into dangerous instability and collapse. Survival depends on the way the systems adapt to behavioral changes, moving forward along the cliff rather than to one side and over it.

Trading is on the very edge of chaos, riding alongside the market. Our survival depends on our ability to define our task and its components to select the right tools and deliver appropriate solutions.

The core of every complex system has a dominant characteristic. The cyclone is defined by wind, the turbulence of a waterfall by water, the clash of market activity by numerical data. We measure the cyclone with an anemometer, the flow of water with a Dethridge wheel and the market with a price chart. No matter how you make your trading selection — fundamental, technical, accounting, financial or news analysis — your trading improves when you know how to read a price chart with its message of probability.

JOINING THE RUSH

Trading with the Balance of Probability, Chapter 1, goes to the core of every trading approach, matching the message of the chart with its implied information about probability. When some price combinations occur more frequently than others they signal a change in probability. The market throws up voluminous data, concealing this vital information. The cipher of understanding is the bar chart. The price bar, or candlestick display, is built on clear market emotions pointing to areas of increased probability. These Messages from the Jungle Drums, Chapter 2, track progress at the market battle front and save financial lives.

Chapter 3, Lasseter's Reef, brings the balance of probability to life in a sample trade, showing how basic understanding is matched with market reality. This is a model of the trading nuggets we hope to find and our search begins when we select the best time frame. Time Bites Character, Chapter 4, shows how we focus short, immediate and long-term pictures into a single snapshot. The detail blurs as the structure emerges. Different time bites are used to confirm analysis across multiple time frames and so further stack the balance in our favor.

PROSPECTING FOR TRADES

Armed with an idea of how our trading opportunity might look and how we might recognize it we are ready to start Searching for Love at First Profit. Some traders choose to follow an accounting path. We give them guide information in No Accounting for All Tastes and explain how their path joins with ours when it comes to assessing and managing the trade.

We plunge into the jungle of technical indicators. This style of trading is a complex activity built on foundations of layered simplicity. We deconstruct some of these complex processes so you can rebuild them in a way that uniquely suits your trading style and financial requirements.

This is database mining at its finest. We consider the value of Eyeball Searches, which provide an essential reference point for every trading decision. We place it near the beginning of our search and also return to it towards the end. Some choose to use this bar chart analysis only at the end of their search but the techniques do not change. Other chartists look for Technical True Love — Searching For Relationships between price patterns and daily price bars. Other technical traders prefer Performance Searches as the best way of quickly finding trading opportunities. All these techniques use common concepts to bind complex groups together. Working with simplicity provides the keys to complexity.

This understanding lets us build effective criteria for speedy searches that quickly find the best trading candidates. These techniques are used by day traders, position traders and investors. Some search criteria are spelled out for you to copy into your charting or market software package. Those who want to fiddle and fine-tune further will find specialist publications listed in the text.

The nuggets uncovered are still untested in the fire of the market. We consider a new indicator used as An Assay Test — Looking for Life in Chapter 10. This combines our understanding of market behavior with data analysis to identify points of explosive price action. Price data is objective, but our analysis of it is not. There are always Two Sides of the Same Coin and we examine ways to identify and ultimately overcome our personal predisposition for gloom or glee. With this ghost acknowledged we finish the assay test interpretation and application with Index Hunting to match nuggets of trading opportunity with markets.

SUPPLEMENTARY NUMBERS

Discovery is nothing without exploitation. Our selected trading opportunities, mined from our database, come in different shapes and sizes. Not all trades are created equal and in This Nugget Goes to Market we examine the calculations required to rank the candidates from good to better and then best. The best satisfy our financial objectives. We breathe life into risk whenever we open a trade so Pinning a Number on Risk gives us an important advantage in validating financial objectives.

The key to successful exploitation of our hard-won trading opportunities comes in the shape of Using the Internet and Electronic Depth of Market. This unfamiliar collection of figures is too often ignored by traders, yet it opens a wealth of tactical information. We show you some ways to understand and use it to your advantage. This puts profit in our grasp and in Trading Plans we are able to step beyond this analysis to show how all the steps are combined in a real sample trade.

FAILURE WAITS UPON SUCCESS

We cannot just go through the motions of trading. It is not a mechanical process. Trading is hard, demanding work. It requires a thorough working knowledge of the market, of trading techniques and of money management. Above all it requires a psychological mastery of ourselves. At some stage every prospecting expedition comes to resemble a pilgrimage. Trading imposes stresses quite different from those experienced in any other job, and many would-be traders find that it is these psychological factors that defeat them.

The way we think about ourselves has a significant impact on the way we trade. Trading slides into Over-Trading when we abandon planning for movement, mistaking activity for purpose. Successful traders recognize this escape mechanism, and put it in the background so it does not distort their trading activities.

Behind every decision the trader makes there lurks a plethora of past sins and prejudices. Failure waits on every trade and there are factors other than the analysis of the trade that have a significant impact on our trading success. Stop-loss is good in theory but difficult in practice. Success depends on knowing the difference between Nerves of Steel — Or Chicken Wire? We look at matching stop-loss points with our nerves to improve stop-loss execution. Some traders, puffed with success from other financial activities, mutate into a market bully, sabotaging their own success.

The market ignores Command and Control strategies so if you find yourself nodding in agreement, then heed the warning.

These are hidden hands driving, or sabotaging, our decision-making. Get to know them well because they are our trading companions always hitch-hiking a ride with success. These are hidden attitudes that cast a pall of darkness over our trading activities, shadowing the way to failure. We cannot eliminate or ignore them, so we must learn to live with them.

The most dangerous shadow of all is the unconscious belief that trading is a game of chance where anyone can walk off the street and take money from the market. Gambler or Trader? takes a professional look at trading behaviors suggestive of pathological gambling. Written specially for this book by an American private trader and psychologist, Paul I Munves, this chapter cuts authoritatively to the core of the gambling trader's self-deception. It is not pretty reading, but nor are the consequences of gambling in the markets.

We are not alone in this expedition. Others search alongside us for nuggets. Some of them are real competitors but most are temporary participants. We want to emulate the survivors but few are initially aware of the Insight and Irony this involves. This book is only an introduction to some of the tools used in trading tactics. It does not complete the question 'I am a trader because ...' That is your task and the prospecting expedition turns out to be as much about this as it is about finding trading opportunities.

AN INTRODUCTION NOT A GUIDE

The procedures detailed in the following chapters are only one selection from many ways to approach the task of analysing the market for opportunities. Our purpose is to provide you with an introduction to a variety of approaches to encourage you to think more clearly about your current methods, or to help you make sense of the bewildering volume of market data. We want to provide you with the tools to finance, equip, explore, develop and exploit your own trading opportunities.

I have endeavored to answer many of the questions raised in readers' e-mail via www.guppytraders.com and in comments from those who attended Trading Workshop seminars. Market data has been supplied by Stock Data Corp in the United States, KeyQuotes in Singapore, Winrow Marketing in the United Kingdom, Electronic Information Solutions and ODDS in Australia. Further thanks must go to David Barnes, Bill McMaster, Will Evans and Nayan Ruparelia who were involved in the international edition of this book. Thanks also to my parents, Ted and Patricia, who labored through the original manuscripts. My wife, Marion, continued to demand an impossibly high standard of plain English, particularly in relation to apostrophes.

If you are reading this book I assume you are a serious trader or that you are serious about trading. This book assumes you have a working knowledge of the language of charting. Computerized charting tools sit, or soon will sit, on your desktop. This book will show you how to use them more effectively and give you search formulas to program direct into your computer.

We approach trading as a business so we must be systematic in the way we go about the many tasks associated with trading. This introduction will help you organize these tasks into a daily routine to take you quickly to the best of the current trading opportunities whether they be found in Lasseter's reef, King Solomon's gold mines, El Dorado or your own private mother lode of market data.

Every journey begins with a small step. We set out to explore for nuggets of trading opportunity but, like every prospector, we also discover a great deal more about ourselves. Trading involves many perils and this book aims to prevent the first step becoming a stumble.

Run with the bulls. Hunt with the bears. Trade well.

Daryl Guppy
Katherine 2000

Part I

JOINING THE RUSH

1

TRADING WITH THE BALANCE OF PROBABILITY

To trade or not to trade is the basic question. But is profit the only answer? Many novice traders think so.

Experienced traders learn that trading is the aggressive management of risk made possible by understanding the process of finding, exploiting and managing trading opportunities, financially and mentally. Traders regularly journey into the market jungle to mine nuggets of opportunity, returning with them to trade for profit. Successful traders understand the landscape and risk, and are properly equipped. The novice, equipped with little other than enthusiasm and a dream, walks into the jungle with an eye fixed on profit. Lacking tactical survival skills, few return.

The client casualty lists from brokerages fill pages with the names of those who thought profit was the only answer, and failed. This book is for survivors. If you want to keep your name permanently off the casualty list you must equip yourself with the best prospecting equipment. Simply aiming for a profit is not enough.

To protect profits and minimize losses you make better use of your tools, use your time efficiently and listen carefully to the roar and whimper of the market crowd. Like Ulysses, who wanted to hear the call of the sirens but avoid being lured onto the rocks, we consider ways to listen to the siren call of greed without coming to grief. We look at how to identify trading opportunities, some methods to analyze only the most promising and how the supplementary numbers from the market are used to confirm the promise of profit.

Later we examine some ways to detect the sound of distant thunder as the crowd stampedes through the marketplace. The market is a master pickpocket and while profit beckons, failure has its hands in our wallets. How much it takes depends on our trading tactics.

This is a prospecting expedition into the market jungle and before taking the first steps we require some understanding of the landscape. What strange shapes await us, what unusual growths, what behaviors? How will we measure and judge them against our own experience? Do we equip for snow, sand or dense foliage? The answers decide the tools, the protective equipment and the way our expedition travels. Consider this first section as an expedition briefing for a land seen but improperly understood.

Our chosen landscape is peppered with probability and shape is delivered in bar charts. In this landscape lie the nuggets, so it pays to spend some time exploring these conditions before stepping into the market jungle. You could skip ahead and start the expedition immediately. When you decide you cannot make sense of the jungle shapes feel free to return to this expedition briefing.

Successful trading means having the balance of probability on your side. Good trading is about achieving financial objectives. Later we will look at some specific ways to identify this balance, set financial objectives and control risk by tilting the balance in our favor. Before doing this we need to renew our acquaintance with probability, and later with the way this appears on a chart.

You cannot control the market, but you can control your entry into the market and your exit from it. Successful trading places these control points near levels of greater probability.

PROBABLE ODDS

Tell people you trade the market, but don't believe in gambling, and you have the perfect stand-up comedy routine. The laughter says a lot about general ignorance of odds and probability, and perhaps why so many 'wanna-be' traders become investors, holding onto losing trades. Trading against the odds, or the balance of probability, is a one-way ticket to financial ruin so understanding the concepts builds better trades.

Probability has an unfortunate historical relationship with gambling. Gambling and trading do not mix, and when we talk about the balance of probability below and throughout the book, we use the term in a very specific non-gambling sense. The concepts of probability did start with games of chance but they now play an important role in understanding risk. The concepts are applied to the construction of bridges, the planning of space flights and understanding the impact of pollutants on the environment.

Forget for a moment the gambling connection because a pair of dice is still the best way to reveal the basic concepts. Between them they have twelve faces and each number from 1 to 6 occurs once on each, or twice between the pair of them.

There are a total of 36 different outcomes. The Renaissance gambler and mathematician, Girolamo Cardano, worked out the combinations and they are shown in column C, Figure A.1 in the annex to this chapter. Experienced traders will note the dominant feature of column C immediately — the bulge in the middle. Most of us will need more time to study the table before we see there are more ways to get to some results than to others. From column A we see that throwing a 7 can be reached by six combinations, or favorable outcomes, but throwing a 12 can only be reached with a single combination.

This information provides the basic calculations necessary for determining the *odds* and probability of any outcome. The *odds* of an event happening is the ratio of favorable outcomes to unfavorable outcomes. These are detailed in column D. Using 7 and 12 again, we see the odds of throwing a 7 are six throws to 30 while the odds of throwing a 12 are one throw to 35.

In contrast, the *probability* of an event occurring is the ratio of favorable outcomes to the total number of possible combinations, shown in column E. Staying with 7 and 12, the probability of a 7 is six throws out of 36. The probability of a 12 is one throw out of 36.

Odds or probability — the distinction is subtle. Those who are unsure of the distinction can find more detailed discussion in the annex at the end of the chapter. This naturally raises the question of trading or gambling. The distinction is important. Get it wrong and the jungle claims another victim. If you suspect you might be gambling then the tests in Chapter 20 will help.

From the trader's perspective, what is important in the dice example is the way results tend to clump in a particular level. Whether we choose to measure the odds, or the probabilities, we still reach the same conclusion. Some outcomes are more likely than others. In market terms, reaching some profit targets is easier than others. We choose to run with probability because, as explained below, trading thrives where the total number of possible combinations is large.

This observation is at the very core of successful trading. When traders look at price action they notice immediately that prices tend to clump in particular areas. This suggests that some outcomes, some price levels, are more likely than others, or at the very least, more persistent over time than others. When we refer to the balance of probability for the remainder of the book, this is essentially what we mean.

The market is more complicated than a pair of dice. In every trade we deal with two aspects of this complexity. The first is the absolute limit in the number of possibilities for the direction of price.

In the market, in one sense, there are only four possible outcomes or events. The price will increase, decrease, remain the same or the company stops trading due to bankruptcy. They are always 1 out of 4. Or to put it another way, the odds of losing money are 3 to 4 because only one result — a rise or favorable price move — will leave us with more than our starting capital. We cannot change these outcomes, so we cannot change the odds. No trading approach puts the odds in our favor so we must look to including probability in the best solutions.

The second aspect of market complexity is the theoretically infinite combinations of possible results above zero. Prices could range from a fraction of a cent, like Australian penny stocks, to thousands of dollars for a single share in Warren Buffett's US-based Hathaway Fund. A theoretically infinite universe of combinations is daunting, but it provides the trader with a solution because some combinations occur more frequently than others.

Whether you feel more comfortable moving with the odds, or considering the probabilities, is not as important as recognizing that building trading decisions around the tendency of some outcomes to occur more frequently than others is a winning strategy. Your primary concern is to find the best way to identify any bulge — the balance of probability — in the market similar to the bulge in Figure 1.1.

Figure 1.1 The probability bulge picture: a pair of dice

Possible results	Number of possible combinations to reach each result	
2	**W**	**1**
3	**WW**	**2**
4	**WWW**	**3**
5	**WWWW**	**4**
6	**WWWWW**	**5**
7	**WWWWWW**	**6**
8	**WWWWW**	**5**
9	**WWWW**	**4**
10	**WWW**	**3**
11	**WW**	**2**
12	**W**	**1**

The graphic presents the same information as the figures in column C, Figure A.1, but is easier to understand. Here the balance of probability is heaviest at 7 because this result can be reached by more combinations than those required to throw a 12. Both the odds and the probabilities are weighted towards 7. Traders look for similar weightings in the market, and price clumps and trends provide the clues. Charting provides the same graphic representation of otherwise abstract figures.

The first clue is the ability of prices to move steadily in one direction for weeks or months.

Now the total number of possible combinations is not open-ended. Some combinations have extended persistence over time, either as consolidation areas where the same price re-occurs frequently, or as trends. These reference points reduce the ratio of possible combinations and favorable outcomes.

This tendency for prices to show trends attracts us to the profit opportunities and tells us where the balance of probability is weighted. If we eliminate gross market manipulation, then what creates this probability?

The probability of one direction of price action over another is not equal and is related to the way prices have behaved in the past. Price has no memory, but the buyers and sellers who decide the price do have memories, some pleasant and many bitter. Just as it takes a long time to forget the theft of money, investors cluster around price levels where they have lost money in the past. A gift of cash is more readily forgotten and levels where profit was taken in the past have less impact than levels where losses were realized.

The strength of these memories and the number of people who have similar memories help to establish the probability of price behavior. Our purpose here is to understand how to recognize this strength and how to use the probability to our advantage.

The way price behaved in the past, and in the future, is a function of fear and greed. Fear paralyses while greed galvanizes. Fear makes us hold on while prices fall, and greed encourages us to chase rising prices. Fear and greed 'load' the dice, and when the trader develops tools for understanding where and when the loading takes place he can make sure the balance of probability is very much in his favor.

Price action is recorded as a database of numbers and the newspaper stock report pages list the results. In elementary school, students sometimes cut up these pages and use them to make cityscapes of skyscrapers. This is as close as many people get to making a picture from printed market information — unless, like accountants and other number crunchers, they are at home with figures.

The mathematician uses numbers to calculate the odds, and the probability. Fund managers use post-modern portfolio theory to hedge against market risk. The private trader finds its difficult to calculate these intensely mathematical solutions. A page full of numbers is difficult to understand.

Mere mortals, traders included, find it easier to see the probability — the bulge — in graphic form. The price chart draws the picture and outlines the cluster of prices in the same way as Figure 1.1 shows the bulge. Deciding when the balance of probabilities is in your favor is made easier on a chart, but only if you can put aside some preconceptions and learn to read the language of the chart.

PICTURE PERFECT

The Antarctic has weird snow shapes sculpted by the wind, the desert sun-blasted rocks. Our landscape resembles that of a little known Disney educational cartoon on maths. It did little to improve arithmetic skills, but its enduring image is of a man in a landscape of distorted numbers, towering 7s and 5s, rather like a Sesame street nightmare. The market jungle replaces vegetation with elegant price bars, thickets of candlesticks and clumps of moving averages against bluffs of charting.

Charts affront many traditional market players, from company directors, to brokerages and brokers, to moms and pops. They appear to devalue their hard-won research and knowledge by suggesting prices can be understood independently from the fundamentals of the underlying company or economy.

Some chartists confirm this divide by relying almost exclusively on obscure number relationships, often expressed as cycles and recurrent angles. Some fundamental traders add their bit to the division by emphasizing that only detailed financial understanding of the company's books, with a dash of informed knowledge about company secrets, can allow the trader to take profitable positions in the market.

The truth lies somewhere in between. I rely primarily on charting and technical analysis as the basis of my trading decisions. This horrifies one of my brokers, but he has learnt to live with it. I use these methods to identify my trading opportunities. You may use other methods, but when it comes to assessing the trade we need information that only the chart can provide. It is beyond question that an ability to read a price chart will improve your trading.

A judicious mix of both disciplines makes for better trading. A price chart conveys very specific information in the same way a balance sheet reveals very specific financial information. Both displays — graphic and numerical — sometimes reveal more than their authors intended. Both displays are easily misunderstood.

No matter how you research, and finally reach, a trading decision you must eventually analyze and assess the trade financially. When the trade is entered, the open position must be managed to achieve financial objectives. The price chart, not the newspaper, gives you the basic information needed to undertake this planning process. Later we will look in detail at these procedures.

For now it is sufficient to understand that neither the entry nor the exit from a trade is determined by changing price–earnings (PE) ratios, by management structures, by product litigation, profit forecasts or food poisoning scares. These certainly are events that trigger a decision to buy or sell, but they do not set the price the trader receives. Better traders make an exit based on the most recent price activity. Except in apocalyptic events, such as October

1987, few market professionals unload stock at any price. Instead they use current price activity to make an informed decision about the best possible exit price. Private traders emulate this and the chart, as a record of prices, is an indispensable trading tool.

Please remember, when a chart is used as some type of computerized ouija board it is just as accurate, and useful, as ouija board forecasts.

Let us very briefly consider the types of information conveyed in a price chart and what it does, and does not, tell us about the security we are considering. We need to decide if the bulge is fat profit, or dangerous flab.

HERE'S HEALTH

When we check our financial health we reach for our wallet. Many market participants check the price chart in the same basic way.

'What causes a stock price to go up or down?' asks a self-confessed rookie trader in any one of the trading chat rooms. Another passenger in the same boat 'SS StockRookie' suggests that price might be linked to demand for products the company makes. Either they are purchased or they sit on the shelf and this affects the price of the company in the market, he suggests. This thinking implies a link between the line on a price chart and the financial health of the company. In this understanding the price chart morphs into a balance sheet in graphic form. The daily cash value of our wallet is put into a graph.

This unsophisticated explanation is usually dressed up more attractively by brokerage analysts. Takeover deals are sometimes described in glowing terms — a marriage made in heaven. Other analysts tell us the deal creates a synergy of size and market share, and analysts include figures to prove it. All too often the result is a slide in share price.

Attractive in its simplicity as this line of reasoning may be, when stripped to the basics the picture is less pleasing. Ashton Mining shows the unattractive side of this simple explanation. It is a diamond producer and explorer working in the Kimberley region of north-west of Australia. Figure 1.2 shows a price chart of Ashton Mining in a standard bar chart format. In this five-month chart period the price of Ashton Mining varies dramatically. In 12 days from point A to point B, Ashton Mining adds 23 percent to its market value. The price increases from $1.74 to $2.15.

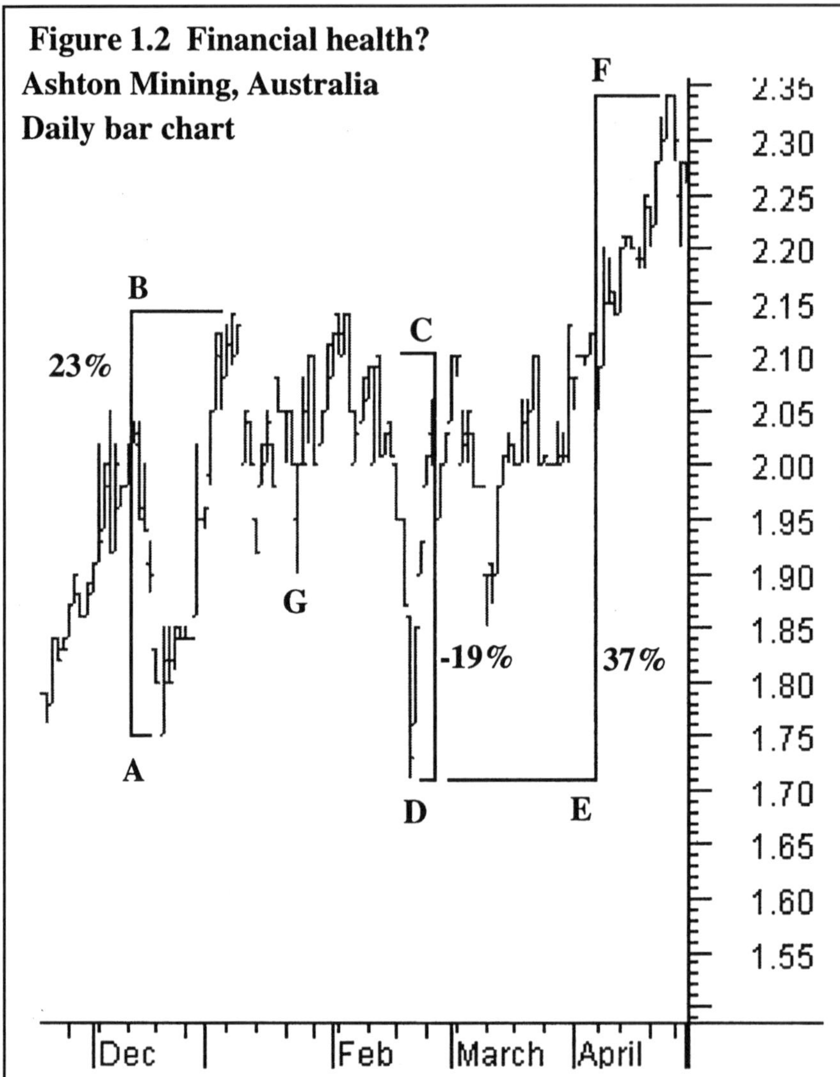

What does this tell us about the health of the company, about the strength of its management, the size of its inferred diamond resources or the state of the cartel market for its products? We can speculate a great deal on this, but it is very difficult to establish a precise relationship between changes in any of these fundamental factors and the share price.

Perhaps they did add significantly to their inferred resource estimates. Perhaps, in this instance, we can accept an increase of 23 percent in the underlying value of the company over 12 days, no matter how improbable it seems.

However, five weeks later this prosperous company loses 19 percent of its value in six days, plunging from point C to point D — $2.11 to $1.71. We are justified in asking if the diamonds added to inventory in December were found to be paste in February? What does this price action tells us about the health of the company, its management and its markets?

To add more confusion to contradiction, the price rockets back to beyond its old level and after nine weeks has grown 37 percent, rising from $1.71 to $2.34 as shown by the rise from point E to point F. Perhaps improved security procedures meant diamonds were no longer being smuggled out the front gate, or that reserve estimates had been upgraded again.

These wild swings in a basically sound company confirm our suspicions that the price chart tells us little about the health of the company. Market price is an accountant's nightmare. The dedicated fundamental analyst, at this point, throws up his hands in disgust and despair, wipes every chart from the screen display, and returns to the raw balance sheet numbers pitting his estimate of the wallet cash value against the market price.

The analyst does this by de-constructing the wallet. The process is described in many articles on how to read company reports, and understanding the balance sheet. They are studded with explanations of 'tricks of the trade' and warnings that a more comprehensive assessment of the financial position requires an analysis of financial statements. Each step takes the trader further from understanding today's market price for the security. The final calculated figure of 'fair value' is not consistent with the price printed in the stock pages so we turn to another attractively simple explanation to explain the discrepancy. In the simple version the calculated figure is used to decide if today's market price is under or over valued.

The further we go down this path, the more subjective the result becomes because vital financial information is hidden, or unavailable, to everyone who wants to attempt these calculations. Many Exchanges now ask for full or continuous disclosure, but this does not apply to commercially confidential material so the analysts must guess at what is concealed. The better analysts often get it right and are paid accordingly.

Getting it right does not mean picking the current market price. This style of analysis is used by brokerages to 'price' an initial public offering (IPO), or 'float'. They have full access to financial details that under other circumstances they can only guess at, or imply from other public documents. They almost decide what goes in the wallet. Yet, the first trades on listing show some spectacular differences between the brokerage valuation and the market valuation. Even in a bull market where a new IPO seems to list every second day the valuation gap remains. Typically, after 12 months about 30 percent are trading at less than their listing price and 60 percent are trading above, while around 10 percent are going nowhere. It makes little difference if the listing is on the New York Stock Exchange (NYSE), the French Stock Exchange, in Hong Kong or Singapore. We tend to remember the spectacular successes, unless we are unlucky enough to have bought stock in one of the losers.

This style of analysis has an important place, but we need firmer footings when we approach the market with trading on our mind. I am suggesting that it is less useful from a trading perspective in the same way that the official valuation on your house bears little relationship to the price it brings on the open market. If you use price charts as a measure of the contents of your wallet, then you miss the advantages charts bring to trading.

Going back to our wallet explains why. If we lose our wallet the insurance value is more than just the cash inside. It includes the credit cards, the sentimental picture, the ticket stub and the PIN card access number ineffectively disguised as a fax contact. It includes some measure of the potential future value of the wallet to the thief, particularly if he uses our credit cards. We readily accept different measures of value and apply them in different circumstances.

The price chart records the insurance value rather than a daily count of the cash in the wallet. The chart display is a barometer of the market's feeling about the company and the potential future resale value of shares purchased today.

THE CHART SAYS SO

The chart is a graphic representation of the market's valuation of the security at a particular point in time. Each point on the chart, such as point D, Figure 1.2, captures in the traded exchange the exact market valuation of Ashton Mining. This is not a valuation of fundamental worth reached after a simple addition of its assets and the subtraction of its liabilities. This is not a simple count of the cash in the wallet or diamonds on the shelves. It is an estimate of how much shares in this company are going to be worth sometime in the future.

When the transaction takes place at D the seller believes Ashton Mining is doomed. He jumps out because he believes prices will go much lower. He takes the loss now before it gets any larger in the future.

The buyer has exactly the opposite conviction. He believes, for whatever reason, be it fundamental or technical, that the price is going to increase in the future. He is happy to get a bargain entry into an improving price. The seller is pleased because the exit saves him from further loss. Time will tell who will be happy and who will be regretful, but for this very instant each person on either side of the transaction believes he has done the best possible in his circumstances.

This understanding of market activity — of this trade — tells us nothing about the current status of the company, about its inferred resources, its management, or its audit report. Point D on the chart is never designed to give us this information. This point tells one thing only — how the market of buyers and sellers felt about the value of the security at this precise point in time in relation to its future potential. Such a valuation is a measure of market sentiment.

When we understand that the bar chart measures market sentiment by using market price, then we have a solution that allows the fundamental trader and the technical trader to make the best use of a chart with a price plot.

Price is primarily a measure of sentiment, not a measure of worth. If we do use it to measure company worth, such as when it is incorporated into a number of financial ratios including price to earnings, price to net tangible assets, or debt to equity, we still end up with a result reflecting current market sentiment rather than a balance sheet.

DEFINING THE BALANCE

Gold fever brings together a rich assortment of prospectors from all walks of life. The portals of the stock exchange building draw crowds in the same way, all impatient to start their expedition. Those determined to survive know at some point they will be called to make, or take, a price in the market. The decision puts the balance of probability with them, or against them. In a landscape shaped by probability, success goes to those who use equipment to make or take this price from within a bulge, rather than those who select a price from more slender territory. Getting behind the price bars offers an advantage.

ANNEX

CALCULATING ODDS

Calculating the odds is the first step in calculating the probabilities. The mathematical groundwork distinguishing odds from probability was done in the Renaissance by Girolamo Cardano. Writing in

Against the Gods, Peter Bernstein maintains that Leonardo da Vinci was fascinated by the concepts, even though he would fail a Year 3 arithmetic test today. Leonardo spent many hours with Cardano until he finally understood the problem. If he understood the concepts then the following primer discussion should not present too much of a challenge to today's calculator and spreadsheet-enabled trader.

Toss two dice, put money on the outcome and we enter the world of odds and probability. And it is not as far from this common wager to trading the financial markets as many people think. The probabilities of any outcome become different from the odds of any outcome in subtle ways.

Before we calculate the odds, we need first to determine the list of possible results. Each of the pair of dice has six faces giving a total of 11 possible results. Throwing a 0 or a 1 are not possible results. The lowest possible result is a 2 (one dot plus one dot). The highest possible result is a 12 (six dots plus six dots). This gives eleven possible results. All the possible results are shown in Figure A.1

Figure A.1 The probability bulge by the numbers: a pair of dice

A Possible results	B Total opportunity set	C Favourable outcomes	D Ratio of favourable outcomes to unfavourable outcomes (must add up to 36)	E Ratio of favourable outcomes to total opportunity set
2	**36**	**1**	**1 to 35**	**1/36**
3	**36**	**2**	**2 to 34 1 to 17**	**2/36**
4	**36**	**3**	**3 to 33 1 to 11**	**3/36**
5	**36**	**4**	**4 to 32 1 to 8**	**4/36**
6	**36**	**5**	**5 to 31**	**5/36**
7	**36**	**6**	**6 to 30 1 to 5**	**6/36 (1/6)**
8	**36**	**5**	**5 to 31**	**5/36**
9	**36**	**4**	**4 to 32 1 to 8**	**4/36**
10	**36**	**3**	**3 to 33 1 to 11**	**3/36**
11	**36**	**2**	**2 to 34 1 to 17**	**2/36**
12	**36**	**1**	**1 to 35**	**1/36**
Total opportunity set is the total of favourable outcomes		↓ 36	**ODDS**	**PROBABILITY**

column A — if only life, and trading, were so amenable to a similar process of neat tabulation.

Calculating the odds of any number between two and 12 appearing after a throw depends on the total number of possible outcomes, or the opportunity set. As our Renaissance scholar Cardano told Leonardo da Vinci, the odds are the ratio of favorable outcomes to unfavorable outcomes. If we want the number 7, a favorable result, then there are 30 other possible combinations in the opportunity set representing unfavorable results. In modern terms the odds of any turning up the number 7 are six (favorable results) to 30 (unfavorable results), or more commonly expressed as 1 to 5 (30 divided by 6).

Why not 6 to 36 (1 to 6)? We are saying that out of a total of six throws one of them will produce a 7 because there are six combinations out of a possible 36 combinations that give this result. The total of throws needed is six — one favorable outcome plus five unfavorable outcomes.

The full list of favorable outcomes is tabulated in column C, Figure A.1. The ratio of favorable to unfavorable outcomes, the odds, are in column D.

CREATING PROBABILITY

The probability of an event is the ratio of favorable outcomes to the total opportunity set. The difference is important. Calculating the odds compares favorable outcomes to unfavorable outcomes. Calculating probability compares favorable outcomes to all possible outcomes. Leonardo, like many high school students and 'wanna-be' traders, had difficulty in understanding the difference. I imagine Cardano dragged the dice out yet again to illustrate the difference.

The divergence between odds and probabilities appears in the ways the outcomes can be reached. There are 36 possible combinations, or ways, of reaching those 11 results. Column C, favorable outcomes, shows the number of combinations required for each result. Some results, such as number 12, only occur from one group of combinations — six dots and six dots. At the other extreme, number 7 is a result reached by six different combinations. They are 6 + 1, 5 + 2, 4 + 3, 3 + 4, 2 + 5 and 1 + 6. For those who do their mathematics simply, the total number of favorable outcomes is equal to the total opportunity set.

From these calculations we create a table of probability. It tells us there are six possible combinations that give a result of number 7. This is six out of the 36 combinations available. This ratio of favorable outcomes to the total opportunity set is written as a probability of 6/36. The probability of a 12 occurring is found in just one combination out of the 36 available and written as 1/36.

We make these calculations because we know the limits of the total opportunity set — lower limit 2 and upper limit 12 — required to produce the total opportunity set.

At a more complex level we can perform similar calculations for a pack of cards, or for the market. The professional card player knows these probabilities, recognizes them instantly and uses them to his advantage. The trader does the same by recognizing market conditions that tip the balance of probability in his favor.

In transferring the discussion of odds and probabilities from the dice to the market, we shift from 'favorable outcomes' to 'events'. The father of Modern Portfolio Theory, Harry Markowitz, showed the mathematics required for this is much more powerful than a simple calculation of odds and probabilities. Although we know the effects of these events it is more difficult to attach a value to them. The extent of a rise is theoretically infinite, and a fall is limited only by zero. The total opportunity set is ill-defined so the calculation of probability that looks at the ratio of favorable outcomes to the total opportunity set is difficult, if not impossible, to complete.

This level of financial mathematics is beyond the scope of our discussion and readers who wish to follow this in more detail should refer to *Against The Gods*, or *Hedge Funds* by Richard Hills. Those equipped with the appropriate guidance equipment can make their way through *A Treatise On Probability* by John Maynard Keynes.

Extended discussions of risk and probability in wider contexts are found in *Taking Risks: The Science of Uncertainty* by Peter Sprent and *Lady Luck: The Theory of Probability* by Warren Weaver. The relationship between odds and probability form the basis of some linked trading and money management approaches. David Caplan in *Trade Like a Bookie* deals with these types of approaches in detail.

Difficult or not, the trader needs a rule of thumb to estimate the ratio of favorable outcomes to the total opportunity set — the probability. Chart tools and chart patterns point the way. What tips the balance of probability in favor of a particular outcome depends on market conditions and the section of the market you are trading. The way prices clump together with reduced trading ranges at particular levels suggests outcomes with a higher than normal probability.

Some trade these clumps for small profits using leverage from options and other derivatives. Equity traders look for trend and break-outs that deliver higher returns. How far does the trend go? This can be calculated using a number of techniques that put the balance of probability in our favor where one outcome is more likely than another.

We shift the balance of success when our trading strategy is based on moves from clump to clump, capturing a break-out as it happens and taking a profit as it slows. This rule of thumb serves the private trader well.

2

MESSAGES FROM THE JUNGLE DRUMS

Jungles give cover for the daily battle 'red in tooth and claw'. In the very best adventure books the battle progress is reported by jungle drums. Our search for trading nuggets in our chosen jungle takes place against a background battle for the bulge.

Unlike the Battle of the Bulge at Bastogne in December 1944 there are no dramatic explosions, no flickering of artillery on the horizon or screeching tank treads through the fog. During those frantic days the airwaves carried desperate, confused and static-ridden messages reporting the progress of the battle. The modern financial market battle for the bulge is fought by silent proxy with numbers dancing across the screen in dealing rooms, brokerages and on home computers. In this battle, progress is reported accurately by the price bar.

People make prices and we would like to know what they are thinking today. If many people make many prices at the same level the bulge gives us clues about probability. If we understand how they thought in the past then we have a guide to their future thoughts. We want to buy at today's prices and sell at a profitable price in the future. Any information that helps to establish the most probable profitable future price is particularly useful so we scan the price bars for messages written by other traders.

Although most people are more familiar with a line chart as a basic screen or newspaper price plot display, it is the bar chart that provides the best starting point for understanding price action. It shows all the important elements of price action for the selected period. Experienced traders are so accustomed to the bar chart they run the risk of forgetting what it means and miss important clues by stepping straight into complexity and ignoring the simply profitable.

Too often we rush into the fray, using analysis to jump from the bar to our favourite indicators. We rush to manipulate price data by smoothing it with averages, by looking at the way today's close relates to the close of several periods ago, we track the momentum in relation to volume, or to its previous rate of change. All of these are valid ways to understand the information provided by the market, but the bar chart — or candlestick chart — is the only price plot combining all the most recent price data in a single screen display along with the probability bulges. The picture is not quite as clear as Figure 1.1 but it is our starting point and time spent here brings rewards.

CONSTRUCTING A BAR CHART

Graphically, the bar on a bar chart — and its Japanese equivalent, the candlestick — is a scratch on the screen. These two styles of price-plotting provide the same information, and despite their cultural differences, are read the same way. Unless noted, the remainder of this chapter assumes bars are interchangeable with candlesticks.

Both plots link the four basic price details — the open, the close, the high and the low — for the selected period. Although the period can be as short as a few minutes, or as long as 13 weeks or more, for this discussion we treat it as a single trading day.

Markets are a moveable feast so traders range up and down the table from the opening price. Buyers entice sellers to lower their prices. Sellers encourage buyers to bid up.

The price bar shows the major points in the course of sales during the day. A small horizontal slash, or bar, is made to indicate the opening price. A vertical line is drawn to the right. It extends down to touch the lowest price where trades actually take place during the day. The line is extended upwards to mark the highest point during the day where trades actually took place. The close of the day is marked by a horizontal slash on the right-hand side of the vertical line connecting the high and the low. These horizontal bars give the chart plot its name and Figure 2.1 illustrates the process. An up day or a down day is shown by the position of the left-hand open bar in relation to the right-hand closing bar. Some screen displays show up days in blue and down days in red.

These construction techniques are slightly modified for traders involved in bond and futures markets, or intraday traders, where there is no open price. We look at these later in this chapter.

Figure 2.1 Daily price plot cousins

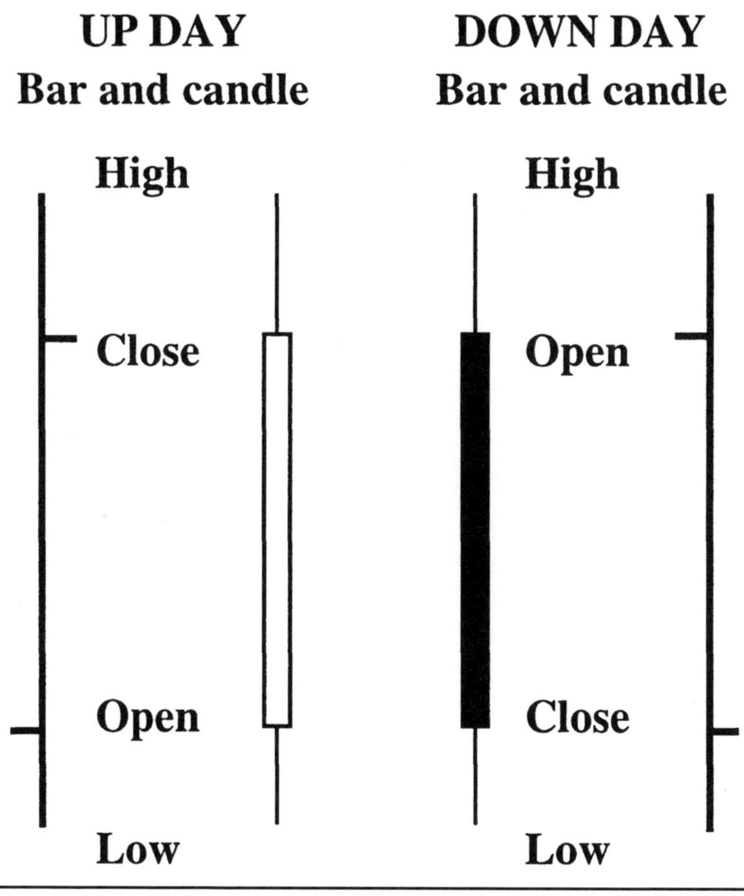

There are always sellers holding out for higher prices and buyers too mean to pay the current price. Their orders are recorded in the depth of market information. These prices, above and below the actual high and low for the day, represent possible prices that were never achieved. We will explore the messages contained in this information in Chapter 15.

READING A BAR BY CANDLE LIGHT

A candlestick price plot is constructed in much the same way as a bar chart plot. Instead of showing the open and close as a horizontal bar to the left and right of the vertical line they are shown as parallel horizontal lines at the top and bottom of a rectangle. These are joined to form a box, or body, of the candlestick as shown in Figure 2.1. Up days are shown as an outline, or white, box. The box is filled in on down days, usually with red ink. Any price movement beyond the open or the close, is shown as a single vertical line rather like the wick on a candle. Hence the European name 'candlesticks'.

The candlestick approach diverges from the European development of charting and analysis techniques. Candlestick charting emphasizes relationships between bars and their placement relative to other individual or groups of bars.

Although the bar remains the basic price plotting tool used in European markets, most of the subsequent developments in technical analysis explore the relationships between the numbers generated by price and volume data. The bar and the candlestick are cousins: one fed on a rigorous diet of mathematics and the other fattened by an understanding of relationships.

We approach the market from a Western tradition so the data series produced by the day's trading is manipulated in many ways. It may be as simple as deriving a moving average, or as complex as Williams' %R. These essentially mathematical approaches are quintessentially European, and although undoubtedly very useful, skip some very important insights offered by price relationships themselves.

The Japanese felt the relationships between prices — the relationships between consecutive candle bars — provided information about the way the market was likely to develop. Their understanding of the market battle places less emphasis on raw figures.

The names given to candlestick relationship patterns sound exotic but they are shorthand for common patterns. If the description suits the mood — dark cloud cover for reversal patterns — then so much the better. Where the pattern name — *harami* cross — is less familiar to European ears, then the ability to easily use candlestick charting as a pattern recognition tool may be diminished for the casual user.

Modern software overcomes this problem to some extent. Specialized software such as CandlePower 5 from North Systems or Candlestick Forecaster scans for many patterns identified by candlestick chartists. Common software packages, such as Metastock, scan for a limited number of patterns.

Modern practitioners of candlestick charting, Steve Nison, *Japanese Candlestick Charting Techniques* and Greg Morris, *Candlepower*, have taken these patterns and explained them in terms of modern European psychological, or demand and supply, analysis. This aids our understanding of candlestick charting, but it should not diminish the importance of the original pattern recognition strengths. The strength of the candle comes from the light it throws on market relationships, not from number-crunching.

No matter how you decide to make your trading decision, the bar, or candlestick, chart most fully displays the price action of the day. In theory, it simply answers the question 'How much is this security worth today?' If the day's price action is encapsulated in a single line — the open, high, low and close are all equal — then the bar chart does give a simple answer to the question.

Understanding the pricing of a security is not as simple as walking into a shop to buy a box of candy off the shelf. We might go shopping for WalMart, but we are not shopping at WalMart. This is not a set price exchange. Although we know the price charged yesterday, there is no fixed price today, and even more disturbingly, there is no fixed price for tomorrow. Price changes during the day, and the slice we select impacts on our future profits. This makes trading both possible and exciting. Trading takes advantage of price differences by using negotiated trade prices to enter and exit a position.

We all have opinions about the market and about particular securities. They are so much hot air until the strength of our conviction forces us to take, or not take, action. The moment we decide to enter or exit the market — the moment we place an order, whether it is filled or not — we condense the hot air into a more concrete activity. The volume of orders sitting in the market provides important information about the commitment of traders. Everyone talks, but only a few commit.

The moment our trade is executed a new slice of information is added to the time of sales or course of trades screen. Our buy or sell order perhaps sets the high, or low, for the day. Our opinion becomes an irreversible part of the day's trading activity.

We expect to make money and we back our opinion with cash. Now our opinion counts, no matter how well-informed or ill-informed it may be. Other traders act independently, and the combined price activity reflects the way a committed crowd of people feels about this particular security at this point in time. This is not a box of chocolates. This price is alive and it changes, grows and morphs in direct response to the urgings of the crowd that buys and sells during the day. The jungle is alive with noise and we use the bar chart to filter our chosen noise from the background static.

UNDERSTANDING A BAR

Each bar or slash on a bar chart measures a different slice of crowd sentiment. To understand how it does this we ask questions about each of the price elements. Who sets the open, the high, the low and the close?

Before we answer the question we must deal with one issue. If there are no trades today, how do we show price? Some data suppliers leave the space blank. As discussed more fully below, some bar charts do not show an open. They start the plot with the first traded price for the day building a high–low–close bar only.

The more common approach is to show the untraded price as the same as yesterday's close and we use this in all of our chart examples. The starting bar on the left-hand side is set at the same level as yesterday's close unless the stock is traded immediately on the open. For the moment these distinctions need not distract us other than to note that the first traded price for the day is the open and the comments below apply to it.

WHO SETS THE OPEN?

This is perhaps the least important of all price elements. It is most commonly set by the novice traders or part-time traders. It is set by those people who download the prices overnight, or read them in the paper, and decide to buy or sell because the stock looks good. They ring their broker on their way to work placing their first orders before the market opens. They act on conclusions based on yesterday's information without waiting for verification from today's initial price action.

Market earthquakes are the exception. When institutions panic they act like novice traders. Anyone who tries to ring their broker on the day after the Dow Jones Index tumbles several hundred points will recognize the phenomenon. The hour before and after the opening of trade is swamped with orders, choking phones lines and rewarding brokers who have three ears. Internet order placement is no exception as the service providers are clogged with on-line traders.

The open is also set by traders who have long-term orders sitting in the market. This includes those trading on support or resistance levels as discussed later. The orders are designed to take advantage of the trader's long-term analysis of the probability of prices reaching a specified level.

Some orders are good until canceled and are simply forgotten. Lazy or inattentive traders may have placed orders days or weeks ago based on price activity at the time. Through inattention they neglect to instruct their broker to remove their orders from the system and when the price returns to this level they unexpectedly find themselves the proud owners of a security they no longer really want.

Generally, the orders filled on the open do not come from full-time traders. This makes the open the least reliable guide to the direction of the market and the feeling of the crowd.

By the end of the first hour the professional traders move fully into the market and set the direction for the day. They confirm overnight trading decisions against the current price action as it develops. These orders are placed by those with access to current market information. The character of the trading day changes as the professionals enter. They help to set the other price elements: the high, the low and the close.

WHO SETS THE LOW?

This is set by the most pessimistic seller — the bears. They believe the market will only go down, so they want to abandon their position as quickly as possible to protect trading capital or to save profits. The buyers are either long-term bulls waiting for a bargain, or institutional traders taking an intraday position at the best price available in relation to the open. Short-term sellers use the same sentiment to make money.

Does your Exchange permit traders to short stocks, or are you limited to contra-trading as in Singapore and Malaysia? If it is very difficult, or not possible to short ordinary shares then this downward pressure is not a result of short selling as it is in the United States. It is more likely to be the result of institutions re-weighting portfolios, fund managers taking a loss quickly, or other traders or investors either taking a loss, or more likely, trying a save a profit.

In markets where short selling is permitted, this downward pressure is driven by the desire to make money rather than to minimize losses. Bears are motivated by optimism rather than pessimism because they want to make money from falling prices. The desire to make money drives the price action differently and the presence of market makers complicates the picture further. In some ways this slice of price action holds a weaker message than the same slice in markets where falling prices translate into losses.

These markets do have equal liquidity in either direction because profit is possible from any price move. In other markets where a loss is the more probable outcome of a price decline, sellers find it more difficult to match with buyers because the buyers cannot immediately benefit from the price decline. Not only are they buying the future, but they are buying a future where prices must increase before they show a profit on the trade.

WHO SETS THE HIGH?

This is set by the most optimistic buyers: those who believe prices are going to keep on rising, so they want 'in' at almost any price. In a rising market, these are institutional buyers who are moving size — share parcels worth $100,000 or more. It also includes enthusiastic private traders; for example, those who have caught the midday news, or who have been watching the price movement on their screens. When the big money agrees with them, this will set an up day.

MOST IMPORTANTLY, WHO SETS THE CLOSE?

This is the most significant of the price elements and is used as a benchmark to assess both the direction of prices for the day, and the strength of the price move. The last 20 minutes of trade is the most hectic period of the day. It is dominated by traders who watch the market because it is their job to do so, or because their primary income depends on it. By definition these are the professionals. The amateur trader is still hard at work on his day job and is unlikely to be able to slip out for a peek at a live Internet trading screen showing depth of market.

The close is also set by intraday traders who usually take their profits towards the end of the day. True day traders do not carry open positions overnight. Short-term traders with a one- to four-day time frame will also close out positions if they feel the market might reverse direction overnight. No matter which way you slice it, the close is set by the smart money, by savvy traders taking profits, or cutting losses, or by those positioning themselves to take profits in the near future.

The close is generally considered to be the most accurate representation of the market's feelings about the stock on the day. So why not use a line chart based on the close?

The range between the price elements gives trading clues vital for the best possible entry or exit. This is the daily reality of the market and it destroys many fancy theoretical calculations. This also applies to groups of bars. The long and the short of it tells traders more than any single line can ever do.

SPECIAL BARS OPEN 24 HOURS

We hinted above that not all bars look the same. These security or equity bar chart construction techniques are slightly modified for traders involved in bond and futures markets, or intraday traders, where there is no open price until a trade takes place. Price bars in these markets look like Figure 2.2, showing the high, low and close for the selected period.

Day traders face a different challenge from position traders and these specialized price bars do a specific job. The Internet day trader is the direct offspring of Jessie Livermore and the other great tape readers. They watch the market action during the day reading the tick information to find the market's intentions, or, in some markets, the intentions of the market-makers and specialists. Gary Smith, a US trader, gives a fascinating blow-by-blow description of this style of trading in *Live the Dream by Profitably Day Trading Stock Futures* and also in the May 1997 issue of *Technical Analysis of Stocks and Commodities*. Other books include *The Electronic Day Trader* and *Secrets of the SOES Bandit*.

The day trader's intention is to enter and exit a trade between the market open and close. They carry no overnight positions.

Figure 2.2 Intraday bars
A 15-minute slice from the 1440 minute global pie

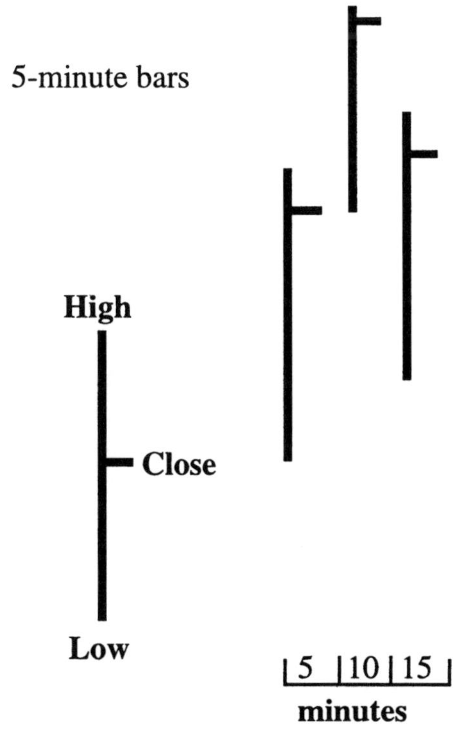

Traders who do carry overnight positions are more properly short-term traders.

A daily bar chart using a single bar to show the action over the six hours of trading is of little use to the day trader. Instead they arbitrarily divide the day into segments and plot the price action in each segment. These segments may be as short as one or three minutes, or more commonly five minutes, and stretch to 10-, 20-, 30- and 50-minute periods. The choice depends on the market being traded.

The first bar in Figure 2.2 is part of an ongoing five-minute price plot. The top of the bar is the high achieved in this five-minute time period. The low is the low traded in this five-minute time period. The close, the right-hand slash on the bar, is the price at the end of this five-minute period.

The next bar in the series does not have an open because the price plot starts only with the first traded price in the next five-minute period, which is not necessarily at the same level as the previous close. The beginning of this period is instantaneous. When the clock ticks to the next five-minute period the chart point moves one bar to the right and makes no entry until a trade is made. What is important in this plot is the lowest and highest points and the final closing price in the selected period.

This style of bar charting offers clear advantages for these intraday traders. For position traders active in bond and other markets where the standard price bars show high, low and close the picture is distorted when some data feed and charting software packages calculate an artificial 'open' for each day. The method used to calculate the 'open' varies and inevitably impacts on the accuracy of the data when shown either as a standard bar or as a candlestick display.

This has several consequences for the way the jungle drums report the battles and the way we search for the balance of probability.

Although not an issue now, the first of these comes with the eventual move to 24-hour continuous markets. This will tend to make many accepted bar charts — open, high, low, close — look more like the bars used in intraday trading — high, low, close. In practice, these bar charts can still be usefully constructed to show an open by using an artificial calculation.

Markets may be traded 24 hours a day, but brokerages are not that active. Futures contracts are traded in the United States on the New York Exchange. International traders participate directly in what for them is overnight trading. The New York Stock Exchange opens day trading at 8.10 a.m. and closes at 2.30 p.m. The overnight session runs from 4.00 p.m. to 8.00 a.m. US traders wishing to trade in this period must participate in what is for them, an overnight market. Among others, they could use the Sydney Futures Exchange in Australia, which provides a continuous open market by trading 6.00 a.m. to 10.00 p.m. local time.

In following this sequence of Exchange hours around the world we find a surge of early orders as trade begins in each local region. This effectively establishes an 'open' and about six hours later at the end of the trading day, in regional local time, there is another surge of orders, effectively creating a 'close'.

In effect, each regional open and close of trading floors creates a distinctive open and close blip on the price action. For all practical purposes these blips can be used in building a bar defining a single 'day' of trading. In any 24-hour period there may be three to four such 'days'.

Trading other 24-hour markets is made more difficult by Exchanges having different procedures for determining the open and the close for the day. This has a significant impact on price data. International traders involved with US markets can follow a full discussion in the annex to this chapter.

The nuances of bar chart construction in 24-hour markets impact on the chart display and on some trading tactics. These changes do not significantly alter our understanding and interpretation of information provided by the bar chart — support, resistance and trend lines — and the subsequently derived and calculated indicator information — moving averages, stochastics and oscillators. Day traders using 3- and 30-minute charts base their trading on the same understandings as position traders who use 6-hour — 10.00 a.m. to 4.00 p.m. — charts.

USING A BAR

Understanding the information in a single price bar, no matter how constructed, allows the trader to make a better entry or exit from a trade. The bar chart tells us how the smart money, the significant money, is positioned in relation to the extremes of emotional feeling about the security. Smarter trading suggests we should be travelling in the same direction as the smart money because it shows us where the balances of probability lie in any single trading period.

These important clues about the attitude and orientation of the smart money are instantaneous and are displayed immediately at the end of every trading day. You get the close at the same time as the institutional traders and every other private trader. You get to act on it at the same time as everybody else — when the market opens the next day. The jungle drums are heard by everybody and the message is in the beat.

The bar chart captures the beat of the market jungle and gives us information to confirm or deny our initial identification of a trading opportunity. For the fundamental trader, the bar chart is perhaps the last stopping point before the market is entered into. For the technical trader, the bar chart is the starting point for all other analysis. The next chapter quickly looks at the way a bar chart builds a trade.

A BAR IN EVERY MARKET

Equity, commodity, currency and the growing derivative markets are different in their rules, procedures, risk profiles and tactics. Many say the great divide between the equity market and other financial markets is the concept of a zero-sum game. Many commentators and traders believe trading any financial market is a zero-sum game with a winner and loser every time — what I win, you *must* lose. This difference is claimed to be so great that any discussion about securities and equities cannot be relevant to other markets. On the surface this makes the bar chart analysis techniques discussed above appear less relevant to these markets.

Every market provides the data needed to build a bar chart. In the same way that gridiron, soccer and rugby are all united by a single common feature — teams chasing a ball — markets are united by price activity. The bar chart as a means of recording price activity is common to all markets so the artificial divide between equity and other financial markets is unimportant because the bar chart always provides us with the same type of information about the player's emotional reaction to current price. It does not tell us who takes money from whom or describe the distribution of spoils.

Nor does it tell us how traders feel about the type of game they are playing — baseball or basketball, equities or commodities — so we don't use a bar chart in this way. In some important ways the philosophical argument about zero-sum games, while entertaining, is largely irrelevant to understanding the message. The bar provides concepts, such as support and resistance, equally valid for equity trading and for commodities or currencies in financial markets. A developing triangle pattern speaks the same language on a five-minute currency bar chart as it does on a weekly equity bar chart.

Our belief about the trading arena we choose, be it zero-sum or not zero-sum, changes the way we approach the market and the trading strategies we prefer. The battlefields are different, but the emotional messages contained in the price dispatches from the front are the same. The balances of probability — the bulges — are exposed in any bar chart. Building a trade from this information is the basic entry point for every trader no matter which market he trades.

All prospectors build a grub-stake to finance the next prospecting expedition. In the gold-mining towns they flash some sample nuggets. Or like the enigmatic Australian prospector Harold Lasseter, they build these into tales of a reef with 'the yellow stuff in it as thick as plums in a pudding'. No briefing on the dangers of the jungle would be complete without a sample nugget to re-ignite those with faltering courage. Chapter 3 gives shape to the nuggets we expect to find. You risk your own capital so it pays to put a more definite shape on the imagined pile of dollars hiding in the market jungle.

ANNEX

WHEN A CLOSE IS NOT A CLOSE

All markets use common terms, but the meaning is not always the same. Sometimes we decide the distinction is not important, but unless we are aware a distinction exists we cannot make an informed decision. The closing price is vital to most charting and technical analysis indicators.

The CNBC feed used by many television stations invariably shows the New York Stock Exchange (NYSE) finish the trading day with the bell. Actual close of trade is not this simple and data showing the close for the NYSE and other markets is not always as accurate as we intuitively believe.

Systematic trading usually requires an entry and exit as close as possible to the target price. Variations in end-of-day data prices affect the results of technical indicators. Delays in real-time data updates on the screen, based on reports of trading activity in the pit, affect profit margins.

A few seconds before the official NYSE closing time all Market On Close orders are executed at the market price. Trading ends only when all such orders have been executed so trading may go some time beyond the official closing time. Trades are settled within a closing range. The simple average of the price range is the settlement price and this may be different from the official close used by data vendors.

To add confusion in futures markets, the closing session for different contracts begins at different times, extends for different periods, and varies from exchange to exchange. New York Coffee's closing session lasts for five minutes, while the Chicago Mercantile Exchange normally starts 30 seconds before the official closing time. Currencies on the same Exchange have about 60 seconds. Traders using Market on Close Orders must know the individual closing times for their contract.

Settlement vs close — does it matter? If your search takes you to this part of the jungle the difference is an additional hazard. A bar chart based on the close can be significantly different from a bar chart based on the settlement price after the bell. The impact of these differences will depend on your style of trading and the way you place orders. You should know which price your vendor supplies — it affects the way your data matches reality.

NOT THE OPEN TOO

If the distinction between the close and the settlement price has not set your head spinning, then rotational openings should do the trick. Futures traders active in US markets using open to set decisions on an intraday basis face significant challenges.

Like the close, all market orders placed before opening time are executed at the market. Prices are quoted as an opening range rather than a price. The closing time of the opening session is when all pending market orders have been filled. The simple average of this opening range is quoted as the official open price.

Many data vendors use the official open price as the open in their daily updating service. Many traders prefer to use the first actual trade as the open. Not knowing which price your data vendor uses is not always fatal, but it is dangerous.

This confusion is compounded with rotational opens on New York markets. The official open starts with trading in the front month contract. Trading opens for a short period, then stops. The next month out is opened for a short time, and closed. This continues until all contract months have established an opening range. Once the rotation is completed trading in all contracts are opened simultaneously and the actual full day's uninterrupted trading commences. The time between the official open and the actual simultaneous open, ranges from a few minutes to nearly half an hour. Off-floor screen traders locked out for 30 minutes are at a disadvantage on days of high volatility.

Phillip York of QBL Funds Management gives an extreme example taken from 27 June 1994. He tells in the QBL newsletter how the Coffee markets opened at 9:15 a.m. after a weekend freeze in Brazil.

> *"The July contract opened at 175.00 and in the next 60 seconds established an unprecedented opening range of 7.00 cents, from 173.00 to 180.00."*

Trading stopped as the opening rotated to the next month out.

> *"A full 35 minutes later, trading resumed at an 'unofficial' opening price of 161.00. The difference was a full $7,125 per contract from the high of the Opening Range."*

Burned by this confusion between official and actual opening prices, some traders only use the second actual open when all contracts are reopened simultaneously. On a tick-by-tick basis the day trader can pick this. The position trader relying on end-of-day data gets unreliable signals unless he knows how the data vendor plots the open. And it is no wonder that it is sometimes easier to draw the bar without a slash on the left-hand side.

3

LASSETER'S REEF

Armed with two concepts — the balance of probability and the structure of a bar chart plot — we are better equipped to find and assay trading nuggets than many of our competitors. Life in the market jungle does get much more complex, but with this information alone we can find and build a better trade.

We know a single bar tells us where the smart money, the big money, is positioned: moving with or against the trend. We enhance the probability of success if we move in the same direction. In the same way, the behavior of a group of bars creates a similar probability bulge. In Chapter 1, Figure 1.1 bulged at the number 7. The same types of bulges are found in Figure 3.1. We have deleted the price scale to make it easier to focus on the way prices move. On the battlefield of uncertainty these are the touchstones of trading success.

Somewhere in the arid centre of Australia lies a fabled, and so far, mythical reef. Harry Lasseter stumbled from the desert and like every prospector he had samples from his reef. These samples were misleading and Lasseter's reef remains elusive. Others are truly exciting. We show you an example below in Figure 3.1, along with ways to judge real gold from fool's gold. This nugget comes from the region we intend to explore.

This sample uses the bar chart alone. We establish profit targets, entry points and stop loss levels based on a framework of probability. A plain analysis of the Australian General Property Trust chart uses this trading framework to give us an advantage over those who do not understand the bar chart. No matter how complex our analysis may later become, the probability bulge is the trading touchstone at the beginning and end of every trading decision.

What stands out from the General Property Trust daily bar chart? Even a cursory look shows information not easily obtained from any other source. Prices seem to clump at particular levels, moving sideways, before moving up, or down. Newspaper price quotations, even when collected together over a few days, do not reveal this information so clearly.

This is the major bar chart advantage. Immediately we see that prices tend to spend some time moving in a tight trading band before taking off, usually dramatically, to establish new levels that later also develop into tight trading bands. These observations give the trader enough information to take advantage of trading opportunities.

General Property Trust support and resistance — the probability bulges — provide a simple trading strategy. Support and resistance are important concepts and we will return to them in Part II. For the moment we only want to take advantage of this behavior so only a brief definition is needed.

Figure 3.1 The probability bulge
General Property Trust, Australia
Daily bar chart

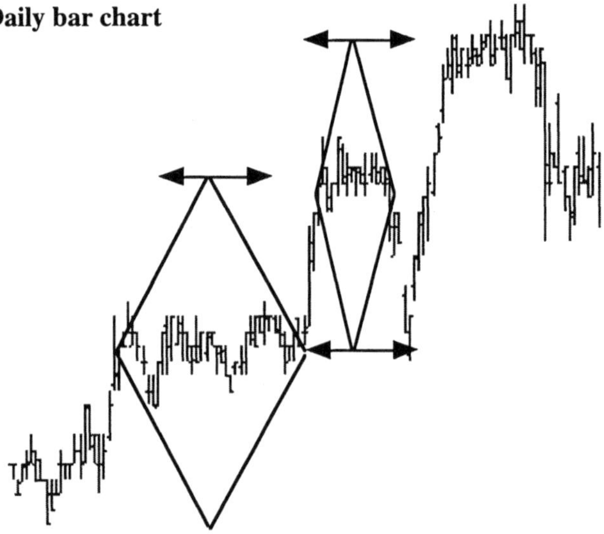

When prices fall, support defines the level where they pause. This level develops when buyers enter the market because they think the stock is attractively priced. With General Property Trust, the lower limits of each band are support levels. They are well defined and easily marked as shown on Figure 3.2.

Resistance is similar to support. It defines areas where prices reach a consistent peak before pulling back. The level forms in the opposite way to support. Resistance levels happen when sellers unload stock because they have made their desired profit, or because they feel the stock will not go any higher. Again, with this chart, the areas are unusually well defined. The middle trading band, or consolidation area, between these upper and lower levels is labeled C. Traders thinking ahead by looking back will note how these correspond to the double-headed arrows in Figure 3.1.

Figure 3.2 Support and resistance
General Property Trust, Australia
Daily bar chart

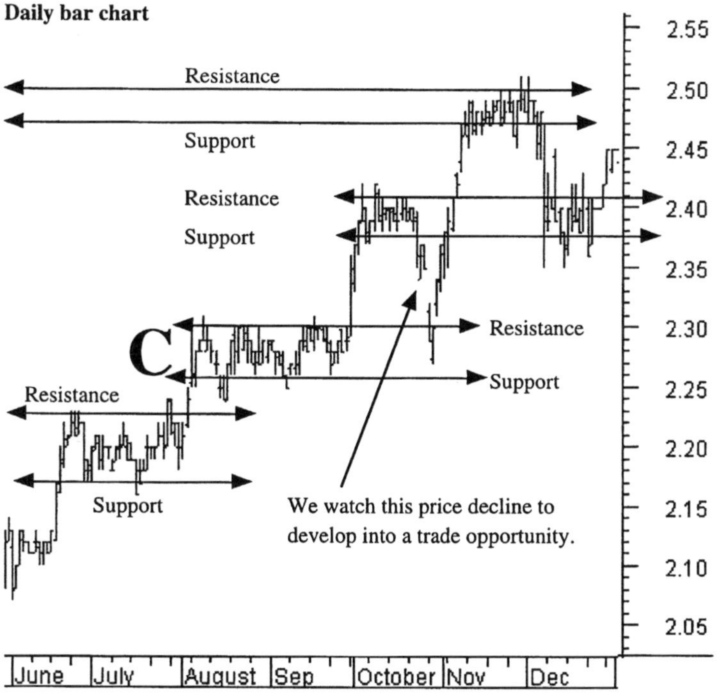

PERSISTENT PROBABILITY

Using the language of probability we observe that there are areas where specific price combinations have persistence — short-term trends — or extended persistence — long-term trends — over time. Gold travels along riverbeds, but gathers in the hollows. The simple vibrating riffle tables in every gold room are built to take advantage of this increase in probability. Our trades do the same by identifying persistent price combinations.

In most cases the support and resistance areas form a narrow price range. With General Property Trust they are only a few percentage points wide, but as we will see later the range is sometimes as wide as 10 to 15 percent. When too narrow in themselves to trade, each area is best treated as a single broad line drawn through the middle of the price action. In Figure 3.3 they are labeled areas A, B, C and D. These match the bands in Figure 3.2.

Figure 3.3 Trading the balance of probability
General Property Trust, Australia
Daily bar chart

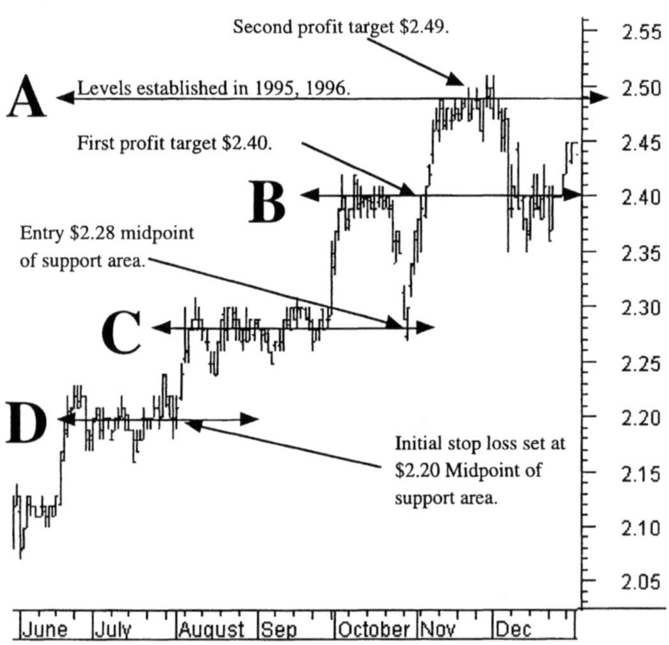

A resistance level, such as the upper line in area C on Figure 3.2, or the centre line C in Figure 3.3 often becomes a support level and vice versa as the trend changes direction. Once the level is crossed there are a substantial number of new stockholders who have made decisions based on this level. They calculate their profits, losses, or break-even points from this level.

Our entry strategy for General Property Trust is simple. As the price drops from $2.40 in October we sense a trading opportunity developing as it moves towards level C. We all want to buy today's high performing stocks at bargain prices so we lie in wait where the balance of probability bulges. The nearest bulge is support level C, and by setting an entry order at the midpoint — $2.28 — we have a good probability of being filled because prices have paused here in the past.

It is important to understand we are not buying the sudden price dip. This does not, in itself, signal a sound trading opportunity. We are buying the balance of probability that the price collapse will pause at one level rather than another.

We are not saying prices will necessarily rally from this pause, although we think they will on balance. We are saying prices will move, and when they do, they will probably move as far as an established support or resistance level and pause for a while. The total number of possible combinations is not open ended. There are areas where combinations persist over time. The use of these clumps or bulges as reference points will place the balance of probability on our side because it reduces the ratio of possible combinations and favorable outcomes.

After striking these levels, the subsequent move will follow a similar pattern, up or down. This is not a rare jungle 'nugget', although it is often well camouflaged. Prices do not move in a random pattern. They do gather at points for extended periods, and thereby provide a smaller range of possible combinations. 'Nuggets' with these patterns are very valuable.

The well-defined support and resistance levels, A, B, C and D, also provide a simple risk control strategy. You should not trade unless you have a fully developed strategy for managing risk in each and every trade. Later we will show how this is developed, but for the moment we want to briefly sketch how this General Property Trust bar chart provides the necessary calculation points.

To manage this trade successfully we must fully plan the risk and the reward so there are no unpleasant surprises. The methods of planning and managing a trade are common to all trades. Whether trading with $2,000, or $2 million, the principles remain the same.

These analysis steps may appear too basic for real trading. In fact they are more than adequate and form the basis of every trade. There is no set relationship between the time consumed by analysis and the trading outcome. Some 'wanna-be' traders fail to understand that hours spent does not necessarily translate into a correct answer and they pursue complex answers when simpler ones are also profitable.

In any trade we first set the conditions to tell us if our analysis is wrong. The second task is to set reasonable profit targets based on the bulges of probability. All of this information comes from the General Property Trust bar chart so we consider each step using Figure 3.3 on page 42.

PLANNING TO AVOID FAILURE

The trader must know when he is wrong. This trade entry is planned at $2.28, just above support and we must decide how much additional price retracement shows we have misjudged. These calculations are the first step and should be completed before the trade is opened so the scope for emotion in later decisions is reduced.

Our trading proposition accepts the basic odds — favorable outcomes to unfavorable outcomes — and measures them. From this pause area, prices will either fall towards the next support level or rally to the next resistance level. There is no shame attached to misjudging the direction of the price move. The real problems arise when we cannot admit the misjudgment because this prevents us from taking appropriate action. Sitting on a loss is not a sign of strength. It is a sign of weakness showing you do not have the discipline to take a loss.

This marks the difference between successful traders and unsuccessful traders. It is not the size of the profits, but the size of the losses. Successful traders control risk by taking small losses early according to a predefined plan. Unsuccessful traders are forced to take big losses usually under unfavorable circumstances because they need the money, because the paper loss is too great, or they need to be able to sleep without worry. It is the loser's law of the market. In Part III we look more closely at planning to avoid failure.

With this simple trade example, to avoid taking large losses we must quickly know when we are wrong. In this case, if the price pulls back below our intended entry around support at \$2.26 — if there is a close below \$2.26 — we are wrong. The current support level would be broken and General Property Trust's past price history tells us that when this happens the price will fall to at least the next support band at D. The midpoint of this band is \$2.20 and an exit here shows a loss of 3.5 percent.

This is within acceptable limits so it sets the initial stop loss point. It is a realistic stop loss because it uses the dynamics of the chart support levels to shift the balance of probability in our favour. If prices do fall, they are more likely to pause in this area than in other areas.

CAUGHT ON THE REBOUND

The second step in any trade is setting reasonable profit targets. What is reasonable? Too often this concept is bounded only by our own greed, or limited by our fear. A price chart unemotionally defines 'reasonable' for each trade. Here we skip the depth of calculations involved because this nugget is just a sample of bigger trading treasures.

This sample General Property Trust trade is based only on information supplied by the bar chart so the price action sets profit levels related to the bulges of better probability as shown in

Figure 3.1. These are also significant support and resistance levels and profit targets set near them increase the probability of a successful exit at our preferred price.

The first bulge in probabilities is around $2.40, shown as area B in Figure 3.3. The return is 5.2 percent. As an initial target this is acceptable. The second bulge, area A, is around $2.48 to $2.50. A midpoint exit at $2.49 for 9.2 percent seems a reasonable target.

This is all very clear in retrospect in Figure 3.3, but not so clear in late October when these decisions about future price action are being made. The higher profit target — the second bulge at level A — was established by previous price action not shown in Figure 3.3. This level formed two years previous in April, and again in June and July of the same year. It was tested one year ago when prices approached this level several times but were unable to breakthrough to new levels. The people who make prices by buying at these levels have long memories so these combinations have extended persistence over time.

Armed with this information from the chart the trader already has a better risk control and profit strategy than those who do not use a chart. The trader was able to exit at a safely calculated $2.49, taking a 9.2 percent return because he knew in advance two vital pieces of information provided by the chart alone.

First, he knew what conditions would signal he was wrong, and he knew the conditions signalling success. Second, he knew in advance how much he expected to gain or lose. Instead of hanging onto the trade in hope, the trader exited cleanly with financial targets satisfied. Trading success was based on understanding how the balance of probability is used to enhance profits and limit losses. This separates the consistent trading winners and survivors from the losers.

The trader used the chart to locate the balance of probability of crowd action, and hence price action. The balance will shift in his favor by setting targets based on the way prices pause and consolidate at persistent levels.

This simple analysis is just the beginning of assessing any trade. Successful trading requires more thorough research, sound analysis matched to preferred trading techniques, and specific methods of establishing the financial objectives and viability of the trade. All trades start with, and return to, this touchstone of the balance of probability.

The search for market gold is similar to prospecting for the real metal itself. Before venturing into the jungle, sensible 'tender foot' or 'greenhorn' prospectors survey the terrain and talk to experienced miners who have worked the ground. They gather clues about what to expect so they can get to the gold quicker than their competitors. This and previous chapters are the market equivalent of this pre-expedition research.

Next, novice prospectors determine the character of the deposits, be they alluvial, placer, or mother lodes. Finally, greenhorn prospectors equip themselves with good tools for exploring the ground, with the best methods for assaying the quality of the find, and with a strategy for protecting the growing bullion. These are issues we will explore in the following sections after we have established a method to define the character of our deposits. There are no shortcuts in this journey — unless you choose to follow Lasseter's footsteps to his mythical reef.

4

TIME BITES CHARACTER

Standing on the site of one of the richest of the historical Australian gold fields is the Sovereign Hill gold museum. On display are a collection of gold samples gathered from the surrounding areas. From nuggetty bits of pure hard cash, to fine flecks of dust and sandy grains, the sheer variety is surprising. This gold has character, be it forged in basalt furnaces, scoured by wind and rain, or tumbled in polished glory along stream beds. Clearly, more than a pick and shovel is needed to extract a fortune on this gold field.

Before we start the search for trading gold we need a good idea of the character of our reef. Does our gold come in nuggets, in rich veins visible in the quartz, or is it scattered like gold dust in a riverbed stream? Although the metaphor is not strictly correct, because our 'nuggets' are living events with character and behavior, it serves as a useful way of thinking about the nature of our search expedition in the market jungle. Character determines the tools we use to detect and mine our potential fortune. Later we use specific tools to discover and unearth trade opportunities, but our search is initially assisted by considering different time frames.

Gold nuggets nestle deep in the wrinkles of local geology and our trading 'nuggets' are hidden in layers of weekly, daily and day-by-day activity. This jungle includes a fractual landscape with small patterns repeated on a larger scale. Stocks have characters, or groups of behaviors, often best seen on a weekly chart. They exhibit individual behaviors, usually best seen on a daily chart. They thrash with emotion on a daily basis. The time bite we choose as a screen display captures character, behavior or emotional activity.

Each chart time bite captures a different glimpse of opportunity and from these we build a better picture of probability. Flip forward a few pages and check the weekly price plot for American heavy equipment manufacturer Caterpillar shown in Figure 4.3.

The 'up trend' character is clear, both for the overall chart and the most recent 12 months. Here is easy money. Most try to climb on board when the trend is well established. 'Get me into something, anything, going up' they tell their broker in the middle and closing stages of a bull market as if the market is a one-way elevator to the roof.

When the same Caterpillar chart is reduced to a few days, shown in Figure 4.6, profit opportunities look less certain as previous days drift sideways. This is an emotional view and events are thrown out of proportion. Unlike other investments, or money-making opportunities, value fluctuates, sometimes wildly. Rationally, traders know if they are on board this simple weekly trend evident in Figure 4.3, price behavior will tend to move upwards. Emotionally they are attacked by the rise and fall of prices shown on the daily chart and listed every morning in the newspaper or in the alphabet soup of the CNBC screen ticker. These contradictory feelings come from different time frames. A better understanding of the links between character, behavior and emotion turns up many rough nuggets.

Securities, like those who trade them, do have character. They range from staid established giants to cheeky little Internet start-ups. Prices develop characteristic groups of behaviors that impact on the probability of future behavior.

Each bar on the price chart is related to, and depends on, the previous bar. Each daily graph of market emotion builds on the behavioral high or low of the previous day. The range of behavioral swings is constrained by the character of the security. Each time bite is a snapshot of market action — minutes, daily, weekly — and signals or confirms different trading opportunities. We need different trading tactics to suit each of them. This jungle includes thickets — daily price bars and open glades where only a few monthly price bars thrive.

TRADING TIME BITES

Dr Elder in *Trading for a Living,* codified these time relationships in the triple screen trading approach. It takes advantage of computer power and modern software to capture snapshots for further study.

The core essential of his approach is to trade in the direction of the prevailing trend while taking advantage of short-term favorable conditions to make the best entry, or exit, possible. Elder suggests we first look at weekly charts; second, daily charts, then at just a few days of at tick data.

In practice we may feel dwarfed in this jungle so we start with the middle view because this is the one most commonly displayed on our trading screens. Some software displays 150 trading days or about seven months of data as the standard default. Other software displays 260 trading days, or just over a year of price history. The size of the screen view time bite is a matter of personal choice but I favor a year, or 260 days, of data. If I want to take a closer look at particular price activity I use the zoom function to expand the detail.

Why 260 trading days? Significant trends develop over extended periods and we want to trade in the direction of the trend. Shorter time bites sometimes give misleading clues. We want to see a wider range of sensible options. At times we might 'fade' the trend by taking an early position in the anticipation of a trend change. As prices head to the bottom, or snatch desperately at new tops, we take advantage of these early warning signs to buy or sell in anticipation of a new trend developing.

Although the turning point might be dramatic, it can also be a whimper. Some stocks break out of the trend and race sideways for weeks or months, trading in a narrow band, forcing our trading capital to take a rest. Stand too close and the action loses significance. Stand too far away and the detail eludes us. A year of daily activity on the screen strikes a balance.

DAILY TIME

The time bite contained in the initial screen view sets our focus in more ways than one. The first subconscious judgments made here heavily influence our analysis of other time frames. If our first look at the data is too narrow, we lose perspective. Significant price moves get lost in a welter of daily price activity. Insignificant price moves gain unwarranted stature because the context of their performance is too narrow.

Just how vital is this, or is it an exercise of academic importance? Impatient prospectors are satisfied with the nuggets they see at first glance. A fortune awaits those who take a longer view. In market terms the following charts of Caterpillar show the advantages of each time bite. The bar labeled A is the same bar in each view. We look for a buying decision based on the analysis of each chart.

I prefer a 260-day time bite but many traders use the smaller default screen display. For comparison we start in Figure 4.1 with a 150-day view. The questions we ask are the same. How strong is the new upwards trend and how long will it last? This chart is dominated by short-lived rallies bouncing off this 'up trend'. The last bar, A, shows price action spiking above the resistance level.

Figure 4.1 Time frames and trends
Caterpillar, USA
Daily bar chart
150 days

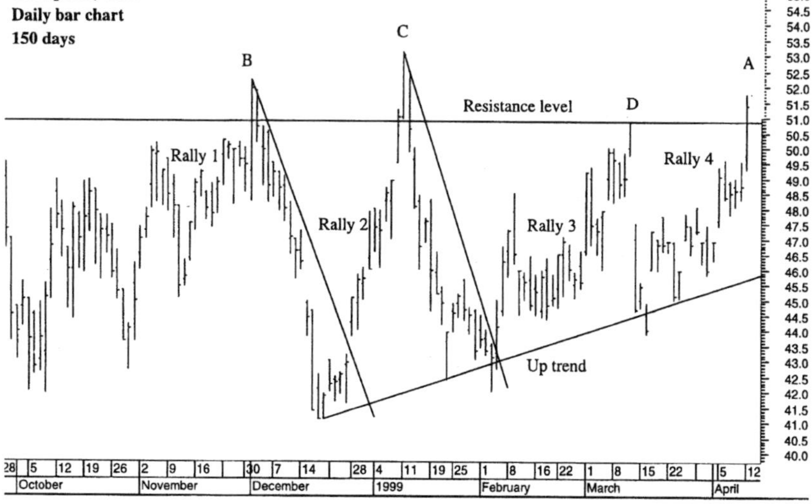

Prices at these levels provided good exit opportunities at points B and C. Most recently, the rally at point D failed to break this resistance level. On this chart in this time frame the action at point A looks like a selling opportunity to lock in profits from the short-term rally. Grab this 'nugget' before it disappears.

Check my preferred screen displaying 260 days of data for the same stock, in Figure 4.2. and the analysis changes. The bar marked A is the same as the bar marked A in Figure 4.1. Now this rally activity is more properly placed in the context of a developing up-sloping triangle. More importantly, the chart now shows the impact of long-term support and resistance levels. These help define future price targets. Additional information available from this time bite includes:

- Two trend lines are in place. A long-term upwards trend shown as line C and a short-term rally trend shown as line B. The short-term rally suggests increasing strength. This is very bullish when added to the projected triangle formed by trend line B and the resistance level at $50. The use of these formations is discussed more fully in the next chapter so here we just have a summary.
  Bar A marked a break-out from the middle third of the up-sloping triangle. This is a powerful buy signal for long-side traders — those who buy low and sell high. For traders who took an early entry in the anticipation of the up-sloping triangle, break-out current price action confirms this as a trade to hold onto and ride.
- A resistance band is established between $50 and $51.50. A new opening above this level is very bullish. This provides a buy signal unlike the 150-day chart that suggests a sell signal.
- Prices have a high probability of running from $51 to the next resistance level of $55. This is an 8 percent return. Traders who bought Caterpillar around $45 as it pulled back to the short-term trend line marked as B have the opportunity to pick up a 22 percent return.
- Upper targets are suggested at $61. These are confirmed by the weekly chart. Buyers at $51 reach for a 19 percent return and will take it once the resistance at $55 is broken. Traders who bought at $45 aim for a 35 percent return.

Figure 4.2 Time frames and resistance levels
Caterpillar, USA
Daily bar chart
260 days

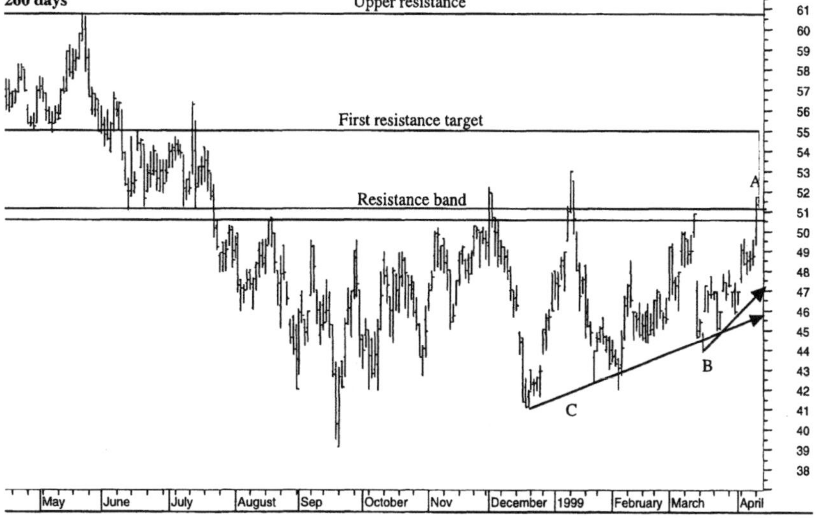

With 260 days of data it is easier to assess the stock against its intermediate trend — weeks and months long — and to reach better conclusions about its short-term trend — over days or weeks. This time bite more effectively shows behavior and identifies the potential buy area around $51. Now this 'nugget' really gleams with potential so we explore its character further.

The daily time bite is the second screen of Elder's Triple Screen approach. The first and third screens display different aspects of character and emotion — both of the stock and of those who trade it.

If the price signals a developing trade opportunity, the trader glances at the longer term time frame before chasing the market into smaller segments of time. We avoid buying a temporary emotional high if we think price will resume its normal behavior.

WEEKLY CONFIRMATION

Moving from the daily chart showing 260 days of data to a weekly chart showing three to four years of data (750 to 1,000 days) on the screen instantly adds additional information about stock characteristics.

The weekly view, Figure 4.3, puts current behaviour into a wider character context. This time bite confirms current behaviour is consistent with a significant break-out and accelerated up trend. Now the combined trading information derived from Figures 4.2 and 4.3 includes:

- The down-side is limited by the long-term trend line shown as B. This is also confirmed by Figure 4.2. The slope of the trend line is consistent across time frames.
- The resistance level at $51 is a major level. A weekly break above this level is very bullish.
- The next major resistance level is around $57 with an upper limit of $61. Here we take the consolidation areas of the 1997 and 1998 peak activity as the lower resistance level. The peaks provide the upper targets.
- The long-term up-sloping triangle puts current price action in the middle third of the pattern. This is a bullish scenario best traded from the long side.

Figure 4.3 Trading in the direction of the weekly trend
Caterpillar, USA
Weekly bar chart
128 weeks

The agreement between these two time bites points to the balance of probability. In deciding how to extract this 'nugget' we make additional notes.

Caterpillar is not an erratic character. From consistent behavior across two time frames we can confidently trade in the direction of the trend and in anticipation of a significant upside break-out. We are prepared to take advantage of a temporary price pullback during the day, but we are also ready to leap on board if the price opens higher than the resistance level at $51.

A note of caution. Computer screens are smart mirrors on top of dumb terminals. When switching to a weekly view make sure the weekly chart displays the time span required. The Metastock default weekly format shows 260 days displayed as 52 weekly bars unless you specify X-axis properties as 750 days or more. Save this as a weekly template for future use at any time.

It does not matter if you turn to a bar chart, a line chart, a point and figure chart or a candlestick chart to get this longer term view. Any longer term view of the market brings important advantages in understanding character. Consistently confirming daily price action with the weekly trend also confirms character. Consistency is important, but so is change because therein lies the real opportunity. For the moment we will ignore the way this usually cloaks risk.

BAD BOYS MAKE GOOD

Bad boys behave out of character, in some cases wildly out of character. This makes excellent trading opportunities as the market is caught unawares by the sudden firing of the stock. Arcadia Minerals, shown as a weekly chart in Figure 4.4 below, is a sleepy stock in long-term hibernation moving between well-established support and resistance bands. A simple trading strategy, buying support at $0.07, selling resistance at $0.14, returns around 100 percent over 12 to 18 months. It is a mining security, but it could also be a high-tech start-up, a bio-tech company or an Internet hopeful. All are noted for sudden changes in character.

Figure 4.4 Sleeping beauty
Arcadia Minerals, Australia, weekly bar chart

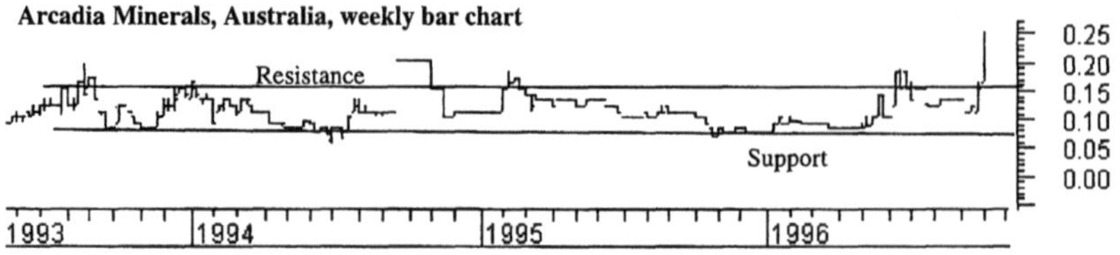

In mid-January the market Prince Charming gave this sleeping beauty a kiss and the price sat bolt upright. This was a dramatic change from the previous characteristics of the stock on a weekly basis, and of behavior on a daily basis.

Several successful trading approaches became redundant overnight. New approaches were recruited and they are outlined in Figure 4.5. When the character of the stock changes, we must change our trading tactics. If we do not understand how to read character we cannot select the appropriate tools and will continue to trade the stock as it was rather than as it is.

Schizophrenic stocks destroy complacency. Arcadia switches character in the February to April period and support and resistance trading is king again. Most times we trade when the behavior of the security is consistent with its character — but not always. Understanding the appropriate context of price activity gives you an important edge.

DAY-BY-DAY EMOTIONAL EXTREMES

The trade decision is based on character and behavior, but the actual trade is based on the emotional activity of the security. This is Elder's third screen and the smallest time bite. Here we zoom in on the immediate emotional dimension. There are many tools used to assess the strength and stability of this emotion, and some of them are discussed in later chapters. Here we consider only how this last, and shortest, time bite helps establish a better trading perspective.

Exactly how tightly we micro manage depends on our trading technique. Day traders use minute-by-minute data drawn from

Figure 4.5 Out of character behavior provides new trading opportunities
Arcadia Minerals, Australia
Daily bar chart

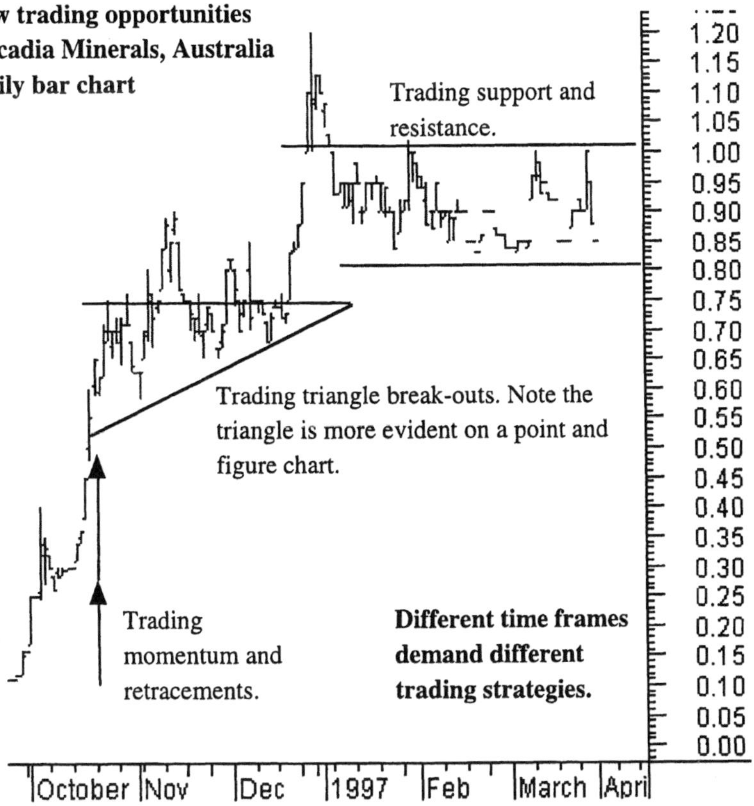

the time and sales, or course-of-trades screens. Some position traders use depth of market information in ways discussed in Chapter 15. Most position traders use the message in the price bars to get a better entry.

As position traders we want the best possible entry into Caterpillar consistent with the current behavior of the stock. The previous time frames suggested $51 as a potential buy area. We refine this decision further by paying close attention to the most recent days' price activity. Using the screen zoom function we bring the last few days into full-screen focus as shown in Figure 4.6 to give a clear view of the emotional balance of the forces of demand and supply over the most recent trading days. This close to the action we smell fear and taste greed.

Fig. 4.6 Taking a trade from the bar

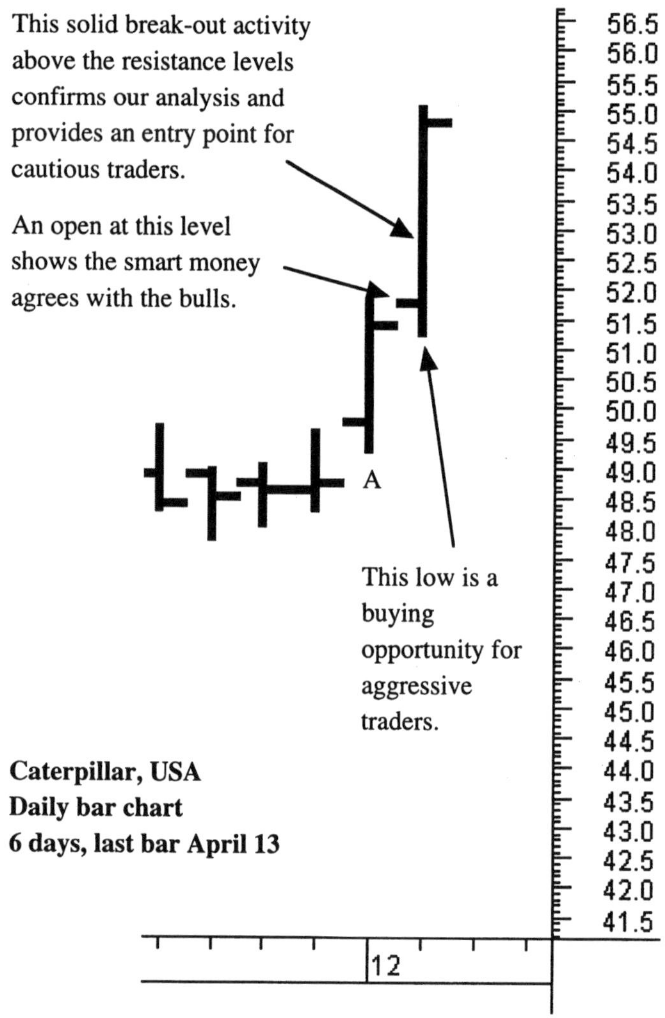

Every tool we use at this level is designed to understand the immediate emotional activity of the stock. We want the most favorable entry or exit point.

Our objective is a favorable entry just above the resistance line. The price bar marked A is the most recent bar in Figure 4.2. Caterpillar opens at yesterday's high and despite the slight fall, is quickly driven higher with buying pressure. The volume figures confirm this. Can we get the lowest price for the day? We have a poor chance because our analysis suggests this stock is moving upwards. We take advantage of any price weakness with confidence. Even the cautious trader reaches out for stock at $52 or $53 because the price activity on the day confirms their analysis of an upwards movement.

An extended view of Caterpillar performance in Figure 4.7 shows how real-time analysis was matched by future price activity. The levels and notations are the same as those in Figure 4.2. Traders who did better than the target $61 made good use of depth of market information available from the Internet and we look at this in more detail in Chapter 15.

Proposed trading tactics are modified to take advantage of the current emotional activity of the stock. The information contained in the last bar of the Caterpillar chart confirms our understanding of the emotional character of the stock giving us the confidence to leave the buy order in place.

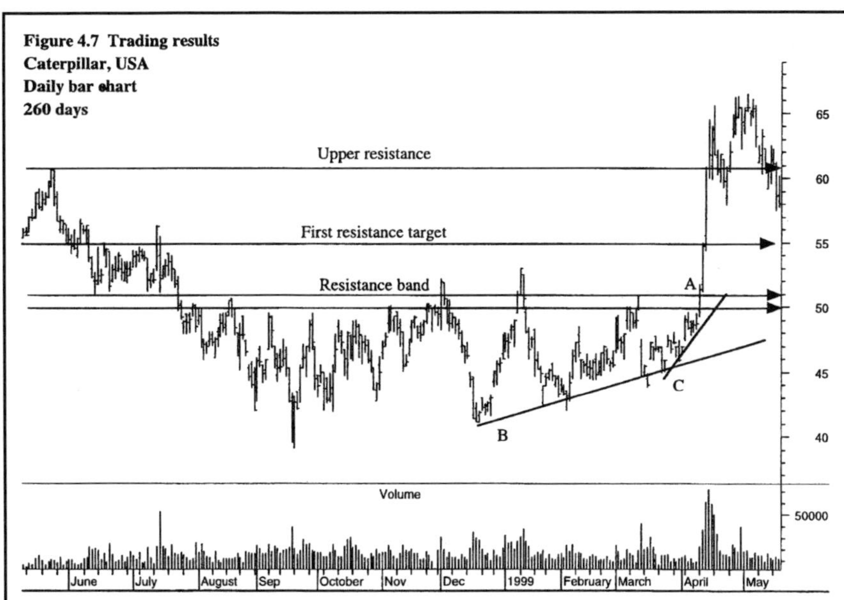

Figure 4.7 Trading results
Caterpillar, USA
Daily bar chart
260 days

CHOOSE YOUR TIME

Most traders start with a daily chart and this sets the focus for our search for trading opportunities. We want behavior consistent with character. The identification techniques discussed in the next section are all based on 260 days of daily chart information.

If your trading approach is based on the character of the stock, weekly charts form the primary basis of your search for trading opportunities. Intraday traders use the daily chart and a real-time data feed to understand the emotional activity of the market crowd mapped by current price activity. Your choice — character, behavior or emotional activity — decides the type of trading strategies you use, and the range of applicable trading tactics.

The choice of time frame is a personal one, but please choose one consistently. When particular trading approaches are suggested by the behavior of the stock a quick check against the characteristic of the stock over different time frames will confirm if the proposed trading approach is appropriate and realistic, or unachievable. We aim to trade in the direction of the prevailing trend by taking advantage of favorable price behavior to make the best entry, or exit, possible given the balance of probabilities.

Our objective is to extract only the best trading opportunities — theoretical, potential and actual — from our market data. For many reasons, what looks good at first glance can prove to be impractical after further study. The next section looks at some ways to separate fool's gold from the real metal and ways to read the assay results.

Prospectors have won gold nuggets with shovels, gold dust with pans, and gold grains with California cradles. We win trading gold by confirming the size and shape of each trading opportunity across multiple time bites. Equipped with this knowledge we know more than our competitors about the market landscape, the lay of the land, the way our 'nuggets' are formed and how they hide. We join the gold rush with a better chance of survival.

Part II

PROSPECTING FOR TRADES

5

SEARCHING FOR LOVE AT FIRST PROFIT

When the gold rush starts thousands flock to the fields hoping to strike it rich. From the Comstock lode in California in the 19th century and Tennant Creek in Australia in the 1930s, to modern-day rushes in the far north of Canada, or the jungles of equatorial Asia, the scene is the same. Armed with everything from spades and metal detectors, steel panning dishes and makeshift cradles to reverse circulating and rotary air blast drill rigs, the hordes rip apart the landscape. Every patch of country within pegging distance of any find is considered prospective. However, digging just anywhere does not bring results so the best prospectors spot the high-probability areas.

Over geological time, nuggets of gold are broken from the surrounding quartz matrix and tumbled along stream beds creating alluvial fields. Armed with a single bit of information — gold is one of the heaviest metals — experienced prospectors select a pile of river sediment, from just the right spot. Inexperienced diggers indiscriminately mine the same ground for profit and find nothing. The difference is not due to luck but to systematic searching for preferred characteristics. The shape of the stream indicates areas of better probability — the shape of market data does the same.

Traders mine market data, searching systematically for chosen characteristics. Although bulges figured prominently in the previous chapters, the weight of the balance of probability is shown on charts in several different patterns. The most significant of these is the trend line, closely followed by its cousins, the family of triangles. Other indicators, calculated from price data, are designed to show when price action moves away from the range of more probable outcomes and towards another set. Oscillator-style indicators rely on oversold or overbought conditions to signal this shift in balance.

The security we want looks good on the chart. This is the first step in selecting the most promising ground. The sorting process can be simple, or it can be complex, but in each case our objective is to identify those opportunities where the balance of probability favors an entry. This can range from spotting a break-out from a downwards trend to finding the best entry point in an established trend. The search focus is primarily on the entry. Once suspected nuggets are selected we clean them up and test them for quality. These processes, particularly with the eyeball search approach, are often intertwined, but for this section we will try to separate them as we look at some search methods and develop some lists.

START DIGGING

Some people claim that the search is so exciting because they don't know what they are looking for. These people are not successful traders. You must know what you are looking for, and in digging through market data there are five necessary steps, ranging from identifying the trade, analysing it and subjecting it to financial analysis, to assessing the potential trade against market conditions and managing the open position until the trade exit. Each step produces a list, each one progressively smaller than before. We will build, use and refine these lists throughout the remainder of this book. Briefly, the first three screening grids in this digging expedition include:

- The size of your trading capital. You cannot trade every opportunity, so you are financially limited.
- The decision you make about the amount of data you include in your initial search. It could be the entire market, or just a market segment.
- Trading style. This rules out some trading approaches in favor of others.

Even if you specialize in a single market segment — Internet stocks, the top 100 banks and property developers — the amount of information available over even just a few years is formidable. This is more so if you have the entire market available to you. And more data are added every day. Miss a few days of data collection and the charts change dramatically — mining the data heap will overwhelm you.

Splitting this heap into a smaller pile is an obvious first step and in taking it you are assisted by a lack of trading capital. You do not have the capital to trade every trading opportunity although this does not prevent some from attempting this feat. Just arbitrarily creating a smaller pile is a waste of time unless you have a system to separate the nuggets from the heap.

Scanning the database to extract trading opportunities aims to build a pile small enough to reasonably handle in a day, and still leave time for trading. The size of the pile, or list, will depend on your analysis skills and the charting software. Programs such as Metastock supply tools to quickly analyze data. We look at how these are used later because these tools are of little use unless you know what you are looking for.

Having a clear idea of what we want to find — a gold nugget — makes our search more efficient. What we are looking for — a heavy metal — will determine exactly how we look. We want to find a trading opportunity so we look for signs showing the balance of probability.

The first database scan aims to weed out stocks not meeting our criteria. The technical trader uses different criteria from the more fundamentally, or financially, based trader. Most traders combine the two styles, but with a greater preference for one. The efficiency of your searching tools should match the size of your database and your style of trading. A bigger shovel will not help if you have no other objective beyond making a profit. Like the inexperienced 'greenhorn' in the river bed, you will find less.

The first search develops a list, or perhaps several lists. These are the stocks that command your closer attention. Later we will look at how the trader puts these under the microscope using a range of indicators and techniques, but for the moment we want to take the first steps in reducing our growing heap of market data to a manageable size.

GETTING COMFORTABLE WITH STYLE

Every trader feels more comfortable with some trades than with others. Some prefer secure trades based on support and resistance bands. Others feel more comfortable trading with long-term trends, while another group takes early positions in the anticipation of a break-out.

Which trading style is comfortable for you depends very much on your trading personality. If the trading style is inconsistent with this, with your overall financial situation, or with lifestyle constraints, then you set yourself up for failure. Good traders are not only in tune with the market, they are in tune with trading opportunities matching their personality and lifestyle. For example, I would find it very difficult to day trade and to write books about trading. As a position trader I have this time.

A person who is more at home with making and taking decisions based on considerable analysis is unlikely to be a successful day trader where rapid decisions are made based on hunches, experience and a feeling for the precise mood of the market at that instant. This sounds so obvious we expect only a few people to fall into this trap, yet the Internet day trading boom shows how successful the trap can be. In fact, many people reach for the money before considering if it is consistent with their style. The goldfields are dotted with inexperienced 'greenhorns' wielding expensive metal detectors.

In a broad sense you have three initial choices for your approach to the market. Matching personal style with choice will determine how you approach the scanning process. The choices are to:

- chase the pot of gold
- use one trading technique applied to multiple market sectors
- master one market sector and look for multiple opportunities using many trading techniques.

THE POT OF GOLD

Chasing the pot of gold is exciting, fast-moving, and most often unsuccessful. Just as a few lottery winners encourage the losers to try again, the few pot-of-gold Internet day-trading successes sometimes receive enough publicity to make it appear this is the rule, rather than the exception.

This approach aims to identify fast-moving stocks with rapidly increasing prices. Jumping on board requires good judgment, perfect timing and nerves of steel. Experienced traders make this approach work very well. By trading with leverage supplied by options, futures or some other derivative instrument, small movements in the underlying stock are multiplied into significant gains.

Inexperienced traders have less success. Their buying helps to drive prices higher. Often they buy from experienced sellers who are selling into strength. The 'blow-off' chart pattern, Figure 5.1, shows this activity. The experienced trader takes it as a warning, while the inexperienced trader sees it as an opportunity.

Chasing the pot of gold is a legitimate trading approach, and later we will look at some specific techniques used in this trading approach.

ONE TECHNIQUE, MANY MARKETS

The second option uses just one, or perhaps two, trading approaches. The entire market is searched for stocks fitting the criteria. The initial search might uncover 40 opportunities, and the next, based on the second technique, might uncover 40 more. The mass of market data is quickly sorted into a smaller pile with a preliminary list of 80 stocks.

The limits of this approach for private traders are reached quickly. Use three or four preferred trading approaches, and you could end up with 100 stocks or more on the preliminary list.

Some traders overcome this disadvantage and look for comparatively rare combinations of market circumstances. When these occur they commit large sums confident these uncommon circumstances will yield predictable results. Some of the techniques described by Peter Lynch in *One up on Wall Street* and attributed to

Figure 5.1 Blow-off top
Walt Disney, USA
Daily bar chart with volume

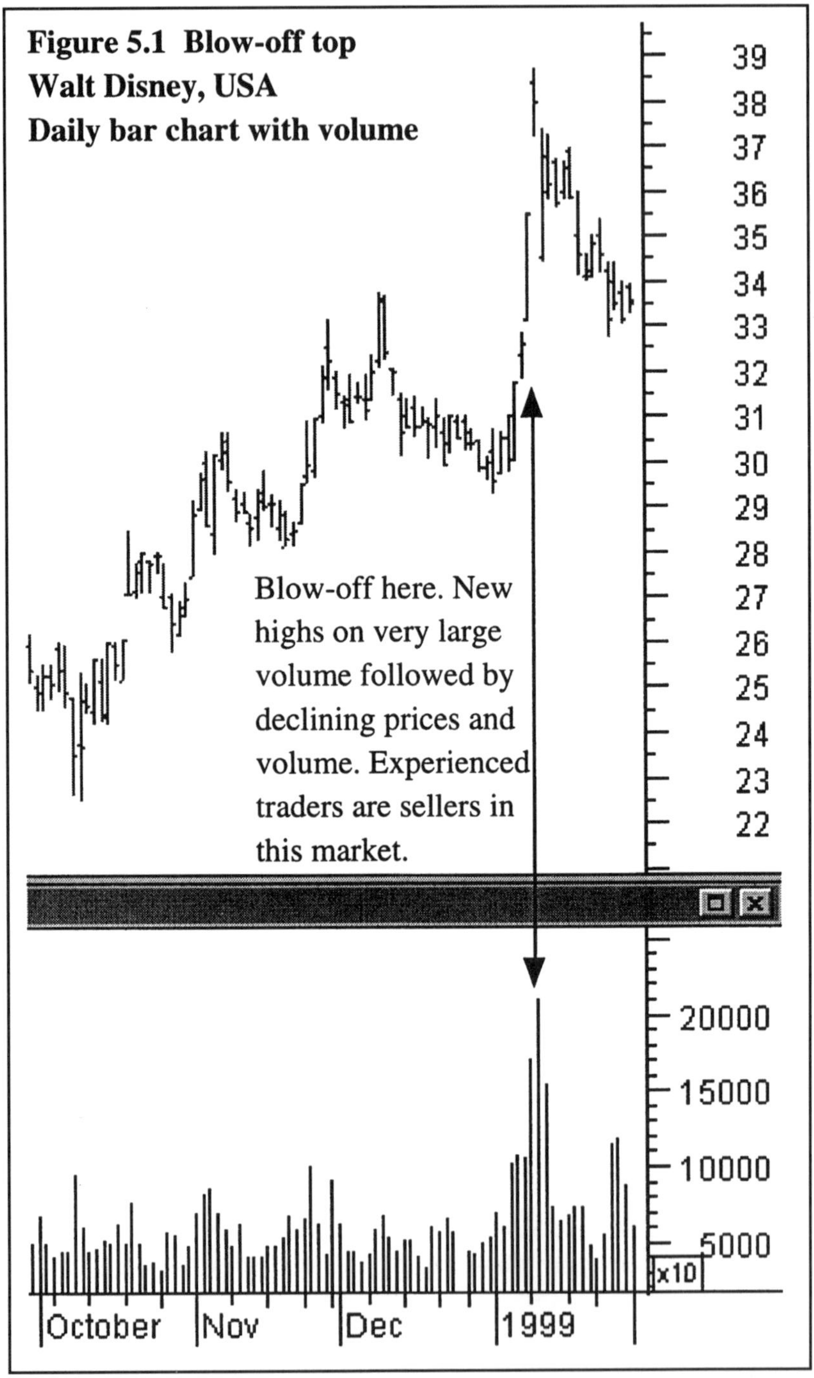

Warren Buffett in *The Warren Buffett Way* by Robert Hagstrom are based on this type of thinking. The trader is out of the market for extended periods, but when he takes a position the returns are large enough to compensate for this time out of the market.

Those who look for trading opportunities across the entire market have to be more selective in their preferred trading approaches to avoid being overwhelmed. Sometimes the market helps by making certain trading strategies less useful. The trading techniques used in a bull market are not suited to a bear market, or to a market moving sideways in a consolidation band.

Comfort also helps the selection. Trading should be a comfortable, relaxed and stress-free occupation. Often it is not because the trader uses methods that do not suit his personality, risk profile or pocket. Finding a trading method compatible with a good night's sleep also reduces the workload of data analysis.

No matter which approach you use the only effective way to cover the entire market is to filter it through a very small number of criteria. The first search list should be small enough to be manageable, and small enough to permit further analysis in sufficient time for positions to be taken today in the market if required.

Identifying a profitable trading opportunity based on yesterday's data is good. Finding it too late to be able to buy the stock at the preferred price is annoying. Watching the stock price move exactly as you thought it would — but without you on board — is vastly unsatisfying.

MORE TRADES IN ONE MARKET

The third option concentrates on one market sector and searches for a variety of trading opportunities.

How you define the sector is not important. It might be on the basis of size — the top 100 — on the basis of industry — E-commerce and banking — on the basis of volatility — stocks with a standard deviation or beta value greater than one — or just your collection of personal favorites and brokerage recommendations. Here the trader makes a prior choice to physically limit the amount of data analyzed and ignore other trading opportunities.

In return he expects to have more time to consider many more trading approaches and to act on this analysis.

By using this approach we can scan for stocks meeting a variety of conditions consistent with a variety of trading approaches. This might include stocks approaching break-out conditions, those hovering near support areas, and those showing unusual price and volume relationships. It does not matter if the we end up with four or five lists. Each list is short because it is drawn from a limited market selection. Invariably, there will be duplicates, so the final combined list is small enough to examine in detail and to apply the results during the current trading day.

More importantly, by limiting our activities to a smaller database we are able to start with the most powerful search method of all — the eye. A chart has one overwhelming advantage — the price relationships are easily comprehended. Instead of a jumble of figures we see a chart that is readily understood at an intuitive level. The trader uses this advantage when eyeballing a chart.

The eye has limits, usually imposed by its owner: fatigue and speed. This powerful search technique cannot be applied to hundreds of charts on a regular basis. It is best suited to a small number of stocks, selected and scanned regularly.

LISTS OF SHOPPING LISTS

We make shopping lists, or sort and reduce market data into smaller piles, so we can focus on the main task without being distracted. Supermarkets have specialists designing shelf layouts to distract us from our shopping list. They are often successful, but nowhere near as successful as the market with its daily specials.

The market distracts easily because scanning the database has one major disadvantage — the shopping list must be prepared freshly each day. Each scan, search or Metastock exploration usually compares the current day's data with previous data. Many software packages allow you to set the parameter dates for the search.

If you do not scan for two days, past trading opportunities will not always be identified in today's search. Trade situations develop and mature over a period and to miss the development of critical points does have an impact on trading. Playing catch-up is no substitute for timeliness; finding the perfect daily special is no good four days after the event.

In developing your scanning routine, factor in the frequency of your searches and the impact this has on identifying the developing and newly emerging trading situations. If you use a weekly shopping list then accept that you miss the daily specials. This does not matter if you did not intend to shop for them. It does matter if your trading techniques rely on daily specials.

Traders must chop market data down to size in a consistent way. By reducing the analysis load to a manageable level we quickly concentrate on only the most exciting and most promising trades showing a better probability of success. Our time frame does not free us from this task. The day trader selects candidates based on end-of-day data. When trading in real time he must know in advance which stocks are gold and which are dross.

Trading success is reached by many different routes, but it helps to follow a consistent path when it comes to identifying trading opportunities. Before focusing on trades with the best probability, narrow the field using any of the four search options covered in the following chapters along with examples.

The options include eyeball, relationship, performance and accounting searches. This list is not an exhaustive or in-depth survey of the search patterns available. It is an introduction to each of the major groups of techniques available so you can more quickly move in the direction that suits your trading style.

Charting software tempts with built-in search and exploration parameters. Metastock users have a small default list of search criteria. Users can adjust, modify and add to these starting lists but searches are more effective if you are aware of what you are measuring with each indicator. The following chapters discuss these directions. Remember, our objective is to find the best opportunities quickly so we have time to assess them and to take action before trading closes for the day.

Finding the nuggets is the first step and before we move off into an unfamiliar financial landscape we consider two paths leading to the mother lode.

6

NO ACCOUNTING FOR ALL TASTES

Copies of the Berkshire Hathaway annual report are snapped up by brokers, private investors and financial commentators as soon as they are released. Warren Buffett, arguably currently among the world's most successful fund managers, uses a fundamental approach and he makes no secret of his methods. Like the renowned Benjamin Graham, on whose style he bases his own, Buffett's approach is succinct: find good companies that are undervalued and buy them. Janet Lowe looks more closely at Benjamin Graham's investment strategies in *Value Investing Made Easy*. Robert Hagstrom brings the approach up-to-date with *The Warren Buffett Way*, while *Buffettology* provides a different perspective to these approaches. Modern treatments of these approaches include *Security Analysis on Wall Street*.

It is this approach, and variants, that dominate the broking industry. Most brokers specialize in buying advice based on a close analysis of fundamental market factors in industry sectors, or the balance sheet of individual companies. Many private traders pit their accounting skills against those of the brokers and the company accountants looking for the discrepancies in valuation. If we use this approach we aim to select a few trading — not investment — candidates from the broad mass of market data.

We suggested in the previous section that no matter how you make your initial stock selection, when it comes to actually buying the stock, and later selling it, the bar chart provides you with invaluable information not obtainable elsewhere. In the following chapters we look more closely at ways to use this information to delve into the mass of market data and locate the best nuggets of trading opportunity.

In this chapter we stand, ready to begin our jungle prospecting expedition, on the edge of an escarpment looking out over the financial landscape below. Like every prospector we hope to see gold-bearing country where we can strike it rich, so we will look for well-worn tracks through the jungle trees. There are two paths leading down into the valley and we will take my preferred path in later chapters.

First, let us consider the choice in paths. Like many others, I place comparatively little weight on the fundamental bookkeeping style of analysis in my trading decisions. It is not my intention to set up a straw-like approach called fundamental accounting analysis only to knock it down. This path does have problems and I choose to highlight these because they confirm my choice of trading approach. As a serious trader you are entitled to understand why I choose to take one trading path rather than another, particularly as this book concentrates on that path alone. In later chapters we explore the dangers and shortcomings of the path I prefer.

Many fundamental traders use charts to back up their analysis, and for market timing. Many technical analysts combine vital fundamental information with chart signals. Jack Schwager, the US futures trader, considers this in two books: *Schwager on Futures: Fundamental Analysis* and *Schwager on Futures: Technical Analysis*. Although in this book we treat this as two distinct paths many traders successfully combine these approaches. Your approach will be an individual blend drawn from each.

Poised on the edge of the escarpment, this chapter provides a signposted summary introduction to the other path. There are many writers more qualified than myself to guide you fully down this path should you decide to follow it. Finding the nuggets using this style of search employs different techniques but, like the technical search methods covered in detail in the following chapters, the paths converge where the nuggets are found. Both have the same objective — to find the best trading opportunities in the shortest possible time, and quickly enough, to be able to buy them before they go up too far or too fast.

FINANCIAL CAMOUFLAGE

For those taking the fundamental accounting path the primary search tool is balance sheet analysis powered by an understanding of market fundamentals and company fundamentals. The search light is provided by insider, or timely, knowledge and aims to capture 'Sound companies that are undervalued'.

Fundamentally sound is a concept torn in three directions.

First, a company requires results to impress the market and existing shareholders. This reflects the core business of the company and a sound bottom line has advantages. Various accounting conventions make this concept more fluid than is comfortable, sometimes delivering unbelievable results. In recent years the cosy accounting practices of many Asian companies have exposed investors to greater than expected risk.

Cosy accounting is not just a foreign term. Too frequently the Wall Street practice of 'managed earnings' involves improper revenue recognition, the abuse of 'materiality', unjustified restructuring charges and accounting artifices such as cookie-jar reserves. They stretch General Agreement on Accounting Principles (GAAP) guidelines and although Securities Exchange Commission chairman Arthur Levitt regards them as very often the equivalent of fraud it has not stopped the widespread use of these reporting practices.

When global competitors merge, profits sometimes shrink as a consequence of new accounting requirements. In some cases the profit becomes a loss. Even within countries changes to the way company results are reported have a dramatic impact. Australian company QBE Insurance was so annoyed with the new Australian reporting standard that for a time it filed two separate financial reports to the Australian Stock Exchange. Using the official accounting standard QBE profits rose in one financial year by 78.5 percent. Using the Directors' preferred accounting standard, profits for the same period rose by only 15.1 percent. It is difficult to decide which report is fundamentally correct.

A brokerage cottage industry is built around correctly interpreting the results delivered by accounting conventions. The shift towards a revised standard on equity accounting based on the International Accounting Standards Committee (IASC) will change some annual multi-national and international company results by millions of dollars. The Securities Exchange Commission responsible for the regulation of American markets will not accept IASC reporting, which it views as inferior to the GAAP. The same company listed in the United States and in Europe may report radically different balance sheets.

When big business and regulators cannot agree on the correct standard the small trader faces a huge task in cutting through a company financial report to find the 'real' fundamentals.

Second, the concept is further torn as the company would prefer that public results did not give away any competitive advantage. Commercially sensitive information is legitimately concealed in balance sheets, company reports and newspaper briefings. Continuous disclosure and conference call briefings do not mean all is revealed. One of the great brokerage games of hide and seek is built around the search for this information before the rest of the market hears of it. Rumors, rumors of rumors and early news breaks are the lifeblood of this game.

TAXING TIMES

Third, and most significantly, the fundamental concept is distorted by taxation requirements. The best financial results are achieved when the costs of production are reduced. Publicly, this focuses on labor costs, but privately taxation is just as significant. Balance sheet items are shifted where possible to minimize taxation impacts.

Personally, most of us have an ambiguous relationship with the IRS and the tax department. You think they want more than their fair share and they think you understate taxable income. This personal battle has more tricks and turns than a barrel full of monkeys.

On a corporate level the battle is fought by lawyers and backed by the best of the big six accounting firms because company accounts correctly presented reduce tax liabilities. When incorrectly presented, the same financial information can create a massive tax bill. The battle on the tax front contributes to bottom-line profits no less significantly than the battle for customer loyalty, increases in labor productivity and commodity price or currency fluctuations.

It is too easy to dismiss the significance of this factor, but those raising capital in the United States, for instance, must prepare financial information under GAAP accounting rules and the impact is significant. When Daimler-Benz agreed to recalculate its 1993 profit according to GAAP rules, the DM615 million profit under German accounting rules became a loss of DM1,839 million. Naturally, national statutory company accounts tend to exploit the most advantageous tax strategy so the same company may be an attractive proposition in some environments and a dog in others. Tax is a production cost and like all costs, corporations legitimately seek to reduce them wherever possible.

From our position on the escarpment, when we survey the landscape this creates a significant problem because corporations do not keep two sets of books. If we could see the set showing true profit as distinct from the set prepared with taxation in mind, we would make better decisions about the fundamentals of the company. Instead, as outsiders we try to unravel the reasoning behind the structuring of specific company transactions into taxable, or non-taxable, categories. We try to second-guess the auditors, the accountants and the taxation official. Some of us, and some brokerage analysts, do this very well and these conclusions can provide a short-cut in our market search. Most of us do not have and cannot reasonably expect to acquire these skills.

Without a guide the financial landscape is covered in an accounting jungle hiding the mountains and valleys. Somewhere the jungle hides a massively wealthy Porgera gold deposit, or equally, a frightening financial hole in the ground like the Bre-X mining company collapse. *How to Read a Financial Report: Wringing Vital Signs Out of the Numbers* and similar other books will help you hack your way through the accounting jungle. They are the first field guide new explorers should carry along with their metal detector.

DO IT YOURSELF RATIOS

With these caveats in mind we turn to an overview of fundamental search material. This 'metal detector' uses financial ratio information retrieved from columns of financial newspapers and market reports on Internet sites. Some of the nuggets are found in the following six ratios.

- **Price/NTA**

  By comparing price and asset backing per share the ratio gives an indication of whether the shares are trading at a premium or at a discount. The theoretical calculated value of the company's tangible assets are divided by the number of shares on issue. The NTA per share figure is divided by the current share price and expressed as a price to NTA value. A figure of one means the company is valued in line with its net tangible assets. If price/NTA is greater than one the share trades at a premium and at a discount if the figure is less than one.

  The search engine, or 'metal detector', starts to screech when shares trading at a price/NTA discount are uncovered.

- **Debt/equity**

  This compares the level of company debt with ordinary shareholders' equity, net of any intangibles. A company with $4 million in debt and $2 million of shareholders' funds has a debt/equity ratio of 200 percent.

  Lower debt/equity ratios are not always better as companies making good use of borrowed funds for expansion can offer attractive trading opportunities. Generally, lower debt/equity readings are noted by our 'metal detector'.

- **Return on shareholders' funds**

  Return on shareholders' funds is measured in cents per share and represents the amount of profit made, equivalent to each share on issue. This ratio is also called an earnings per share or return on equity.

As a way of measuring current performance this is often listed as Current RSF and Latest Year RSF. The current period includes the latest financial reports while the latest year is the final figure for the last financial year.

Stocks showing an increase in Current RSF register on our 'metal detector'.

- **Dividend and dividend yield**

  This is a simple rate of return calculation from dividend payments. It is calculated by dividing the rolling yearly dividend per share by the share price and expressing the result as a percentage.

  Dividends per share is the historical rate of dividends paid per ordinary share. Results are shown as Current Final and taken from interim reports. Previous Year results are taken from the last full financial year.

  Bigger is usually considered better and these bumps are noted in our search.

- **EBIT**

  This is earning before interest and tax and when divided by the figure for sales we have an EBIT margin. This shows the proportion of sales contributing to company profit. Appropriate margins vary across industry groups so we must fine-tune our 'metal detector' for each sector.

  EBIT is also used to calculate the company's ability to generate profits from its assets. As with the EBIT margin, generally higher is better, but our 'metal detector' should be tuned to the general level applicable to each industry group.

- **Current and quick ratio**

  The current ratio measures the theoretical ability of the company to repay short-term debt. A ratio of less than one suggests the company may have difficulty so again bigger is generally better. The same outcomes apply to the quick ratio, but this is calculated by dividing current assets less inventories, by current liabilities.

These ratios, and a number of others, are derived from the relationship between market price and the internal financial activity of the business as reported to the Exchange or as inferred through other accounting announcements. Many of these broadly form the basics of a capital asset pricing model (CAPM) approach. *Modern Portfolio Theory and Investment* is an introduction to the intricacies of the CAPM approach. Readers looking for greater detail about this style of analysis for individual stocks can turn to *Investments: Analysis and Management*.

You might decide the CAPM approach does clear the jungle. If so, use the analysis methods discussed in detail in the books mentioned above, but remember when the time comes to make your buying decision, and later the selling decision, that the bar chart provides you with invaluable information unobtainable anywhere else.

BALANCING ACTS

Reading a balance sheet has more twists and turns than a modern thriller and we do not intend to re-invent this particular plot. The financial sleuth uses *How to Read a Financial Report: Wringing Vital Signs Out of the Numbers* as a detective's bible.

The balance sheet is a snapshot of the company's finances at a single point in time, typically the end of the financial year. The profit and loss statement covers a selected period, a quarter, a half year, or a financial year, and shows how profitably it has operated in the period. In a broad sense, the profit and loss report tells us if the company has made money in the last six months, while the balance sheet lets us know if it still has a lot of debt left to service, thus requiring high profitability to continue. The cash flow statement is a summary of cash received and paid out by the company.

Some thriller-style balance sheets use many twists and turns developed in the 1980s, including:

- Improper revenue recognition.
- The abuse of 'materiality'.
- Unjustified restructuring charges.
- The capitalization of interest on projects of uncertain value when completed.
- The valuation of share holdings in associated companies at market value when the share prices of those companies is influenced by the market activities of other associates.
- Unrealistic valuation of assets, particularly property, so book value is poorly related to market value.
- Using 'equity' accounting to inflate profit figures when little of the 'equity-accounted profit' is actually available to the company.

The balance sheet search for concealed golden opportunities is painstaking, time consuming and, for those like Warren Buffett and Peter Lynch, ultimately very profitable. In addition to the books mentioned above, *The Economist Guide to Business Numeracy* and *Numbers Guide: The Essentials of Business Numeracy* are useful references for those who put the latest thriller to one side in favor of a night with company reports. The topic is a hardy perennial in investment magazines and in the financial pages, so I do not intend to duplicate the excellent work done by others.

Compared to the demands of trading, these balance sheet and ratio searches are leisurely pursuits and ideally suited to an investing approach that does not place as much emphasis on timing market entries for short- and intermediate-term trades. Despite this investment emphasis, many traders are looking to link CAPM-style analysis with trading tactics. They want to trade the best stocks rather than the best trades so our purpose is to find the most efficient means to search through masses of market data to identify the best stocks. Some affordable software packages work with the CAPM and balance sheet approach.

SOFTWARE BLOODHOUNDS

This idea of finding undervalued stocks and staying with them until they sell at their true value, or perhaps even beyond, is a constant theme of established investment advice. The financial relationships are old. What is new is the development of extensive databases and the software to access them. This not only makes the search easier and cheaper, it puts the tools into the hands of clients, rather than advisors, and gives an advantage to traders, rather than brokers.

Indeed some software packages, such as the most recent version of Windows on Wall Street, use these factors in scanning stocks.

Some of these packages are close to a 'gray box'. Buy and sell signals are generated automatically, but unlike a black box trading system, the relationships between each of the factors is clearly explained. Additionally, the user is given limited opportunity to manipulate the parameters. The user is presented with results determined by the software but he must decide whether to buy the recommended stock or to perform further toolbox technical analysis.

We believe the recommendations made by such software trading programs need to be further analyzed against the specific financial and trading objectives of the user. The ways to do this are discussed more fully in Part III.

Windows on Wall Street, and similar programs, are toolboxes. The user manipulates the parameters to suit his favorite ideas; and the software scans, sorts and ranks the data according to these user-defined criteria. They are a more powerful analysis package for those who wish to combine chart, technical and fundamental analysis.

However, there is a major shortcoming. Both these software packages, and others operating in the same way, require more than just a data stream that provides open, high, low, close, volume and perhaps open interest information. The data provider must also supply the basic information necessary for the calculation of PE ratios, NTA, EBIT and so on. Emerging software packages in some countries are finding difficulty in obtaining this information in electronic format and private traders will have trouble accessing this relevant information for the entire market.

TAKING A DIFFERENT PATH

For many people involved with the market, this fundamental and accounting approach is the primary source of trading information. Our purpose here is to understand that if you use these factors as part of a trading decision, they need to be ranked and sorted in much the same way as other important price and volume data. This ranking will help to identify the better trading opportunities.

The significance and weighting you attach to each of these accounting factors will depend on your trading objectives. When you prioritize these to your satisfaction the search to create the initial list of trading opportunities is rapid and effective. Chapter 13 will show how to bring the trade to fruition using charting information and Chapter 14 will outline how to assess trades against our financial objectives.

From where we stand on the escarpment at the beginning of our journey there are two paths leading down into the valley. Although not mutually exclusive, most traders choose to take one path more closely than the other. If you decide to take the path outlined above then I cannot guide you, so please read the recommended guidebooks. The other path, my preferred one, follows R-plot, performance and eyeball signposts. This path will be explored more completely in the following chapters.

Both paths meet wherever gold is found. Readers taking the CAPM and associated paths should rejoin us in Chapter 11.

7

EYEBALL SEARCHES

The bulge of probability concept, shown in the grouping of number combinations based on a dice throw, was transferred to the support and resistance levels shown in the General Property Trust chart in Figure 3.1. This plot used a visual chart pattern to highlight probable entry and exit points. Identifying and understanding such patterns relies on eyeball recognition.

The eyeball search rests on simplicity and when completed, it presents a short list of the best trading candidates. A sample typical eyeball list with notes, drawn from the Singapore market, is shown in Figure 7.1. Everybody owns eyeball software and it is very powerful when used in conjunction with a computer screen.

Figure 7.1 Extract from an eyeball search of Singapore stocks with notes

	A	B
1	**Stock name**	**Comments**
2	Armstrong	Support 36 - Breakout?
3	Avimo	Support 2.20
4	Bonvest	Support 85 Resistance 1.20
5	C K Tang	Down slope triangle
6	Chuan Hup	Strong trend Buy 1.25 Target 1.55
7	City Dev	On support 9.30. Next 8.00
8	Comfort Corp	Trend break 89 Target 1.20
9	Gen May	Spike - informed buying?
10	Haw par	Channel trade 2.65 - 3.10
11	IFS	Breakout 1.00 target 1.70
12	Kepfels	Strong trend - buy weakness
13	Pacific Century	Up sloping triangle 6.50 target 8.00

The eyeball search is the simplest of all the search techniques and it must be used at some stage in the trading process. Those taking the entire market defer this eyeball search until the last steps in assessing trading opportunities. For them this is when the number of candidates is reduced enough to make an eyeball search time effective. Traders who rely on fundamental analysis eyeball the charts to select timing clues.

I choose to track a small segment of the market — 200 to 300 securities — so the eyeball search is always my starting point. It takes ten minutes to flip through these bar charts. With such a small number I manage to know each of them so I quickly skip those that have been out of contention for weeks.

Despite claims from the computer industry, the eyeball has not been replaced by a software replica. Pattern recognition software is improving and some traders use it to search their database and identify a multitude of patterns. Here the danger lies in the large jump between recognizing the pattern and building a causal link between past and future price activity.

SuperCharts software lets you 'paint' a series of bars to show other occurrences of the same pattern. It is a very powerful feature, but fails to establish any causal link between the pattern and future price action. Metastock contains a similar feature. We use other tests to prove the validity of the links. The computer helps but it cannot do these tests automatically. Use this type of pattern recognition software to supplement the eyeball scan by expanding the number of securities that are scanned quickly. The resulting list should be subjected to a further eyeball evaluation before moving on to other techniques.

THE EYES HAVE IT

What do you look for? The most powerful technical patterns are trend lines, support and resistance levels and the triangles they produce. They point the way to high probability outcomes. Some triangle patterns are much more likely to move up than down. These are the four basic pillars of technical analysis, and although they sound complex, they are usually easier to see than they are to describe. The chart examples used below are typical examples drawn from a variety of market sectors.

Recognizing any of these patterns is a judgment call. Recognition of the patterns is difficult to program in a mathematical sense. A trend line is a basic concept so software developers have grappled with mathematical descriptions. Many software packages feature automatic trend lines, but rarely do they look 'right' so most packages also allow you to draw them by hand.

Hand-plotted trend lines follow five construction rules:

- The line is placed along the lows of the price bars in a rising trend. An upwards trend is defined by higher lows each day. This is the price element we want to track, so the line goes underneath. If prices fall below this then the trend may change into a downwards trend.
  A falling trend is defined by the failure of prices to make new highs each day. We track this by placing the down trend line along the highs.
- The trend line starts with the extremes of the price bars — the high or the low. These extremes really count because a close beyond the extreme tells us the trend might be changing. This is an entry, or an exit, signal.
- The trend line starts at the very extreme high, or low. This is called a pivot point. The pivot point can only be determined retrospectively.
- The trend line should touch the maximum number of price bar extremes from the available choices. This means we do not exclude too many extremes, nor do we go for the maximum number of hits. We want to use the trend line as a trading signal, so we are interested in closes beyond the extremes of the existing trend because these give the best trading signals.
- The more often a trend line is hit by price extremes, but not broken, the more powerful the trend line signal. A trend line hit ten times, but not broken, is very strong. So when price does close beyond this it is a very strong trend change signal.

Later we do strictly apply these rules, but in the first eyeball scan we look for a general idea of the trend. The eyeball is still supreme and a search for these simple patterns filters out many unattractive trading prospects. The search is rapid, it is judgmental and by its nature it is approximate — limitations are willingly accepted in return for a small bundle of stocks that warrant much closer attention.

Finding these patterns does not require an advanced degree in mathematics. Good software speeds up the eyeball scan. Metastock users flip through charts by clicking the Next Security button. Starting with the first security in their database, experienced eyeballers spend three seconds or less on each chart searching for visual evidence to support intuitive conclusions about the nature of price activity. They look for a definite trend, a support or resistance level, and for obvious triangle formations. They navigate towards the balance of probability using weekly patterns to point the way. When behavior is consistent with character the probability of selected outcomes is enhanced.

BUILDING ON SUPPORT

Support and resistance offers significant information about the balance of probability as shown in Chapter 3. Remember support is formed when buying pressure consistently overcomes selling pressure at a particular price level. Resistance is created when selling pressure overwhelms buying. When prices reach the resistance level so much stock is on offer that buyers need not bid any higher. These levels show a consistent valuation over time.

To find these levels start with a weekly bar chart. Note where prices hit a level several times and rebound, and you find support or resistance. The chart of American retailer Sears Roebuck in Figure 7.2 shows a clearly defined support level at $39.00. This is a clear cut line, but more often it is a narrow area a few cents wide. This is not a triple bottom as the support line also defines price activity in previous years not shown on this chart extract. Point and figure charting is a very useful way of confirming support levels. This is discussed in more detail in my book *Share Trading* and *Study*

Figure 7.2 Finding support
Sears Roebuck, USA
Weekly bar chart

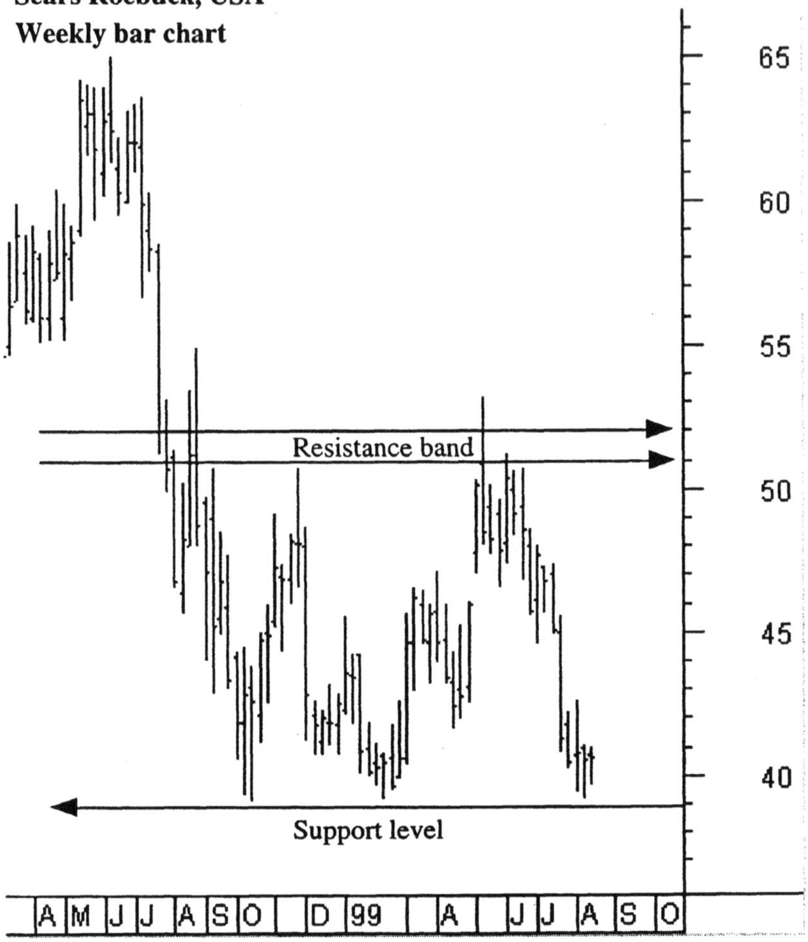

Helps in Point and Figure by Wheelan. For traders unsure of how to use point and figure, the weekly bar charts also show support and resistance fairly clearly.

In establishing these lines the key factor is the limit of the price bars. The lines are plotted with the cursor where price bars consistently finish, or start, their price moves. The line in Figure 7.2

is drawn just under the extremities of the down price moves from October 1998 to August 1999. On all charts in this chapter, for clarity, the line is drawn slightly below or above the actual level.

As Sears Roebuck comes up in our eyeball scan we note the support area of $39.00 on a scratch pad. Two additional observations are needed before adding these stocks to your preliminary list.

First, look for a nearby resistance line or level and write down its value. Sears Roebuck shows a resistance band at $51–52. This is a price target for any future rise and sets a return of around 31 percent.

In some stocks the support and resistance levels are very well defined. First Pacific listed in Hong Kong shows support at $6.60 and a resistance band around 7 percent above this at $7.10. A fall below $6.60 is arrested on the strong support level at $5.60.

A stock on support and moving sideways in a consolidation pattern offers few trading opportunities. When the trading band — the distance between support and resistance — is only a few ticks high, the trade is unprofitable. The upper trading band in Figure 7.3 shows almost a 7 percent gross return. The lower trading band offers an 18 percent return on a recovery from the support level 1 with resistance on the old support level 2.

We look for securities actively bouncing between support and resistance. We want consistent volume, price activity and enough room for a reasonable profit. We will build on these analysis steps in detail in later chapters. In this quick eyeball search all we want is confirmation of the resistance level. When confirmed, we add the security to our preliminary list.

If there is no easily defined resistance area then do not add the security to the list — unless it passes the second observation discussed below.

Figure 7.3 Using support and resistance
First Pacific, Hong Kong
Daily bar chart

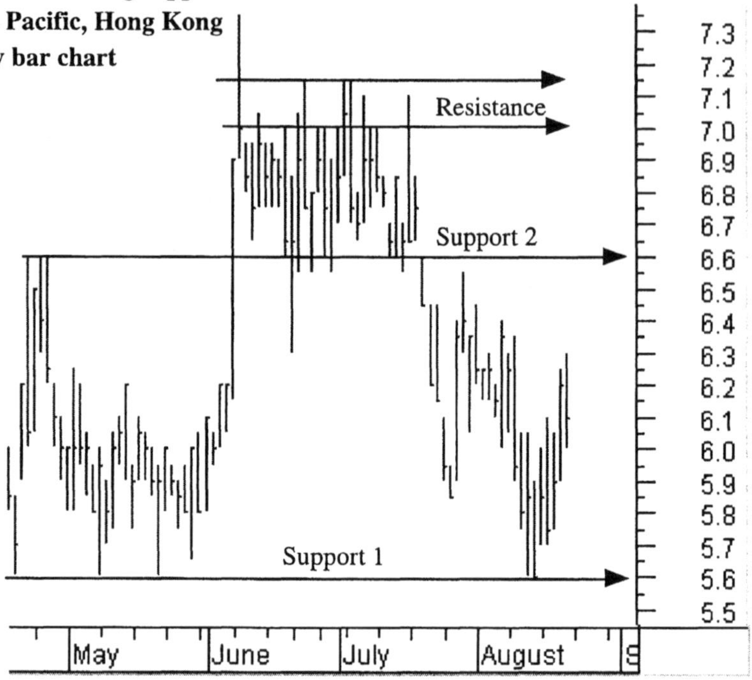

A BALANCE TIPPED

The second observation looks for the other primary chart pattern — the trend of a stock, which is like a support or resistance line, but tipped to one side. This shows the way the market consistently adjusts value over time. Establishing the broad trend is an intuitive process. The short-term trend shown in line A on the price chart for Eastman Kodak in Figure 7.4 is never in doubt. You might argue about the exact positioning of the line, but Eastman Kodak is in a down trend. The conclusion is inescapable.

We look for a close outside the trend line because this tells us a break-out may be taking place. Which side of the trend line we use depends on if we want to trade long or go short. In a down trend, a long position is taken on a break-out to the right-hand side of the trend. A short trader looks for breaks on the right-hand side of an up trend.

Figure 7.4 Finding trends and break-outs
Eastman Kodak, USA
Daily bar chart

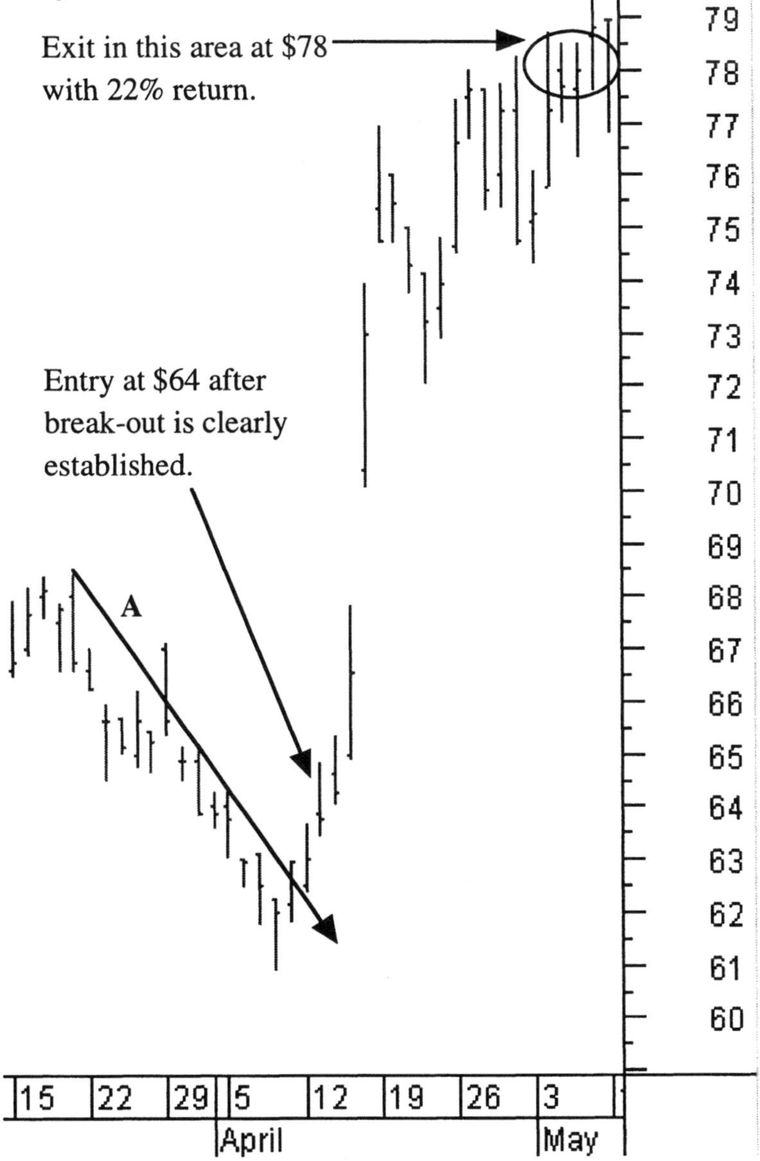

List only securities with definite trends and, at first glance, unequivocal break-outs. This simple and effective process selects only the best and the most obvious trading opportunities. This does not mean they are unprofitable. The obvious is often surprisingly profitable.

In April 1999 Eastman Kodak clearly changed direction. Spotting the break-out from the down trend is easy and we do not need to confuse the issue with high-tech charting techniques and advanced technical analysis. The obvious is often profitable, with an entry at $64 and an exit at $78 returning 22 percent over four weeks.

Later in the analysis process you might decide the stock has moved too far to make a good trade, or perhaps there is too little upside. These decisions are made at other steps in evaluating the trading opportunities. In this first search we build a broad list reliant on our judgment. If the trend is not immediately visible, then it is probably not there, or if it is, the trading opportunity is weaker.

Trend line break-outs sometimes last for several months, or years, as property and vehicle distribution company Cycle and Carriage indicates in Figure 7.5. Break-outs are often sudden and decisive. To catch them we must eyeball the charts regularly: two or three times a week. This is not a time-consuming chore when applied to a small list of stocks but it can be very profitable. The Cycle and Carriage trade returns a comfortable 200 percent. We develop the small list either by initially selecting a small market segment to follow, or by using the last list culled from a search of the entire market using the methods covered in the following chapters.

Trading is more of an art than a science. Trend lines can be defined mathematically, but if they don't look right we have little confidence in the signals they generate. This is not a magic picture where we squint and half focus our eyes to see the hidden image. If it is not there at first glance, it is not there. Do not lose sight of the objective of this first search. We want a short report listing all major trading opportunities.

Figure 7.5 Identifying simple trends and break-outs
Cycle and Carriage, Singapore
Weekly bar chart

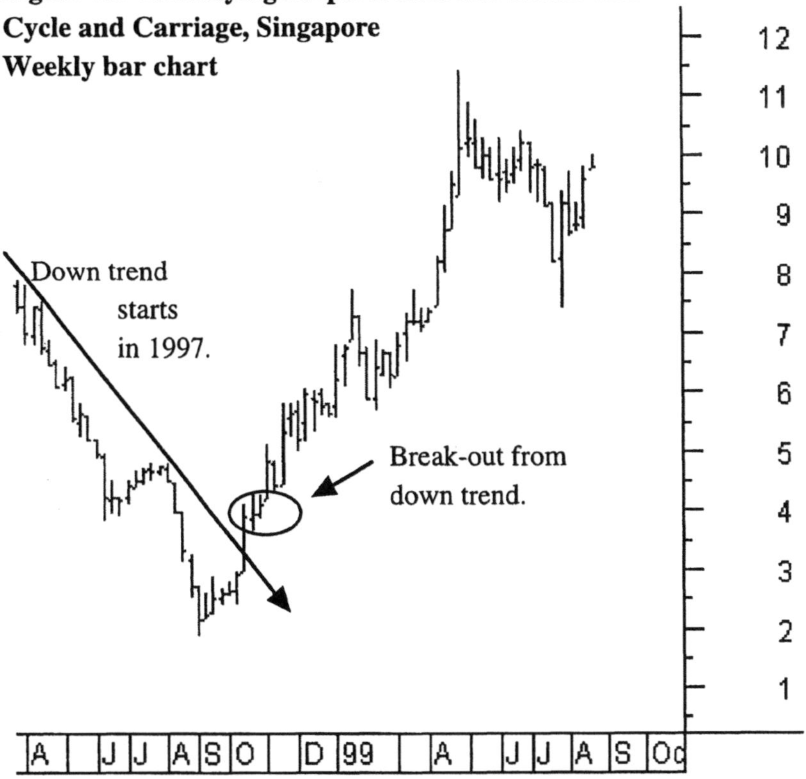

HOT TIPS

When sloping trend lines intersect horizontal support or resistance lines they form triangles. These are the focus of our second qualifying observation in the eyeball search for support and resistance levels. If the support level is well defined, and it forms the base of a triangle defined by the trend line, then add the security to your list.

Triangles are attractive because they suggest increased probability of price action and to a lesser extent, direction. The horizontal edge of the triangle is divided into thirds. On each of the remaining figures in this chapter these divisions are marked '+'.

The probability of strong price action is highest, and strongest, towards the end of the middle third of the triangle formation. Apple Computer in Figure 7.6 shows a successful break-out from this area of the triangle. Good break-outs often develop in the last third of the triangle but they have reduced probability of success. Price break-outs from the very tip of the triangle tend to be weaker. This is a judgment call and if your initial list overflows with trading possibilities the securities moving towards the very tip of a triangle pattern should be ignored.

Figure 7.6 Finding up-sloping triangles
Apple Computer, USA
Daily bar chart

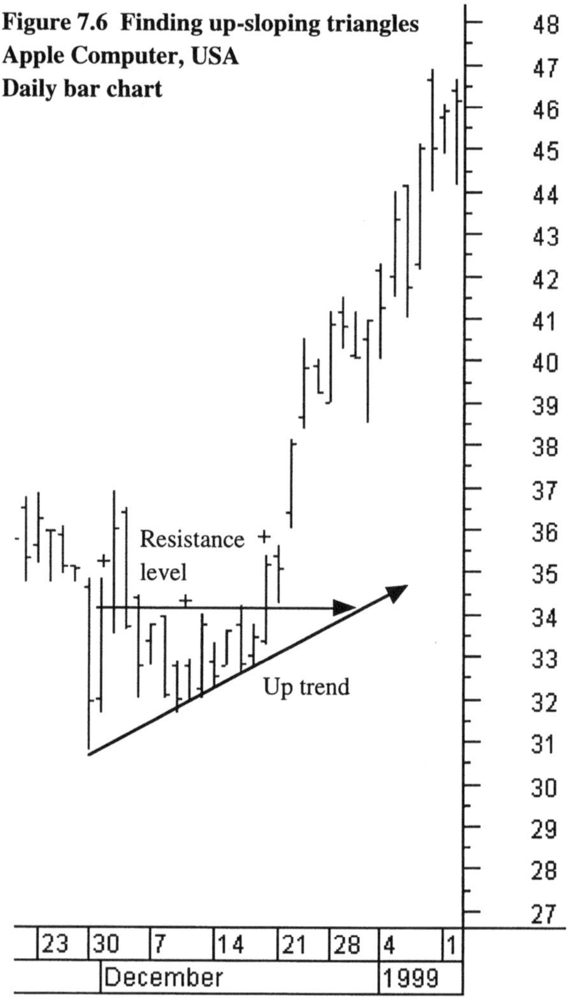

Two of the triangle patterns, up-sloping and down-sloping, feature a horizontal edge created by either support or resistance levels. Computer manufacturer Apple Computer shows the way the top of an up-sloping triangle is formed by the resistance line at $34. The sloping side of the triangle is formed by the trend line.

This is a simple visual pattern, and as it develops the full triangle is projected into space. Watch future price activity to confirm the projected triangle. The break-out from the Apple Computer

Figure 7.7 Finding triangles
Mintye, Malaysia. Weekly bar chart

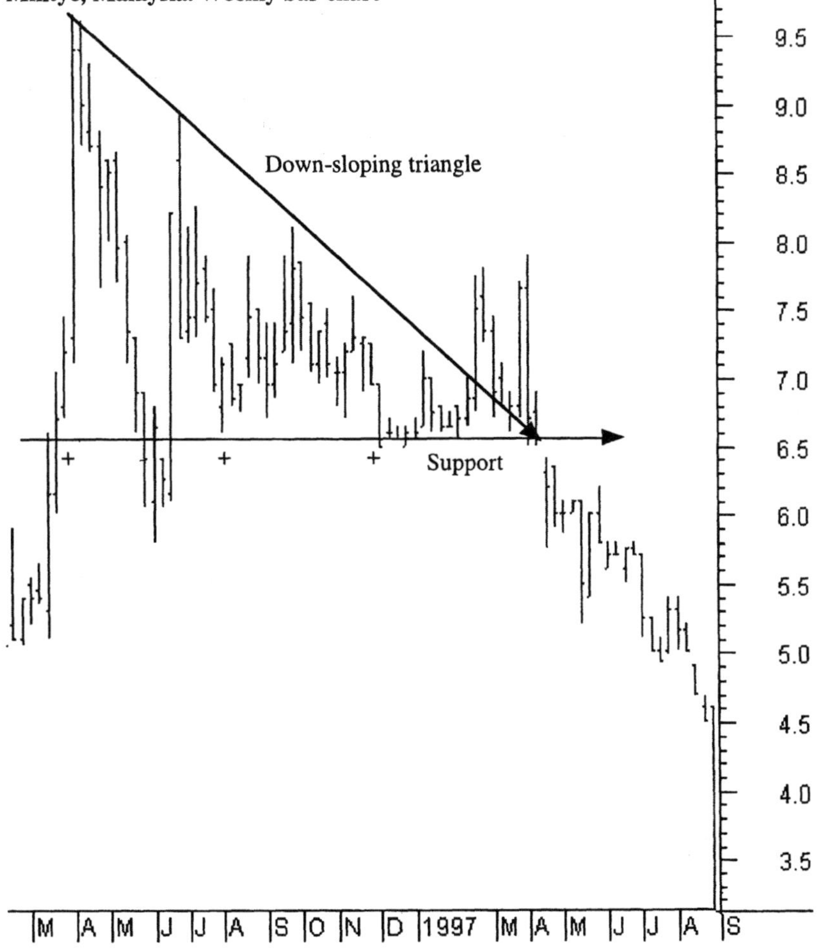

triangle in December is substantial with a 35 percent return. It takes place at the end of the middle section of the formation.

Automotive component manufacturer Mintye shows the full impact of a down-sloping triangle in a falling market. The break-out from the very tip of the triangle is weak. Once support is broken it is a long way to the bottom. An aggressive, and optimistic trader, may have taken a position at $7.00 on the break-out, but once the rally failed and dropped below support at $6.50 prudent traders abandoned the trade. This is not a perfectly formed triangle, but there is no mistaking the shape or the intention of the market. These chart patterns are a guide for traders and we ignore them at our peril.

Eyeballing these patterns built from the interaction of support and resistance lines, and trend lines, is not a complex process. As the patterns develop, the securities are noted on a scratch pad list for further analysis.

The third pattern, an equilateral or symmetrical triangle, forms when two contradictory trend lines meet. When it is almost as easy to draw an upward-sloping line as it is to draw a down-ward sloping trend line, we have contradictory trend lines. The pressure down seems to balance the pressure up, creating two converging trend lines. This indecision can extend for weeks, or in the case of Chevron shown in Figure 7.8, just a few days. The market is just as confused as we are about the direction of the trend and there are usually better trading opportunities available. The subsequent price direction is often closely related to the general direction of the market. The Dow took a tumble and Chevron took an 11 percent bath.

Triangles are hot tips because they flag an increase in price activity and indicate the most probable direction of future price activity. A matrix of probability and price direction in prevailing market conditions is shown in Figure 7.9. This is covered in more detail in Chapter 12. The trader fits this into the charting context, matching probability of action with probability of reaching price targets.

Figure 7.8 Finding equilateral triangles
Chevron Corp, USA
Daily bar chart

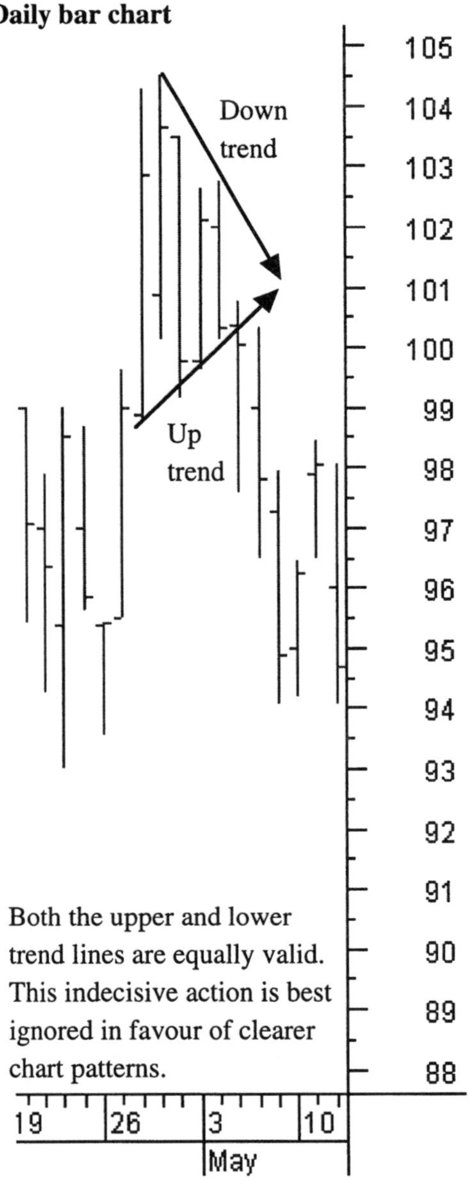

Figure 7.9 Reading hot tips

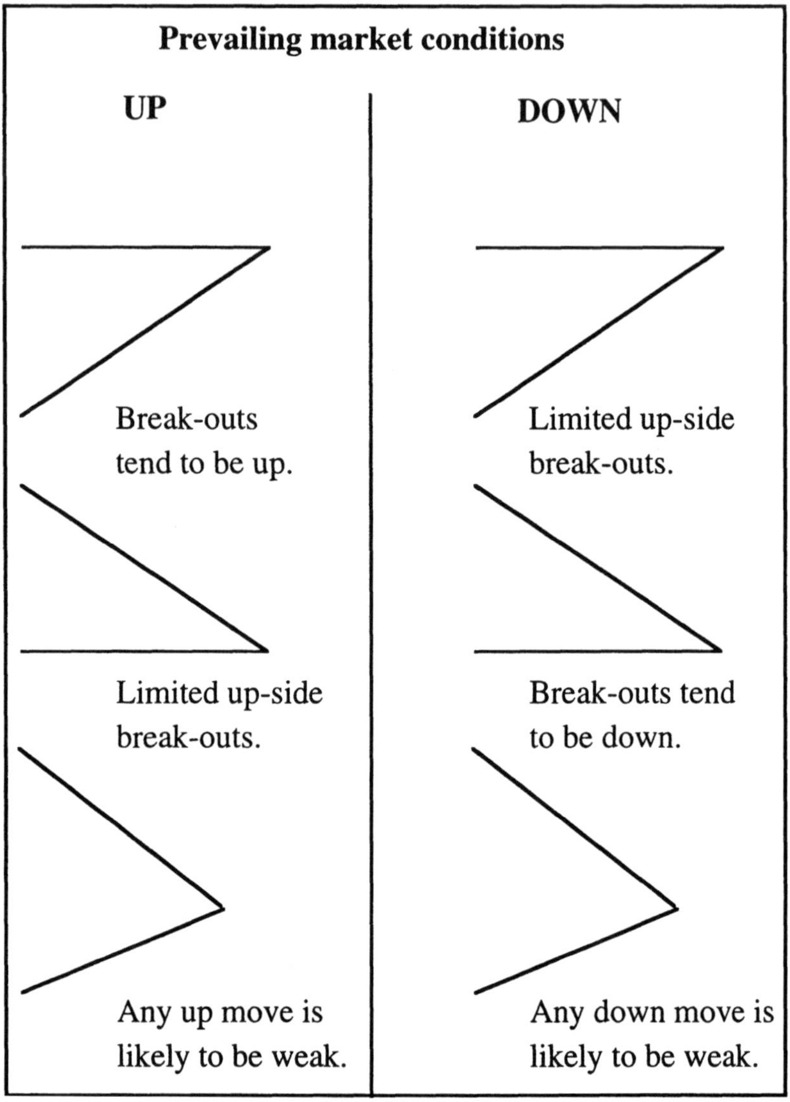

EYESTRAIN

Useful as it is, the eyeball search has some serious limitations, usually imposed by its owner. Fatigue, wishful thinking, or seeing, and the upper limits of speed mean this powerful technique cannot be used with hundreds or thousands of charts on a regular basis. Use it to regularly search a small number of stocks.

Beginners have more success searching for one feature each time — support, or trend lines, rather than both. With practice it is easy to check for both features in a single glance.

The eyeball search effectively develops an initial list of trading candidates but searching a database with more than a few hundred stocks is impractical. In later chapters we will show how this list is reduced further by better analysis. Searching larger databases calls for software able to evaluate each stock against selected specified criteria. These selections are next eyeballed before moving to a deeper level of analysis.

The eyeball scan is so useful it is included in every trading decision. We all look at charts, but really seeing them is a different skill.

BEYOND THE EYEBALL

Let us not lose sight of our objective. Confronted with massive amounts of data we must establish methods to separate the nuggets from the overburden. Failure to do this means our working day, or hours, are consumed by fruitless activity, forever tantalized by missed trading opportunities. There are nuggets in this jungle, but finding them is generally hard work.

Traders downloading the entire market use software to uncover stocks meeting specific criteria. Judgment is apparently elbowed to one side by rigid formulas. Unless we are very clear on our trading objectives the software-driven search lets us build fantastical myths. Remember, no matter how complex we make this process, this search expedition simply aims to develop a short list of the best trading opportunities rather than a long list of possible trading candidates.

8

TECHNICAL TRUE LOVE — SEARCHING FOR RELATIONSHIPS

As with every prospecting expedition, many traders are consumed by the belief that some tools will help them to see beyond the surface to the reality beneath. A good mining geologist has a reputation for spotting surface blows indicative of deeper geology and mineralization. Modern alluvial goldfields vibrate with the screech of metal detectors searching for the reality below the surface clays. Eyeballing the charts is only one of many ways to mine our database. The remainder of this section deals with mining much larger fields, usually the entire market. The techniques are also applied effectively to smaller market segments.

The nuggets we seek are securities where the balance of probability suggests a change in direction. We cannot use the power of the computer to mine our database of price and volume history unless we know what we are looking for. There is no signpost reading 'Profit here'.

The software manuals provided with Metastock, SuperCharts and other charting programs have extensive sections devoted to search formulas. A multitude more are available from Internet sites including *www.guppytraders.com*. They are all valuable tools but not particularly useful in unskilled hands. This, and the following chapter, are not toolboxes. We show some sample tools, but only to explain how they work effectively with one type of market geology rather than another.

Which ones do I use? I use all of the techniques mentioned here, but the exact combination depends on market conditions. There is no single trading answer that works all the time in all markets. Our intention is to understand some of the tools and techniques available so we are in a better position to select the right combination to match our preferred trading style with the current market conditions.

Effective database mining relies on two significant types of market geology: relationship or R-plots and performance-based plots. Both use raw price and volume data. Most tools belong in either one of these categories. Selecting the best tool from the correct category box is an important step towards trading success.

R-plot approaches rest on simple relationships between the open and close, and volume. They rely on the price plot and price patterns visible on the charts rather than on indicator results. Every result is a market price that could have been traded.

These are the geologists' surface blows indicating a deeper reality.

Performance-based approaches manipulate, smooth, average or extrapolate the data. Like an aero-magnetic survey the search is for numerical results indicating a probability balance. The search looks for a distinctive signature hoping the owner is nearby.

When we look at the value of a moving average, typically used in performance-based approaches, we come up with a figure that is not necessarily a price traded in the market today. The moving average may give a value of $59.00 with the stock trading between $60.00 and $61.00. Traders could buy or sell at these prices, but not necessarily at the moving average price of $59.00.

These performance, or indicator, results are one step removed from the market and give the trader a different category of information about market activity.

In contrast, R-plot searches give the trader information drawn from the range of price activity actually experienced on the day. These results are much closer to the actual market activity, and are more useful in some circumstances. Although the line is often blurred, it is a useful distinction to remember.

CHARTING THE BASIC R-PLOT

The basic R-plot tells us which stocks have performed best over a selected period. This is simply a powerful application of the computer's capacity to search, compare and rank information in a database. This basic scan trawls through our stock list, ranking them by comparing today's price with previous points. The search identifies nominated high, or low, achievers, but leaves the task of interpretation to the trader.

There are many basic ranking criteria. Among the most commonly used are:

- Best performers today compared to yesterday.
- Best performers over the past three or five days.
- Best performers over the past week or two, or three weeks.
- Stocks making new highs or new lows.

Remember, we use the power of the computer to identify potential trading opportunities so we can analyze them at depth at a later stage. The list should be small enough to make in-depth analysis possible. Figure 8.1 lists the top five selected from all listed stocks in Singapore. The results show the first two search criteria.

Figure 8.1 R-plots. Finding the top performers. Singapore Stock Exchange
Metastock exploration results

	1 Day performance		3 Day performance		5 Day performance	
1	PCI	17.3	Roly Intl	30.6	Roly Intl	52.8
2	K Kellas	11.3	Chew Eu Hock	28.2	Jacks Intl	41.5
3	Show Pla	10	Jacks Intl	25	Chew Eu Hock	34.7
4	FCC	8.9	Seaview	23.6	Drangon Land	34.6
5	Austland	7.8	Tong Meng	21.7	Tac	34.2

Metastock users can modify the default Performance, Daily exploration in the Explorer Module to scan the periods they prefer. The exploration formula is:

```
Column A
CLOSE
Column B
ROC(CLOSE,1,percent)
Column C
ROC(CLOSE,2,percent)
Column D
ROC(CLOSE,3,percent)
Column E
ROC(CLOSE,4,percent)
Column F
ROC(CLOSE,5,percent)
```

Results are sorted by performance over a selected number of days.

At other times it is useful to find all those stocks making new highs for the year. This suits trading strategies designed to buy strong stocks in a bull market. Figure 8.2 shows the results of this Metastock search for the entire Hong Kong market. The exploration formula is:

```
Column A
High
Column B
HHV(High,260)
Filter
(Col A – Col B) = 0
```

Just knowing which stocks are moving quickly, or making new highs, is useful trading information not easily extracted from other sources. The information published in much of the daily press is taken from a reduced database built from the most popular and

Figure 8.2 R-plots
New yearly highs
Entire Hong Kong Stock Market
Extract only

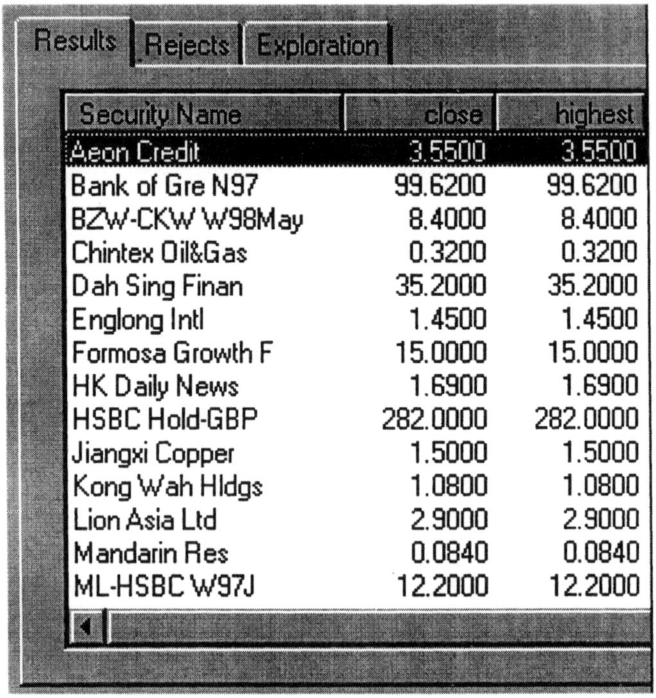

Security Name	close	highest
Aeon Credit	3.5500	3.5500
Bank of Gre N97	99.6200	99.6200
BZW-CKW W98May	8.4000	8.4000
Chintex Oil&Gas	0.3200	0.3200
Dah Sing Finan	35.2000	35.2000
Englong Intl	1.4500	1.4500
Formosa Growth F	15.0000	15.0000
HK Daily News	1.6900	1.6900
HSBC Hold-GBP	282.0000	282.0000
Jiangxi Copper	1.5000	1.5000
Kong Wah Hldgs	1.0800	1.0800
Lion Asia Ltd	2.9000	2.9000
Mandarin Res	0.0840	0.0840
ML-HSBC W97J	12.2000	12.2000

well-known stocks. In large markets with thousands of listings this pre-selection is inadequate for trading purposes because it excludes too many stocks.

In most cases the trader will want to examine basic R-plot results a little more closely before committing his time to further in-depth and time-consuming analysis.

ADVANCED R-PLOTS

All R-plot searches compare price activity against a predetermined pattern, or another data element, such as volume activity. They do not compare indicator results.

The most commonly used advanced R-plots include:

- inside days
- gap days
- out of range days with a close near the high
- price and volume break-outs.

Advanced R-plots usually compare one day's price activity to a previous day or group of days. An inside day, shown with the Dupont chart in Figure 8.3, is created when the high and the low are within the high/low range of the previous day. The significant feature is the way the price bar relates to other price bars — smaller, larger, or built on changes in volume.

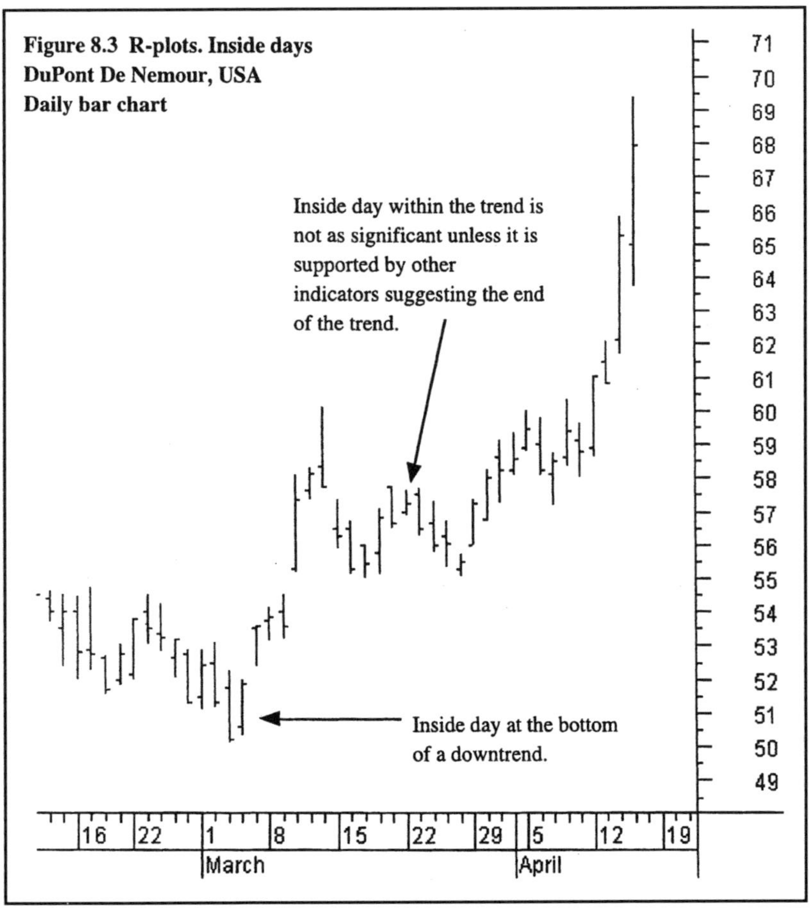

Figure 8.3 R-plots. Inside days
DuPont De Nemour, USA
Daily bar chart

There are many other R-plots. The equivolume chart, for instance, uses changes in the width of the bar to plot changes in volume. How useful these other R-plots are depends on your trading style and technique. The key is to decide what you are looking for before you select the search criteria.

Most modern charting software comes equipped with default search criteria. Many people use these defaults indiscriminately and by using something different you may find a useful corner to give you an edge over the main crowd. Equally, by using the defaults as a starting point, the trader further refines the initial selections by assessing them against his own specialist criteria. The examples that follow are not a complete list of possibilities. The purpose is to show how such R-plot factors are incorporated into a data search so you can make better use of your favorite factors.

INSIDE DAYS

An inside day is when the day's price activity — the range from the low to the high — falls within the range of the previous day's price activity. The bar chart display of American chemical company Dupont De Nemour in Figure 8.3, has two inside days marked. This is an important reversal pattern when it occurs near the end of an established trend. Further confirmation of the end of the trend is required, but by searching for this relationship we add the security to our watch list.

The inside day often acts as a leading indicator, giving the trader advance warning of a price volume break-out. The warning is derived from the relationship between bars of price activity. Dupont shows an inside day at the very turning point of the down trend. This relationship is enough to add Dupont to a watch list of potential trading opportunities.

Some R-plots are also readily identified as part of a candlestick bullish and bearish Doji-day pattern. On a Doji day the open and the close are equal. The bullish or bearish character is created by the length and direction of the 'wick' above or below the Doji.

Using a daily candlestick approach and trading from the long side, we are interested first in a Dragonfly Doji, shown in the bottom section of Figure 8.4 with the Malaysian-listed counter Maypak. This is most significant in an established down trend, particularly so when the end of the trend is signaled by a particularly disastrous day. Prices dip dramatically, appearing on the chart as a very long tail, but there are only a few frightened sellers left, so prices close equal to the open. This price action shakes out the last sellers, setting a new low. Find this, and we watch the stock the next trading day for confirmation.

The significant confirmation is when prices open and close within the range of the previous day. This suggests sellers are refusing to participate in the market unless they get a better price. This is a change from a market dominated by fear — 'I'd better sell now in case prices go lower' — to a market discovering greed — 'I will hang on because things are going to get better'.

Figure 8.4 Using candlesticks
Maypak, Malaysia
Candlestick daily chart

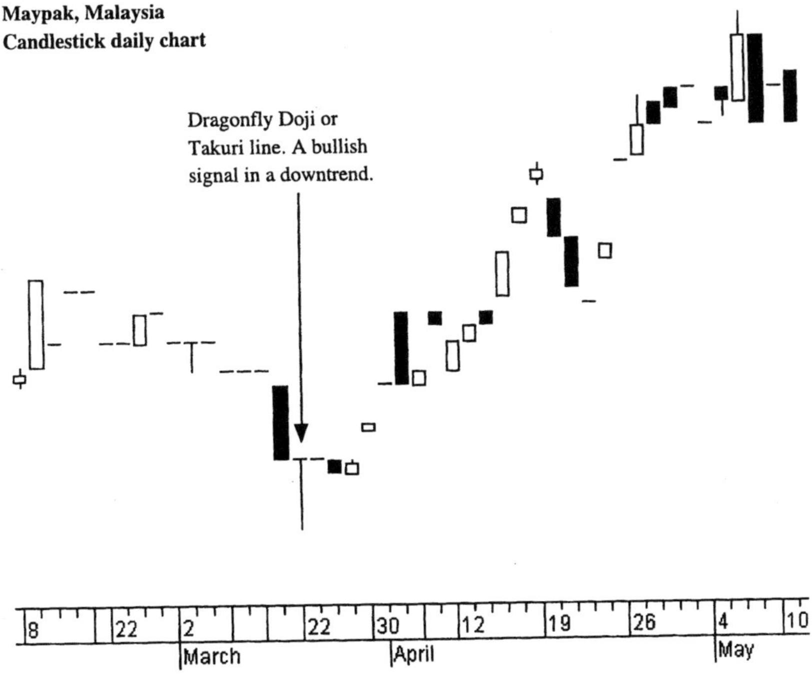

As a long-side trader you want to select those opportunities developing into worthwhile entry positions for new trades. Scanning for an inside day uses the Metastock Explorer function. A search formula is as simple as selecting Inside() from the Analysis Tools.

Searching for Candlestick patterns is usually straightforward but in this case Metastock does not have a default Dragonfly Doji day tool. We have to build one using logic and several Candlestick categories in the Functions list. The following Exploration formula shows the construction process for this and other custom formulas.

```
Column A
Close
Column B
If(LongLeggedDoji(),1,0)
Column C
If(LongLowerShadow(),1,0)
Column D
If(Doji(),1,0)
```

This Metastock Exploration will return a boolean answer for each stock examined. Stocks meeting the search criteria appear as 1, while those failing the test return a 0 result. The formula element — ,1,0 — tells Metastock to do this, but in everyday English the 1 is read as Yes and the 0 as No.

The logic of three simultaneous searches defines the dragonfly day. In plain English, any stock that returns 1 in each of the columns must be a dragonfly day because:

- The day will have a very long tail above or below the Doji — a LongLeggedDoji in Column B.
- The tail is below the body of the day — LongLowerShadow in Column C.
- The open and the close are the same — a Doji day in Column D.

These logical conditions define a Dragonfly Doji and are included in the Explorer Filter Column as:

```
When(colB,=,1) AND When (colC,=,1) AND When(colD,=,1)
```

Complexity is built from levels of simplicity: an issue that becomes more important in the next chapter. Our purpose here is to show how Japanese candlestick charting is particularly adept at identifying R-plot patterns. If you feel price R-plots are important, or perhaps the most important factor, then learning how to construct search criteria is important. If you do not have this skill, specialist software such as North Systems CandlePower5 may save a lot of time.

GAP DAYS

A gap occurs when price closes, at say, $62.00 and opens the next day at $64.50, as in area E on the Coca Cola daily bar chart, Figure 8.5. This gap is $2.50 wide. In area F the previous bar closes at $67.00 and the next bar opens at $68.00 — a gap of one dollar. This chart extract shows seven gaps, all marked by a letter. All except the last, gap G, have been 'closed'. Closing the gaps means prices subsequently cover the gap in price activity. This is shown by the arrows in Figure 8.5. Prices can gap up, or gap down, and some analysts believe that each gap must be closed or covered. This leads to specific trading strategies, but before they can be applied the trader must isolate those stocks showing gap activity.

A gap is a chart set-up, or an R-plot, between one bar and another. A gap up is created when buyers are so eager to get stock they bid ahead of other buyers in the market. During the day, prices leapfrog forward as selling dries up. When sellers see hordes of buyers at $61.00 the sellers know they can probably ask for $62.00 or more. In this boiling market someone among the buyers will break ranks, meeting the offer price.

When trade closes for the day, both buyers and sellers review the situation. Not all market participants watch the action during the

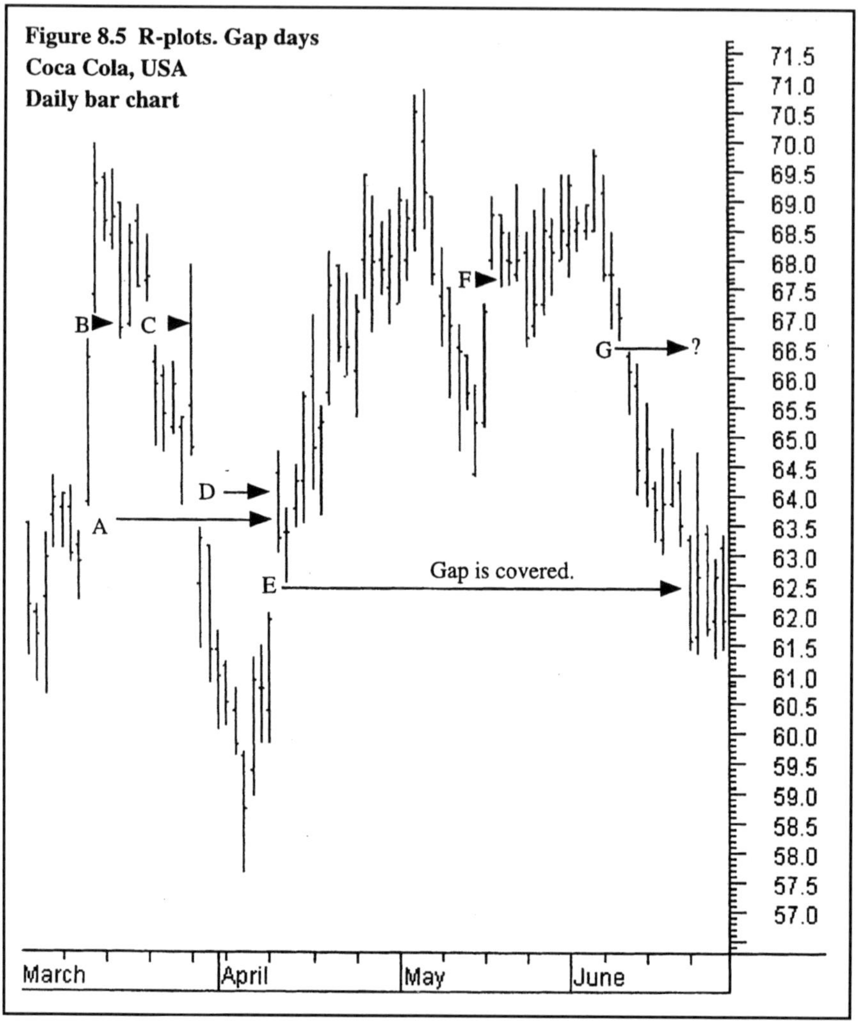

Figure 8.5 R-plots. Gap days
Coca Cola, USA
Daily bar chart

day. Many are position traders, or investors, taking positions based on end-of-day data, on broker's advice, and on the information they glean from the television or financial press. Sellers who were in the market withdraw their orders when they see the acceleration of prices. They hope to get a better price. Buyers who know nothing about the stock decide to join the action. They jump the order line with bids at a higher price for the opening of trade. Other informed buyers who particularly want a position place opening bids higher than the previous day's close.

On the next open the first sale takes place when bid meets ask. Higher bids create a price gap up. The price gap is confirmed only if all subsequent trades for the day continue at prices higher than the previous day's close. As Coca-Cola shows, this action does develop in blue chip stocks, but it is most profitable in mid-cap stocks where liquidity is more erratic.

Of course, when the same thing happens in reverse — a gap down in a down trend — a short trade opportunity is signaled.

This price action is often associated with price and volume breakouts, but it does not have to be. In a stock with moderate liquidity, sales may take place at gap prices without an increase in volume. Sellers move their ask prices up in response to a whole series of factors, not necessarily in response to being chased by a large number of buyers. It is useful to search for this data relationship in itself.

Metastock allows users to scan by applying the GapUp() or GapDown() formula to the exploration. Candlestick users search for Rising Windows.

Edwards and Magee in *Technical Analysis of Stock Trends* presented the classic interpretation of the gap phenomenon. They included specific trading strategies for each. You may decide to concentrate on common gaps, exhaustion gaps or runaway gaps. Analyzing and categorizing the gap is a later trading decision. In this initial search we look for any gap because selecting them hones the list against our specific criteria.

This is not a useful method when dealing with all stocks. Stocks with extremely low, and intermittent volume activity, often show gap-like behaviour. With so few sellers and so few buyers, sales are irregular, and often without any intervening price activity. Many of these stocks will show up on a search based on gap criteria. Weed them out by looking at the charts to determine if the gap-like activity is the usual price behavior.

Although the textbook understanding of gaps works well in American markets, it is sometimes less relevant to other markets.

Traders need to be careful, in particular, of building trading strategies around closing the gap. Some gaps are never closed, while others remain unclosed for months or years.

OUT-OF-RANGE DAYS

When the range of daily price movement is greater than normal it points to an imbalance between buyers and sellers. If the direction of the imbalance is upwards it suggests prices will be bid higher to satisfy the demand because the supply — sellers — is limited. If the supply was greater, all buyers would buy at lower prices.

Out-of-range days blur the distinction between an R-plot and an indicator. This concept considers the 'range' of price activity between the open and the close and compares it with the previous range. This is sometimes a straightforward intuitive process. With small Australian miner Carpenter Pacific shown in Figure 8.6 there is no doubt price bar A is much larger than the normal range of price activity.

This is an extreme example and although very easy to see, such price activity provides few useful signals to the trader. The price has moved too fast for the trader to jump on board. If we use end-of-day data we are disadvantaged because the spike may be a singular event, and not the beginning of a prolonged up move. Only future price action tells us if it is worth jumping on board after the inevitable retracement. However, this type of development, as shown with Carpenter Pacific, is a frequent occurrence in mid-cap and speculative stocks. A single massive out-of-range day provides the clue and trading this type of move is hair-raising, but very profitable.

This finger chart pattern is a price spike. Prices show massive ranges, accompanied by substantial volume. The pattern is completed by a dramatic fall bringing prices back to under the midpoint of the initial spike. Often they pause around a quarter of the spike distance and traders enter on this retracement. The halfway point of the spike provides an exit target.

Figure 8.6 R-plots. Out of range days.
Finger chart pattern
Carpenter Pacific, Australia
Daily bar chart

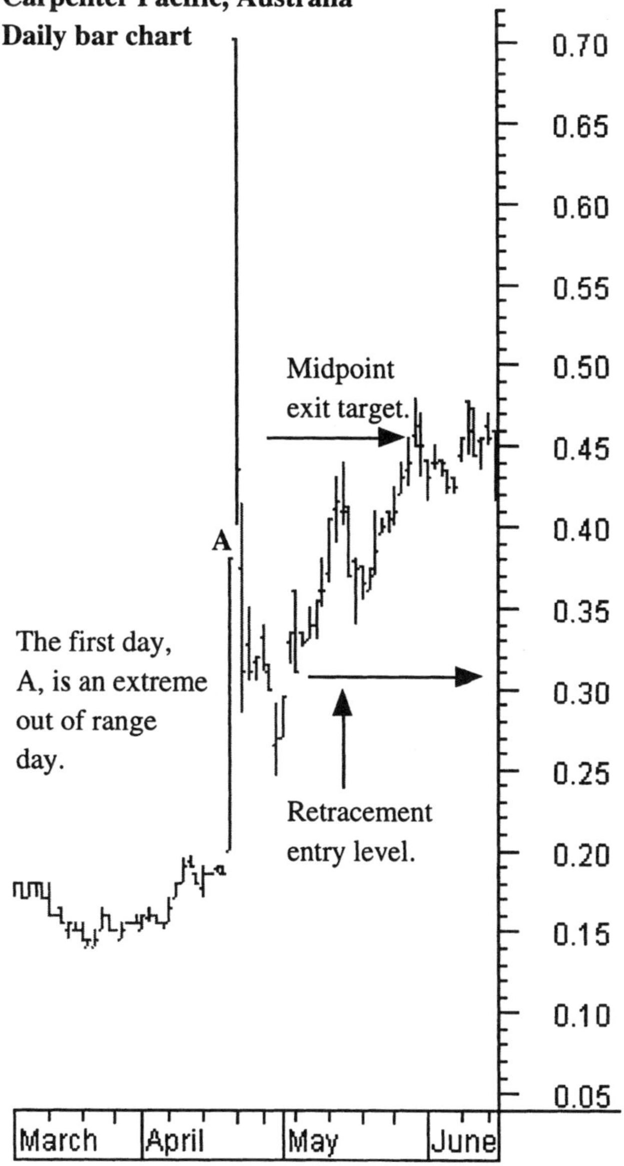

These are dramatic exceptions. Normally we look for the situation where a day's range is significantly greater than the previous day's — or an average of a series of preceding days — but not so great that the trading opportunity is missed. There are several ways of identifying this. In the first R-plot today's range is compared with the previous day's range. The second approach blurs the line between R-plots and indicators by using a calculated average and comparing today's range with it.

The standard R-plot approach makes use of Japanese candlesticks because it provides a useful way to compare today's range with the previous day's range. The Big White Candle provides this R-plot for Metastock users. When used as a search criterion the user must rely on the judgment of the software to identify a Big White Candle. That judgment is sometimes faulty, and those charts are discarded quickly.

The second approach compares today with the calculated average range of previous days, reached by taking the difference between the high and the low over the previous 5, 10 or 21 days, and converting this to a single figure. Today's figure — also the difference between the high and the low — is plotted against this average. A higher figure suggests the day's range is larger and future price action might be building. Indicators that work like this include Average True Range and ADX-style analysis, which plot the difference between today's range and the average range over a defined previous period.

Notice how we are drifting from R-plots to indicators. This drift alters the way we search the data and effects the search results. The constant danger is when the search delivers a result different from the one we intended. There is nothing wrong with searching for gold nuggets and ignoring the odd valuable streak of silver exposed in the process. There is something wrong when the search ignores the gold and only selects the silver. If we use indicators to find what are essentially R-plot conditions, we sometimes miss the nuggets and find the silver instead. The silver ADX indicator reacts slowly because it is based on averages. The gold R-plot trading opportunity is signaled sooner with a Big White Candle search. The search must match objectives with methods.

The R-plot delivers a simple visual message flagging the potential for further price action and suggesting an appropriate entry price. The performance indicator moves away from this simple message, placing today's price in a wider context more suited to a different style of trading.

For our purposes it is enough to know you can make this criteria as simple — a Big White Candle — or as complex — an Average True Range indicator — as you wish. Adjust the parameters to suit your trading needs.

PRICE AND VOLUME BREAK-OUTS

Financial writers make some rather artificial distinctions between market information: fundamental, charting and technical. Good traders use a combination of each to enhance their trading style by identifying those perfect, or near perfect, opportunities matching their ideal trading conditions.

Volume is the fuel driving the market. An up trend, to survive, must be nourished by new buyers and fed by cautiously reluctant sellers. Consistent volume is important. To topple the existing trend there must be a surge of buyers, or sellers, capable of changing the price.

The change in price and volume provides the groundwork for this R-plot, but to explore it the trader needs indicator-like tools.

Volume is usually shown as a histogram, with solid bars. Volume charts yield clues when volume is out of character but this is hard to decide. The jagged pattern needs smoothing so in this case a mathematical solution is better than a visual one.

The key in using volume as search criteria is to measure today's volume against consistent past volume calculated on a long-term average; for instance, where the volume is 50 percent above the 50-day moving average. Price break-outs are selected on a percentage approach basis, perhaps where price has increased 5 percent or greater over yesterday's close.

The search is not meaningful unless we define the criterion to match our trading intentions. A search of an entire market may need to be repeated several times using slightly different criteria. I look for short-term break-outs where the price increases 5 percent or more over yesterday's close. I match this with stocks where volume is 50 percent above the 50-day moving average.

The Metastock formula is:

```
ColA CLOSE, ColB REF(CLOSE,-1), ColC
ROC(CLOSE,1,PERCENT) ColD VOLUME, ColE
MOV(VOLUME,50,EXPONENTIAL), ColF ((VOLUME-
MOV(VOLUME,50,EXPONENTIAL))/
MOV(VOLUME,50,EXPONENTIAL))*100, Filter
WHEN(COLC>=5) AND WHEN(COLD>=COLE*1.5)
```

With around 846 securities, including warrants, listed in Hong Kong, the Metastock Explorer takes less than two minutes to identify all securities meeting these default criteria. Figure 8.7 lists the top 14 selected from a search of the entire Hong Kong market. Not all are real candidates. Some may be too far advanced to be

Figure 8.7 Finding price volume break-outs
Entire Hong Kong Market
Metastock exploration results

"Price and Volume Breakout"

Results | Rejects | Exploration

Security Name	Close	Previous	% change	% above
Nam Pei Hong W01	0.8900	0.6800	30.8823	348.9117
Capital Automatn	0.1680	0.1360	23.5294	444.4616
HSBC Hold-GBP	282.0000	236.0000	19.4915	82.1070
Tian An China In	0.3000	0.2550	17.6471	547.2927
HSBC China Fund	7.9000	7.0000	12.8571	285.1385
Qing Ling Motors	1.7000	1.5200	11.8421	112.4649
Founder (HK)	2.3250	2.1000	10.7143	213.3460
Leung Kee Hldgs	0.1700	0.1570	8.2803	146.5071
Mei Ah Intl	0.6000	0.5600	7.1429	200.7835
MANYUE	0.3200	0.3000	6.6667	354.4949
Jilin Chemical	1.0200	0.9600	6.2500	183.4278
Perfect Treasure	0.5600	0.5300	5.6604	57.9110
BZW-CKW W98Ma	8.4000	7.9500	5.6604	174.3218
Ocean Grand	0.2950	0.2800	5.3571	272.7139

worth trading. Others are rejected due to weak chart patterns or because other indicators fail to confirm the break-out potential.

From this list we select Qing Ling Motors. This chart in Figure 8.8 displays the relationship between price and volume that signals the start of a trading opportunity and the entry point. The remainder of the chart shows how this trade developed to deliver around 80 percent return.

My trading style determines the structure of the R-plot and the Metastock search parameters that I use. These are not default search formulas. They are modified to reflect my particular beliefs about market behavior. Your beliefs about the market, and your trading style, will differ from mine so the final formula settings you use will be different as a result.

My objective in setting the cut-off figure, such as 5 percent or a 50-day volume average, is to eliminate as many stocks as possible, and to include only those with a real possibility of becoming useful trading opportunities. Some bigger fish will slip through the net, but we ought to catch enough to give us a feed for the day.

The choices we make in setting the search criteria should all assist in excluding those stocks that are least likely to develop into trading opportunities in the immediate future.

BUYING INTO COMPLEXITY

We look for nuggets, and the search can be as simple, or as complex, as we choose to make it. The search is productive as long as we do not lose sight of our objective. In the same way that a 180-ton capacity Caterpillar 5230 Excavator is just a pumped up spade, the search for NR4 conditions used by US futures traders Linda Raschke and Larry Conners is conceptually in the same R-plot class discussed above.

The NR4 conditions understand that a market tends to move swiftly from periods of price consolidation to new levels. The high volatility, narrow four-day range conditions, help traders recognize this market set-up before the market moves.

Figure 8.8 Price volume break-outs
Qing Ling Motors, Hong Kong
Daily bar chart with volume

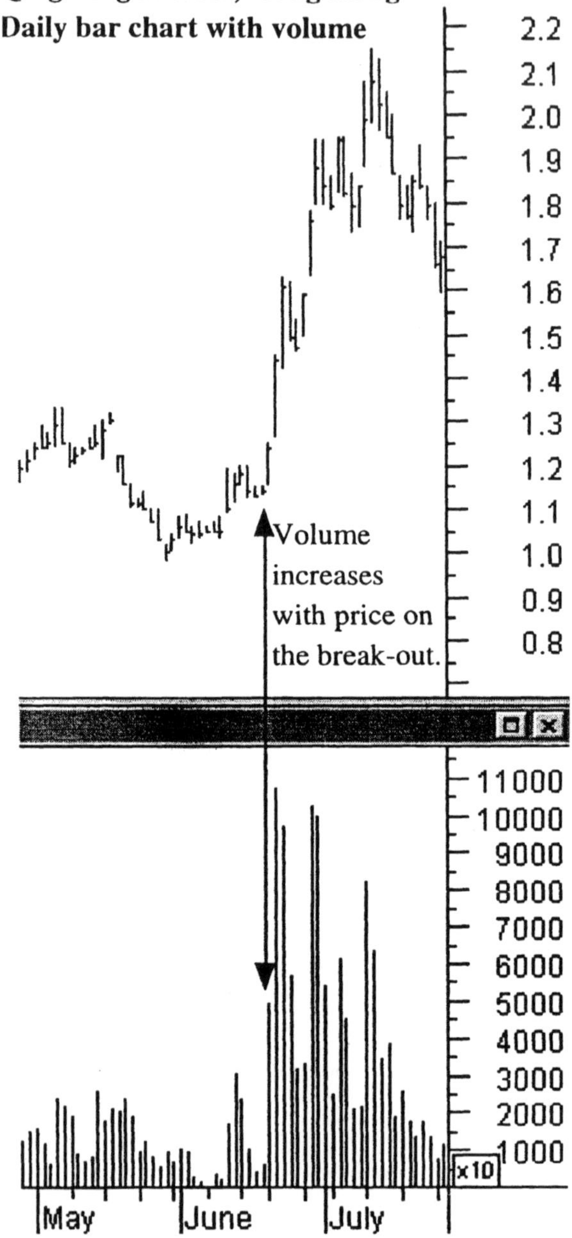

Raschke and Connors combined the narrow range four-day pattern discussed by Toby Crabel in his *Day Trading with Short-Term Price Patterns* with historical volatility and inside days. The relationship they use looks at the 50-day average volatility. When this reduces, it signals market agreement on value and a narrow price range compared to the last four days, which confirms this. The equilibrium cannot last so it signals a price break.

This is a swing trading technique based on an R-plot relationship. Defining it is mathematically complex, but the essential process is the same as for any R-plot. The process is discussed in the August 1996 issue of *Technical Analysis of Stocks and Commodities* magazine and developed more fully in their book, *Street Smarts*. Readers who would like to explore this concept further should read either the article or the book.

Our purpose here is to illustrate the way complexity is derived from common basic concepts. The exploration formula below is a long way from our first search for gap days, yet it builds from the same concepts.

The Metastock formula for NR4 with high volatility used by Raschke and Connors is:

```
Column A
Std(Log(C/Ref(C,-1)),5)/Std(Log(C/Ref(C,-1)),99)
Column B
HIGH-LOW<Ref(LLV(H-L,3),-1)
Column C
HIGH<(Ref(HIGH,-1)AND LOW>Ref(LOW,-1))
Column D
HIGH
Column E
LOW
Filter
colA<.5 AND (colB= 1 OR colC= 1)
```

Column A shows the ratio between 6-day and 100-day volatility. Column B shows a 1 (yes) if today is an NR4 day. Column C shows 1 (yes) if today is an inside day. The high and low, Columns D and E, help determine entry points.

Complexity does not guarantee success, but if complexity is built on a firm understanding of the concepts, it can be a very useful tool in identifying situations of high probability. By developing better search criteria we reduce our time in mining the ore body so we can spend more time polishing the nuggets.

THE PRELIMINARY LIST GETS BIGGER

Where to look and what to look for? The answers depend on the market you select, the tools you prefer and your trading style. The results can be selected after a search based on patterns most easily selected by the human eye, or on relationships between price, price ranges and volume. This *a priori* — before the fact — decision determines what is included in our preliminary list and how large it is. A free list of ready-to-use Metastock exploration formulas is available from *www.guppytraders.com* and they are updated regularly.

Before returning a single cent of profit the trader must expend a fortune in search and analysis time. Performance-based searches, discussed in the next chapter, provide the last component of this constant search for trading nuggets.

9

PERFORMANCE SEARCHES

So far we have looked for nuggets of probability using direct evidence — the eyeball — and by spotting surface blows characteristic of gold-bearing country — R-plots. The boom in modern mining is built on inferred results. Geological activity conducive to the formation of gold leaves a signature. The signature is an indicator, and often easier to find than the gold. When this approach is applied to our market search the danger lies in being so distracted by the signature indicator that we walk over nuggets in plain view.

In this chapter we look at the family of indicators and search approaches based on price performance. These performance indicators suggest a strong probability that price action is developing but, like modern gold exploration techniques, we need additional digging to confirm the resource. I cannot tell you which combination of performance indicators is best because your trading style is individual. Instead I will show you how your choices determine the search results. If your choices are inconsistent with your beliefs about market activity then the nuggets will be elusive. Understanding the process builds a better search mechanism for identifying the balance of probability.

Unlike the R-plot, an indicator takes price data and manipulates it to reveal additional 'hidden' information about the development of price action. For instance, by comparing the standard deviation range to previous trading days we build details about the speed and momentum of price that are not available through R-plot or eyeball searches.

The difference between the R-plot group and the performance indicator family is that an indicator reading is not a market price.

It is a numerical value obtained from the result of a calculation. This is the key to working with technical analysis indicators.

Elder suggests in *Trading for a Living* that indicators fall into one of three categories: trend following, oscillators and miscellaneous. This chapter concentrates on the way we use the first two without discussing a host of individual indicators at significant depth. Additional reading references are noted where appropriate. Later we provide a test for indicator success.

The way the indicator is constructed tells us what it is trying to measure. If it measures the same factors we want to measure, then it is safe to use it to set our scanning criteria. If it does not measure our preferred factors, we should not use it because the results may become a dangerous threat to our trading. Powerful indicators give enticingly complex results and it is too easy to second-guess our otherwise sound analysis. Many traders succumb to the temptation to use a range of sometimes contradictory indicators because the names sound interesting, they are available on the software, or other people talk about using them.

Very broadly, these two groups of performance indicators — trend following and oscillators — are designed to answer two simple questions:

- Where are we? — These are the trend-following indicators.
- Are we breaking the speed limit? — These are the oscillators.

The first part of this chapter considers trend-following indicators. These are all based on moving average concepts and we show how this simple idea is layered into some of the most complex of indicators. All of them are designed to answer a single question: Where is price now in relation to price in a previous period?

FROM ZERO TO ONE AND BEYOND

Using the power of the computer to search an extensive database of securities is as simple as a few mouse clicks. Understanding the report results is more difficult.

Depending on the software used, some scanning results deliver a numerical value. Others use boolean logic returning either a 1 = YES or a 0 = NO. It would be a major step forward for Metastock and others if they could convert this 0 and 1 to plain English equivalents. By using the 'sort' function in Metastock the responses are ranked from the highest to the lowest. This groups all the 1s — yes responses — together, making it easier to develop a useful list.

The 'Yes' results suggest turning points where the balance of probability bulges at its thickest. These points are not always supported by the bar chart price action, but the idea is that the indicator either confirms or anticipates the shift. The initial task is to find the securities at turning points where an entry is signaled. Judging the next turning point for the exit is a different task: see Part III.

WHERE ARE WE? AN AVERAGE ANSWER

The old prospectors looked for specks of gold. By collecting enough specimens from several areas they determined an average concentration and the potential location of the mother lode. More recently, some modern geologists watched Dyak tribesman panning specks of gold and extrapolated the Bre-X disaster. Other modern prospectors fly over a larger area, gathering extensive aerial data that is manipulated to give a better average indication of the size and location of the ore body. We have the same choice of market search techniques using performance indicators.

The trend-following group of performance indicators plot the current position of a stock against some previously calculated average position. The result tells us where we are.

Prices fluctuate, sometimes erratically. A plotted price line is constructed by snapshots of one price element — perhaps the close — and is a little like joining the dots. This line is made more useful when compared against past prices, on average. We want to know where we are in relation to a range of previous price activity. Simply looking back at past history is one solution.

Another compares today's price with the moving average of prices. Unfortunately, price has four parts — open, high, low and close — we must choose one to base the average calculations on. Most times we take the close, and create a pre-defined average range from this data. Many traders use 3-, 4-, 5-, 7-, or 20-day moving averages. Choosing a single element — the close, or high — immediately reduces the amount of information available. As discussed in Chapter 2, a line chart is not as useful as a bar chart.

An alternative solution combines the four price parts into a single 'average' figure. Choosing the median price — the mid-point between the high and low for the day — captures additional information about price, more than any other single data point, such as the open. This price–data relationship has a value plotted on a chart as a single point. Calculate the value for each day in the past, join the dots, and the screen display plots a line in the same way as a closing price line.

We can further manipulate the median price by plotting the 10-, or 15-, day moving average of the value. We then have a data point against which we compare today's median price. Conceptually, this is no different to a closing line display plotted against a 20-day moving average. The difference is in the detail. We plot a median price against its 10-day average and learn something different about price behavior.

This is essentially a simple calculation concept using an average of an average. The mathematics is more complex, but this calculation task is ideally suited to the computer's form of high-speed idiocy. Often we make this calculation even more complex by the calculation method chosen for the moving average.

DATA MANIPULATION

The choices include a simple moving average (SMA), an exponential moving average (EMA) and a weighted moving average (WMA). Your choice may be based on simplicity and ease of use, or it may be more closely related to a specific belief about the market. With modern software all choices are equally easy so it pays to think carefully about the impact of each approach.

Does it really matter? Figure 9.1 lists the results of two Metastock Explorer searches using an EMA and an SMA. The database of Dow index securities searched are the same, but the membership of each list is subtly different. One of these lists gives you a head start. Which one it is depends on how you match your choice with your beliefs. The search results should support and reinforce your trading strategy.

In the *Lion King* the wise old monkey hits a young lion across the head with his staff. He tells the angry lion that the attack was in the past, so, according to the young lion's philosophy, it doesn't matter. Rubbing his head, the lion concedes that the past does have an impact on current and future events. In the same way, I believe recent price data is more significant than less recent price data.

What happens today has a greater immediate impact on what happens tomorrow than do events of 10 or 20 days ago. As a result, I use an exponential moving average calculation because it is consistent with my understanding of the market. My trading list comes from the first column.

Figure 9.1 Performance indicators. Moving average crossover 3/10 Dow index stocks. Metastock explorer results (first 10 only)

EMA results		SMA results	
1	AT & T Corp	1	Union Carbide Co
2	Alliedsignal Inc	2	Minnestota Mng &
3	Aluminum Co of A	3	Aluminum Co of A
4	American Express	4	Chevron Corp
5	Boeing Co	5	Exxon Corp
6	Caterpillar Inc	6	Procter & Gamble
7	Chevron Corp	7	Goodyear Tire
8	Coca Cola Co	8	Johnson & Johnson
9	Disney Walt Co	9	Eastman Kodak Co
10	Dupont De Nemour	10	Caterpillar Inc

Applying any of these styles of average calculations to a single data element — open, high, low or close — gives useful results, but they are not a simple traded market price.

The level of complexity increases when we use a relationship between price data. We might manipulate the data by selecting a median price. In this example if the low is $40 and the high is $80 the median is $60.

Others prefer to use the mean price or what we commonly call the average. Continuing the example above, if the open is $42 and the close $64 we have four observations: open 42, high 80, low 40 and close 64. The total is 226. To find the mean the total is divided by the number of data points giving a result of $56.50.

Plotting the mean against the median leaves a $3.50 gap. This is not insignificant if your trading method relies on signals generated by moving average crossovers.

The levels of complexity are almost infinite, and addictive. Other manipulations calculate the standard deviation and compare today's price activity with past activity. Some use the mean deviation to find the average absolute value of the difference between the population of data points and the mean.

Again, does it matter? The answer is yes. Figure 9.2 lists exponential moving average crossover search results from the entire Malaysian market using the close, the median and the average, or typical price. The results are ranked by the value above or below the crossover point with zero values identifying the exact crossover. We have only shown the candidates' names. The difference in the makeup of and order within the lists reflects the relationship between the price data selected as the basis of the EMA calculation. Opportunities noted in one list such as Commerz, PSCI and Ptgtin sometimes do not appear in either of the others.

When Walter Scott lamented 'O, what a tangled web we weave, When first we practise to deceive' he wasn't talking about price data manipulation but the effects are the same. If you use an indicator based on complex calculations and price data

Figure 9.2 Performance indicators. Moving average crossover 3/10 Entire Malaysian market. Metastock Explorer results (first 10 only)

Close price results		Median price results		Typical or average price results	
1	Kluang	1	Kluang	1	Kluang
2	Dialog	2	Repco	2	Repco
3	Repco	3	Dialog	3	Dialog
4	Ekovest	4	Ekovest	4	Ekovest
5	SPK	5	SPK	5	SPK
6	Imcken	6	Incken	6	Incken
7	Amolek	7	Amolek	7	Btota
8	Kossan	8	PSCI	8	Kossan
9	Btofo	9	Btoto	9	PSCI
10	Commerz	10	Kossan	10	Ptgtin

manipulation make sure you understand and agree with the reasoning behind the structural choices.

Complexity is not always the best answer so do not select an indicator just because it is complex. Nor should indicators be selected purely on simplicity. The computational power of modern software makes the mechanics of calculation an insignificant factor in our ability or inability to construct and plot indicators. The choice of indicator should be made on the basis of the combination and approach that most closely matches your understanding of the market, and that brings out the relationships you think are important. The signature of the nugget you look for is subtly different from other signatures.

CROSSED SIGNALS

Averages, in all their forms, help establish where today's price is in relation to prices as they were, on average, in a predefined past period. They help build the balance of probability and show the trader if his contemplated entry price is a bargain, or fully priced, when compared to a previous period of price behavior.

Traders are a suspicious lot. Among the rabbit's feet, lucky coffee mugs and winning routines is a strong feeling that more is always better. Within reason this is true. Confirmation of any indicator result helps 'prove' the initial conclusion. For confirmation many traders plot two moving averages, using the crossovers as trading signals.

By overlaying a longer term moving average — one that gives very reliable signals — with a shorter term average — one that gives less reliable signals, but which is more responsive to changes in the market — the trader gets confirmation and he hopes for the best of both worlds. When the current price is higher than the short-term average, and when the short-term average has crossed over, or turned above, the longer term average, a buying opportunity is signaled.

The simple strategy identifies a bulge in the balance of probability and, as expected, we can make it more complex in steady degrees. The Moving Average Convergence Divergence (MACD) indicator explores changing relationships between averages.

This impressive-sounding and popular indicator measures the distance between two averages, usually a 12- and 26-day EMA. The difference between the two values is calculated and plotted as a solid fast MACD line. Next a 9-day EMA of the fast MACD line is calculated and plotted as a dashed line.

Briefly, the trading rules for MACD are:

- Buy when the fast MACD line crosses above the signal line.
- Sell when the fast MACD line crosses below the signal line.

Building further complexity gives the MACD-histogram indicator. This gets its name from the vertical histogram bars used to plot the value of the fast MACD line minus the signal line. Figure 9.3 is an example of this indicator histogram plot in a Metastock format applied to the United Kingdom listed book and music retailer WH Smith.

Figure 9.3 Performance indicators
Daily bar chart and MACD histogram
WH Smith, UK

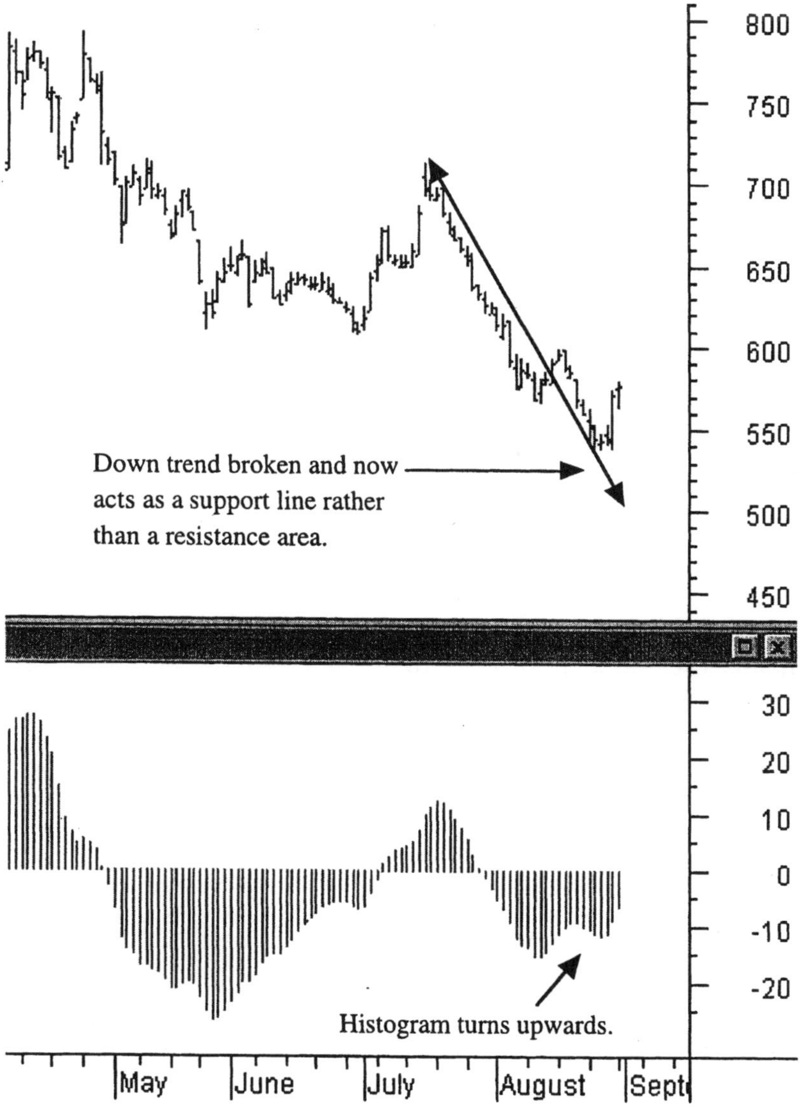

In screening the database to identify stocks meeting these criteria, Metastock users can select the default MACD Buy Signal. A selection of results of an entire search of the Hong Kong market for MACD crossovers are listed in Figure 9.4. Out of 846 securities this scan identified 30 meeting the criteria. This list must be reduced further, either by comparing it with another list, preferably one based on a different group of indicators, such as R-plots, or perhaps the trend following performance indicators discussed below. Ultimately, we cannot get away from the task of eyeballing the final candidates.

Our intention is to show how these groups of performance indicators are used to find specific types of information about market activity and build a list of trading candidates for closer study. Readers who wish to further explore the construction and use of this and other related trend-following performance indicators are referred to Colby and Meyers' *The Encyclopedia of Technical Market Indicators*, or Elder's *Trading for a Living.*

The trend-following indicators tell us where we are. From simple beginnings, where we recognize the neighborhood, we layer levels of complexity until we reach the equivalent of a military strength global positioning system. The objective of the search remains the same: find securities where, on balance, the current trend is changing. Effective screening using indicators has clear objectives and a clear understanding of the message each indicator is delivering.

Figure 9.4 Performance indicators. Moving Average Convergence Divergence (MACD) Entire Hong Kong market. Extract of results ranked by % above crossover point

1	Kowloon Dev	Liu Chong Hin Bk	GOLDEN POWER
2	Daido Concrete	China Assets	SOLARTEC
3	Leung Kee Hldgs	Cosmos Machinery	CL Fin-FPac W97
4	Nam Pei Hong W01	Recor Hldgs	Magnificent Est
5	Mandarin Orient	Chaifa Hldgs	Herald (HK) Ltd
6	Theme Intl	K M Bus	Peaktop
7	Cafe de Coral	Chevalier OA	Asia Comm Hldgs
8	Shaw Brothers HK	Same Time Hldgs	Mansion Hldgs

FROM ZERO TO 100 PERCENT

The remainder of this chapter deals with the second group of indicators: the oscillators.

Knowing the position of today's price relative to a previous range of prices is useful, but the market does not stand still. Good trading moves in the same direction as the market, and at the same, or greater, speed. The momentum of price movements is important, but so too is the speed.

When we drive beyond the speed limit we run the risk of making an involuntary contribution to reducing the State debt and this encourages us to slow down. Put on a well-worn tractor cap, chain a dog on the back of the pick-up and drive below the speed limit and some road rage maniac will encourage us to accelerate to match the flow of traffic. The smooth flow of traffic is bounded by those who drive too fast and too slow. A driver may oscillate between these extremes, but the pressure is always to return to a middle speed.

This pressure represents a probability bulge. At the extremes of oscillation there is increased probability that events will swing in the opposite direction. This observation is at the core of the way oscillator-based indicators are used in trading and the way we include them in performance-based screening criteria. Trading presents two problems for oscillators. First, how to measure the speed limit and, second, how to find the middle or equilibrium point when extreme speed limits change.

On the road we measure our speed in absolute terms — from zero to 100 miles an hour or more. There are no absolute terms in trading so we measure momentum, or speed, results as a percentage — the lower limit 0 percent and upper limit 100 percent. In a percentage calculation the equilibrium point is always 50 percent. In extreme situations these indicators sometimes give readings above 100 and below 0, but this is most unusual.

Within these upper and lower limits, experience, and testing, suggests most price activity takes place within a very broad band. The software standard Stochastic indicator is ideal for this measurement. It compares where today's price closed relative to its highest and lowest trading range over the last ten trading days. By adding a slow period we select an average figure for the high and low over the last ten days and compare today's against the average range. This gives %K slowed by, for instance, 5.

Some Stochastic plots step straight into complexity by plotting a %D line. This is an average of the %K line and conceptually no different from any other ten-day moving average, except that it is a moving average (%D) of a smoothed moving average (slow period) of an average calculation (%K).

Simple or complex, the Stochastic plot sandwiches these values, expressed as percentages, between an upper and lower band usually placed at 20 percent and 80 percent. The Relative Strength Index (RSI) uses the average upwards price ranges and average downward price ranges. This value is compared with today's price range. The RSI sets speed band levels at 30 percent and 70 percent.

Most price activity, or speed, is within an equilibrium range. The Stochastic plots the current calculated position within this range. The upper and lower chart bands define the areas approaching the extremes, rather like the thick line in the high-speed areas on a speedometer. The momentum or velocity of price is also limited within an equilibrium range. The RSI style of performance indicator red-lines the extremities.

In the equilibrium range the buyer's mood almost exactly matches the seller's mood so there is high agreement about current market value. There are fewer trading opportunities in this equilibrium range. All things being equal, prices will return to this state of rest and when activity reaches extremes there is an increased probability that it will swing back towards, not to the other extreme, the point of equilibrium. Just like the speeding driver, speed slows to within the normal speed limit and his location changes.

SPEED BUMPS

Oscillator indicators surrender information about speed, but not about location. Activity in the lower extremities is termed oversold. On the balance of probabilities price will move upwards. The indicator suggests an underlying shift in the demand and supply situation.

In trading terms, there are less sellers and more buyers.

An overbought reading, above 80 percent, suggests the current price will return to normal. This implies prices will steady within their established range before moving out of equilibrium again. In trading terms, there are now more sellers than buyers altering the balance and forcing prices down.

Securities moving towards extremities are candidates for a return to equilibrium, and perhaps, even overshooting towards the opposite extremity. Figure 9.5 is an extract from a Metastock Explorer full Australian market RSI search. These are candidates moving into the oversold area. This full market search of nearly 3,000 securities took around four minutes. This list is further refined with eyeball examination of bar charts to find those stocks that have started to recover from oversold positions and move upwards towards the equilibrium point. This distinctive signature points to possible nuggets.

Figure 9.5 Performance indicators. Relative Strength Index (RSI)
Entire Australian market. Extract Metastock explorer results. Extract shows RSI over-sold and moving up

1	A.I ENGINEERING	HARRINGTON GROUP	CORDUKES LIMITED
2	ADVENT LIMITED	HARTLEY POYNTON.	CORNWALL RESOURC
3	AJ LUCAS GROUP	INMOB INDIAN MIN	CPCN CARPENTER P
4	ALPHA HEALTHCARE	INNERHADDEN LIMI	CSR LIMITED
5	AMP LIMITED	INTERNATIONAL AL	DATA ADVANTAGE
6	ANACONDA NICKEL	INVESTOR GROUP	DEVEX LIMITED
7	ANGLO AUSTRALIAN	IPYCA INDUSTRIAL	DIAMOND ROSE NL
8	ANZOIL NL	ISPOA ISP NL	EASTERN GOLD COR
9	APER A.P. EAGERS	IXLA LIMITED	ECTEC LIMITED

Oscillator performance indicators show three bulges in probability and search criteria are adjusted to identify them. With a bulge at each extremity and a very large bulge in the middle, the trader can position all trading candidates on a performance curve. Most securities spend most of their time in the middle area and this suggests a strategy based on fading the trend. This calls for trades from the extremity towards a return to normalcy. Charting this, as shown in Figure 9.6 with Pacific Dunlop, is the first step in assessing the further viability of the trade. Knowing where we are, and how fast we are travelling sets the scene for a trade. A database search based on performance indicator results provides this information.

Oscillators revel in complexity. By manipulating the calculation parameters, price element and time periods, percentage or point change, the user builds more subtle indicators. Some traders look for disagreement, or divergence as an additional distinctive oscillator signature. When the bar chart price makes new lows and the RSI plot does the opposite, developing a series of new highs moving up from the oversold level, the indicator signals divergence as shown in Figure 9.7 with HIH Insurance. Some traders use this as a leading trend change signal, both at market tops and bottoms, believing it uncovers performance relationships obscured by the bar chart. The road to complexity is easily opened but users are warned of blinding clouds of confusion.

In selecting indicators, the choice between a specialized, flighty thoroughbred, or a robust general duties hack or ranch horse is yours. The market yields winning outcomes for each, but whether you ride them to the finish depends on your trading style. Complexity is not a panacea for profits so do not confuse the search for increasingly subtle signatures with the search for nuggets.

THE INDICATOR SUCCESS TEST

Performance searches clarify the trend and its strength. Use them to find candidates for closer analysis, or to confirm initial conclusions based on eyeball observations. The lists provide candidates, but not solutions. We build better lists by applying search tools correctly rather than on the basis of complexity alone.

Figure 9.6 Performance indicators
Pacific Dunlop, Australia
Daily bar chart and RSI

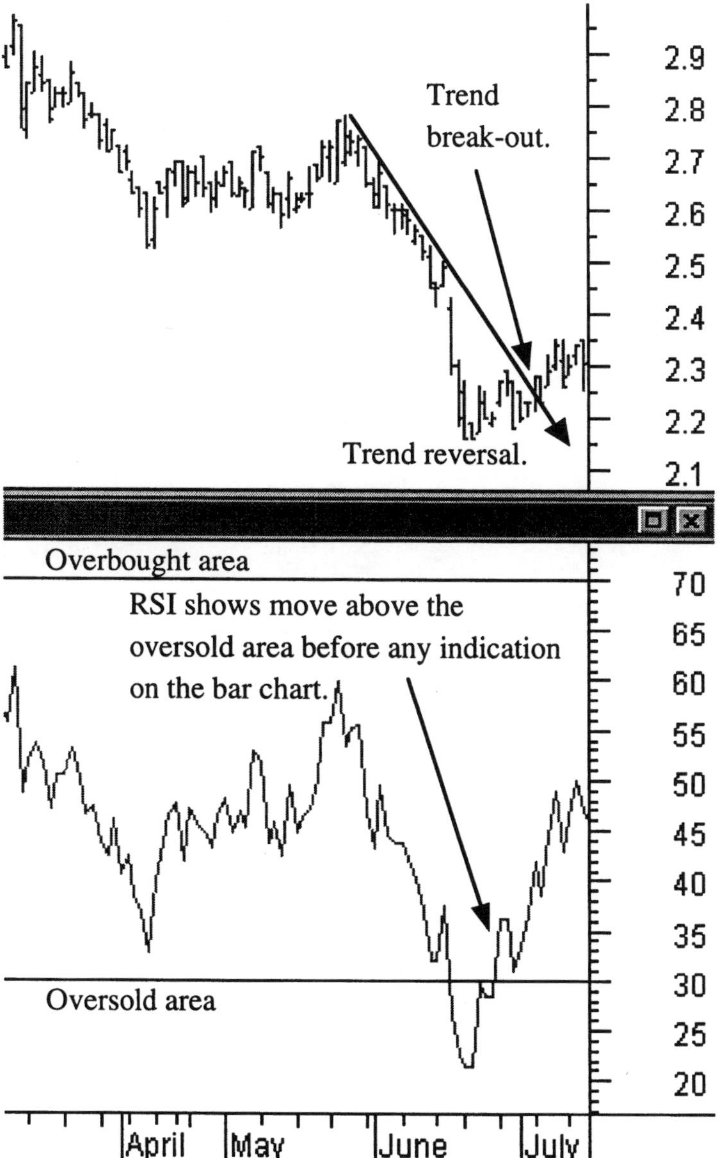

Figure 9.7 RSI divergence
HIH Insurance, Australia
Daily bar chart and RSI

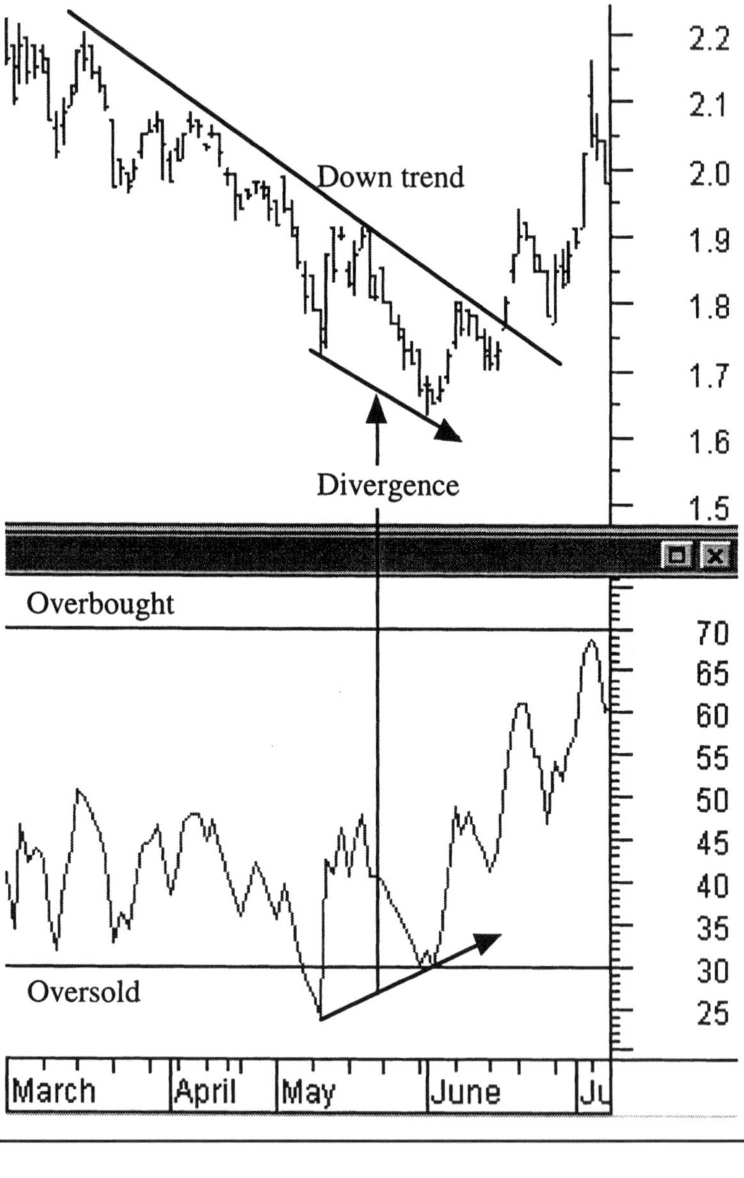

By comparing a screen display of our chosen indicator, and parameter settings, with a bar chart of the stock being analyzed, we assess the effectiveness of our choice. All indicators must pass this test. Past bar chart activity shows the very best trading opportunities. If our selected indicator signals these historical opportunities then it is likely to signal future opportunities.

Traders must get this relationship correct. The indicator reflects decision points already on the bar chart. Indicator signals fit the bar chart, not vice versa. It is a sad trader who moans, 'The indicator signaled a trend break but price continued to fall.' Price validates indicator results and the further you move away from market price — the more complex the indicator calculation — the greater the danger of losing touch with the market.

The United Kingdom listed De La Rue shows this problem in Figure 9.8 when the bar chart is compared with the RSI indicator display. Normally, traders keep a keen eye on divergence signals. Initially, the new price peaks for De La Rue are matched with new RSI peaks shown as lines A and A1, and this confirms the up trend. The next price peak at B is not matched with a new RSI peak at B1. This divergence pattern continues with price peaks C and D. In this case the RSI divergence signals take the trader out of a strong up trend robbing him of substantial additional profits. The RSI divergence does not identify a change in the De La Rue trend. Building trading decisions around RSI divergence alone is not a useful strategy in trading this stock.

If your chosen indicator does not pick historical turning points it certainly will not select future ones. Any database search built around such an indicator turns up fools' gold.

JUGGLING LISTS

Mining the database using performance indicators to identify particular signature activity is not a substitute for further analysis. Like the previous searches, this search helps to manage our time effectively by eliminating irrelevant price activity. Those candidates passing the test are not necessarily good trades.

Figure 9.8 Matching bar chart reality with indicator signals
De La Rue, UK
Daily bar chart with Relative Strength Index (RSI)

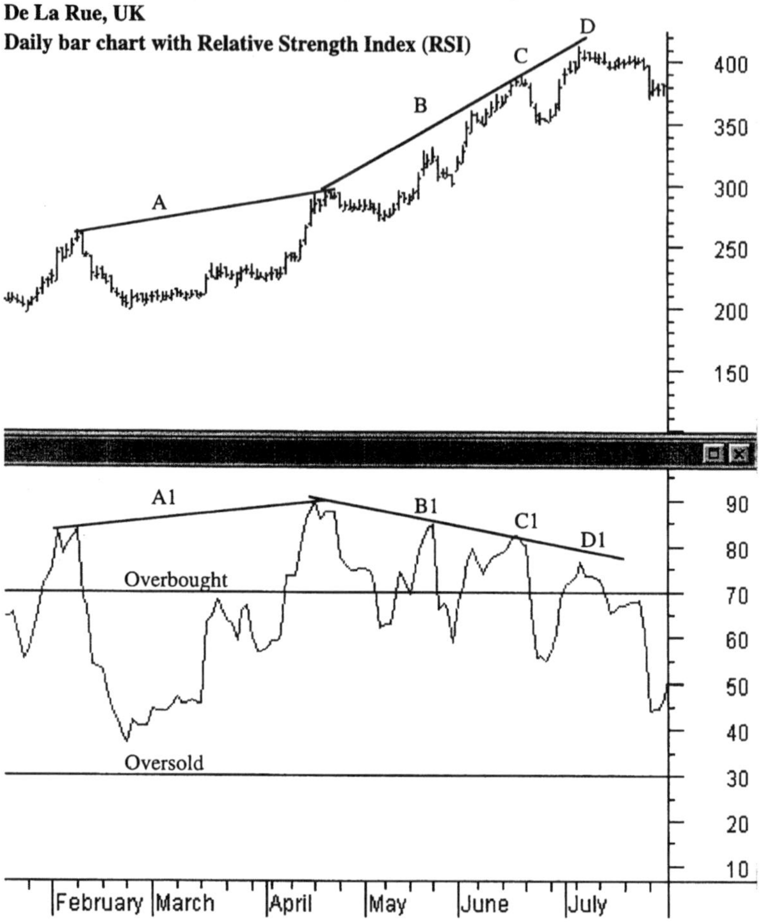

Each candidate on the lists, as shown above, is finally eyeballed on a chart. This way the nugget is cleaned and inspected to discard any made of fools' gold. The chart gives additional information and the first set of supplementary numbers needed for any trading decision. When other market numbers confirm the balance of probability, the trade is opened, or closed.

Some nuggets are counterfeit so we need some simple tests for real gold before we start converting the nuggets into dollar signs. The following chapters describe these tests.

10

An Assay Test — Looking for Life

In the 18th century suspicious merchants bit gold coins to make sure they weren't made of soft gilded lead. Our first list of trading nuggets must undergo a similar quality test because some potential trades are counterfeit. Sometimes every indicator flashes a buy signal, but the trade goes nowhere or prices do move, but not far enough or fast enough to satisfy our trading objectives. We need to determine if the market sees imminent price action because some break-outs move sideways rather than upwards. We tighten the search focus, looking for signs that the market thinks the stock needs revaluing.

Although it pays to be patient in trading, it is also dangerous to wait too long for a trade to turn in a profit. In assessing the shrinking list of candidates we need a means to assess the probability of price action developing within a reasonable time.

The stochastic and momentum-style indicators point us in this direction, but we need additional confirmation. We get this by exploring some further relationships between moving averages and applying one further observation about the nature of the market.

For this we use a Guppy Multiple Moving Average (MMA) indicator to confirm the market is coiled for action. Like a compressed spring the market sometimes explodes into action and we can be ready for it. Other indicators tell us the direction of movement, but the Guppy MMA tells us it is imminent. This indicator tells us the balance of probability is tipped in our favor because price is about to get a kick along.

This kick does not come out of nowhere. The operation of the market demands that price gets booted under specific circumstances.

FIXED PRICE

Travelers are often bewildered in tropical resort islands when they discover that shopping really means haggling. 'Fixed price' stores have sprung up to cater to this insecurity. The market stalls and beach front tourist markets are a confusing babble of hard bargains. For many, shopping is unpleasant because there is no fixed price.

This is one of two different market approaches. We are accustomed to the fixed price model. When we talk of bargain hunting we usually mean finding the store with the best bar-coded pricing for the goods we want. Shopping for the same basket of groceries at American Stores may cost less than shopping at Safeway, and there may be differences between suburban and country stores. But in every case the price of the goods is marked on the shelf and encoded in the bar code. There is no room for negotiation with the assistant on the checkout.

A bargain hunter searches for the best location offering the best price. Some investors try to use this approach to finding buying opportunities in the stock market but the financial market rarely works this way.

The financial markets are built on the island resort model. There are no fixed prices and buyers and sellers constantly argue with each other about the trading price of every security. We label them bulls and bears as shorthand to describe how optimism attempts to triumph over pessimism. As we show in the next chapter, the market has morning prices and afternoon prices, it has special prices and tourist prices. The one thing it does not have is a fixed price.

This important observation tells us the market is constantly in a state of unstable equilibrium. Like a ball balanced, or resting, on the top of a flag pole, the slightest puff of wind will send it plummeting. The tendency is to move away from the resting point towards another balance point.

In contrast, a stable equilibrium is when the ball is at the bottom of a valley. It takes a fair amount of pressure to push it up the sides. The tendency is always to fall back towards the resting point.

The stock market shows an unstable equilibrium. It has to. If it did not, there would be long-term agreement on pricing and, effectively, no stock market. Without disagreement about prices and value, traders are reduced to shopping at American Stores or Safeway, tracking down the best fixed price offerings.

This pricing instability means when prices pause it is an unusual event. Paradoxically, when prices are apparently stable — when there is a high level of agreement about prices — it is the time when they are most likely to change. The dynamics driving the market zero in on stable prices because someone inevitably sees an opportunity to do better, or worse, than the current price.

In the same way that fixed price stores broadly agree on pricing an item, most of the time the market broadly agrees with the valuation of a stock. This does not provide a trading opportunity where we can exploit the difference between our entry and exit prices. But every now and then the market comes into near-perfect agreement about value. This stability cannot last.

It is usually a signal for a violent disagreement and this disagreement is what we trade. Points of temporary stability and agreement imply a greater probability of imminent instability. The MMA indicator discussed below is used to find this point of agreement.

A BOOT UP THE MARKET

Stability and stable prices are relative terms. When we talk in this way about the financial market the trader frequently reaches for a moving average to compare today's price with some average of prices in the past. Moving averages in all their forms tell us a great deal about current price in relation to a previous price series, or about the behavior of price over a selected period.

At this level of analysis we would like to know what the market is thinking about the stock, and if the current price is in tune with that thinking. If the current price is below market thinking, we have a tougher decision to make because we are pitting our conviction against the common opinion of the market. If current price is above market thinking we have to decide if the security is overpriced, if it represents a bargain entry price when compared to the potential for the stock, or if this is merely an enthusiastic bubble that will not last.

Essentially, any combination of moving averages is equipped to provide us with information and answers for these questions. Taking it at its most basic, a common grouping compares a 3-day moving average with 10-day moving average. To recap briefly, the 3-day moving average tells us how today's price is situated in relation to the previous 3-day period, on average. This comparison with today's price tells us if the stock, on a very basic level, is overpriced, or underpriced. The 3-day average gives us a reference point for American airplane manufacturer Boeing, Figure 10.1, but the trend, or price activity it measures, is too short for most trading purposes.

Hence, we smooth out the sudden bumps and lumps with, say, a 10-day moving average, using Boeing for base data. This gives us an additional reference point so we can more effectively compare the placement of today's price in a context of a more established trend. For those who are involved in investing rather than trading, these figures are often shifted from 3 days to 3 weeks, and from 10 days to 10 weeks. On the other extreme, intraday trading, we could use a 3-minute and a 10-minute tick chart. The principle remains the same in all cases. By using two reference points, plus a known point — today's close — we can triangulate a position.

The trading signals given by most moving average approaches are usually based on crossovers; that is, when the short-term line crosses the long-term line, and when both lines are heading in the same direction. This is usually understood as a good indication that prices will continue to move in that direction.

But, additionally, each crossover point also indicates a moment of agreement on prices and this is the aspect we want to draw out. In

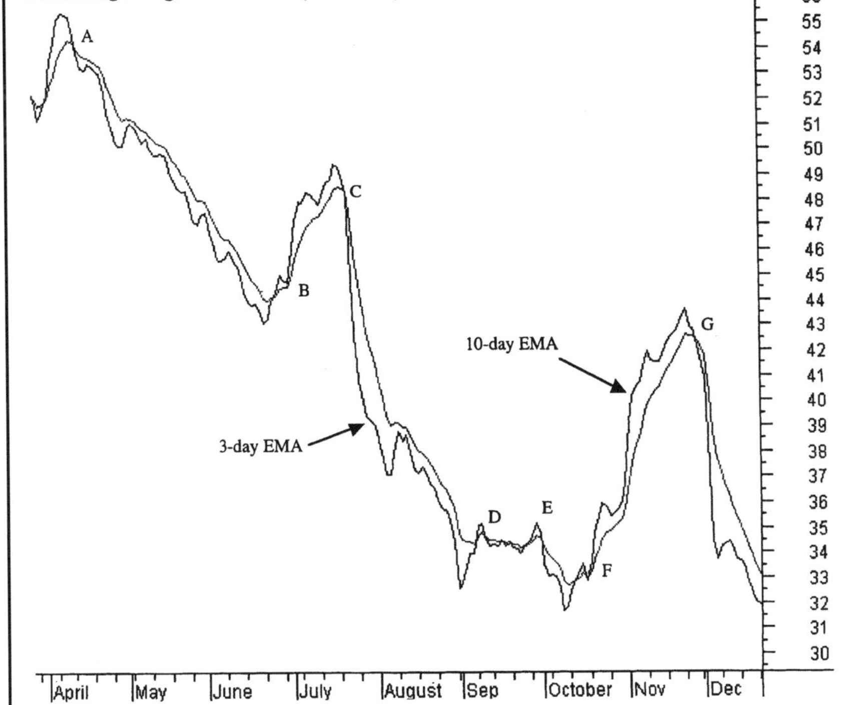

Figure 10.1 Boeing Co, USA. Daily chart.
Two moving average crossovers 3-day and 10-day

two time frames, two valuations are synchronised, shown as points A through G in Figure 10.1. This momentary agreement cannot last, and it is usually fleeting. Usually we ignore this message because we are looking for different trading information.

Let's pause for a moment, forget that we use two averages to smooth out whipsaws by confirming signals from the shorter average with a longer average, and examine this crossover point. We subconsciously use the crossover as a signal to confirm valuation because we compare current bar chart price with the crossover point. Very few traders use more than two moving averages, but when they do a significant relationship develops.

The US futures trader, Linda Bradford Raschke, noted these relationships using momentum charts and negative feedback loops on short-term and intraday charts. Pursuing the relationship between momentum, oscillator signals, fractuals and critical points, while eliminating market noise, she developed some swing trading techniques and risk control strategies incorporating this information.[1] Another example from this type of work was used in Chapter 8. Our purpose here is at a less complex level so we use one of these concepts in the context of a basic Exponential Moving Average (EMA). Our intention is not to solely manage positions according to the market's subsequent behavior, as in swing trading, but to use this information to confirm previous analysis of points where there is increased probability — a bulge — of imminent price action.

By plotting a group of six short-term averages — 3, 5, 8, 10, 12 and 15 — the emerging relationships are clearer. Figure 10.2 shows Boeing with this group of moving averages. Here we combine multiple short time frames on a single screen display. It does not include a closing price line.

As expected, each of these different time frames, or moving averages, give us additional useful information about the nature of the price activity. We might expect the crossover points to lean to the right as each point develops a little later, depending on the length of the average used. Instead the crossovers are almost simultaneous, shown as points A, B, C, F and G. The crossover signals generated by each are roughly in the same place no matter which time scale — 3, 5, 8 etc. — is used. The entire collection of short-term averages all converge and cross within very short time spans at points A through to F, which are placed in the same locations as Figure 10.1. Note how the indecision at points D and E is eliminated by the display showing the group of short-term averages. We return to this later.

1 Swing trading is about entering trades with minimal risk and managing positions according to the market's subsequent behavior. It does not try to predict an outcome in the same way that pattern recognition or trend-based strategies do. Swing trading is a useful approach to markets where traders can take simultaneous long and short positions.

These concepts, and others, are applied in *Street Smarts: High Probability Trading Strategies for the Futures and Equities Markets* by Linda Bradford Raschke and Larry Connors. This is available direct from Oceanview Financial Research, fax US 818 353 2099.

Figure 10.2 Boeing Co, USA. Dailychart.
Short-term group of moving average crossovers: 3, 5, 8, 10, 12 and 15

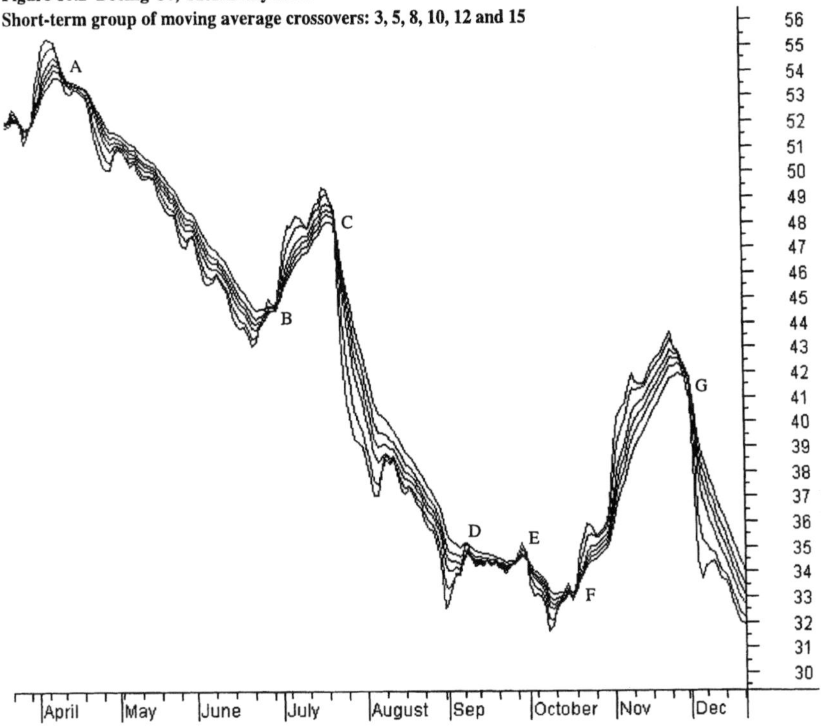

The moment of price stability captured by two moving averages is confirmed by every other short-term average, at about the same time. The action of the group of moving averages tells us something that the individual averages cannot. This convergence of average calculation across multiple time frames pinpoints important market turning points.

This happens in a time window that is not significantly out of step with the current price action. The convergence does not signal the direction of price. It alerts us to increased potential for price movements because we know that agreement on value cannot last for long in the market.

This combination of short-term averages suggests that at significant turning points the strength of the revaluation of the stock is so strong that it draws every previous valuation together. The short-term averages do not, as we might expect, streak ahead because they are measuring only the revaluation in a very short-term time span.

THE BOOT ON THE OTHER FOOT

Using a group of short-term averages, the trader sees an increased potential for price action as the temporary agreement on value disintegrates under market pressure. The investor, with a longer time horizon, also sees the possibilities in this approach.

The investor usually takes a longer view of the market but he still wants to select the significant turning points. Identifying these points, but not the direction of the turn, is assisted by using a group of long-term moving averages. The logic of the construction of the averages and the interpretation of the results is exactly the same as above.

When plotting the averages from an investment perspective we have two choices. The first is to shift to a weekly display, using 10 as the time value. This is automatically read as 10 weeks because we are using a weekly display. The second choice is to use the daily display. When we do this we must change the weekly time periods into the daily equivalents. So 10 weeks become 50 days.

Why 50 days? Ten weeks on a weekly chart means 10 trading weeks of five days each. The daily equivalent is 50 days, not 70 days.

In selecting short-term averages we used a mid-week starting point and shifted to a full week. In selecting a long-term group we double the last of the short-term group and start with 30 days. Moving one week at a time, we add 35-, 40-, 45- and 50-day moving averages. I choose to end with a 60-day moving average that I use as a last resort confirmation line.

Traditional market theory lists late entry and exit signals as a penalty attached to long-term averages. They are late because the time scale is too long. We expect any convergence, or coming together, of this average group will be spread over days and weeks.

Instead there are sudden and decisive shifts in the relationships, mirroring the activity of the short-term group. Staying with Boeing, Figure 10.3 paints the picture clearly. The crossover points are just as dramatic as with Figure 10.2, but now there are only three: points 1, 2 and 3.

This chart message tells us that when the market reaches long-term agreement on valuation the long-term averages converge. At this moment of convergence, when the lines crossover, the market undergoes a significant revaluation of the stock leading to a major price change. The investor can use this type of information for investing in the same way as the trader uses the short-term information for trading.

Figure 10.3 Boeing Co, USA. Daily chart.
Long-term group of moving average crossovers: 30, 35, 40, 45, 50 and 60

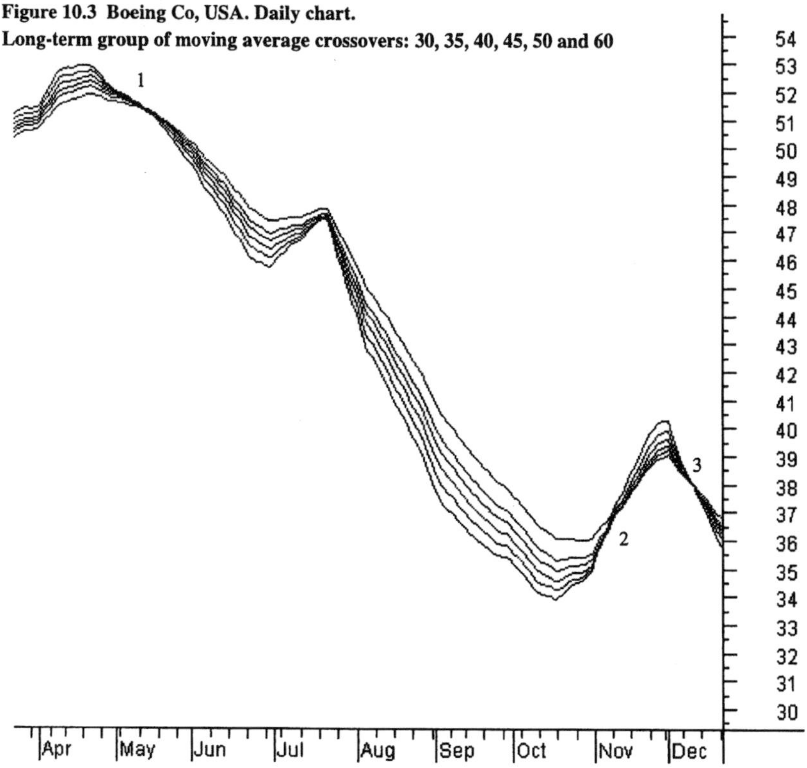

But, surprisingly both charts have an unexpected application for the trader.

BOOTS AND ALL FOR THE TRADER

Counter to our intuitive understanding of the lagging impact of averages, both the short-term group and the long-term group identify significant market revaluations as they happen. The potential lag is reduced because the signal we read is not price, but behavior.

The implication is startling. When Figures 10.2 and 10.3 are combined in Figure 10.4 we see the market reaches agreement on value across multiple time frames at major turning points. This is a fractual repetition where activity is duplicated in increasingly larger scales. The pattern of agreement and disagreement is evident in both the investors' long-term averages and the traders' short-term averages. When agreement coincides in both time frames it leads to a powerful price change. The letter and number notations refer to the same positions as in the previous Boeing charts. Areas A1, F2 and G3 are major points of agreement giving specific and unambiguous timely trading signals.

Area A1 signals an exit, but only in conjunction with other indicators. More properly, area A1 confirms the agreement on value suggested by the short-term group of averages.

Contrast this to points B and C. Despite the powerful up thrust, it is not fully confirmed by the long-term group. The short-term traders cannot convince the long-term holders of a higher value for Boeing. The sell off at point C is rapidly endorsed by the long-term investors. This is not to say there is no trading opportunity in this area. This is a rally opportunity. The MMA does suggest the move is likely to collapse fairly quickly because it does not have the powerful support of a general agreement on value.

Area F2 signals an entry, but only when the direction of the price move is confirmed by other indicators. Again, more properly, this area shows a high level of agreement on valuation, and therefore an increased probability of violent disagreement. This was suggested a

Figure 10.4 Boeing Co, USA. Daily chart.
Guppy MMA indicator
Using two groups of moving average crossovers

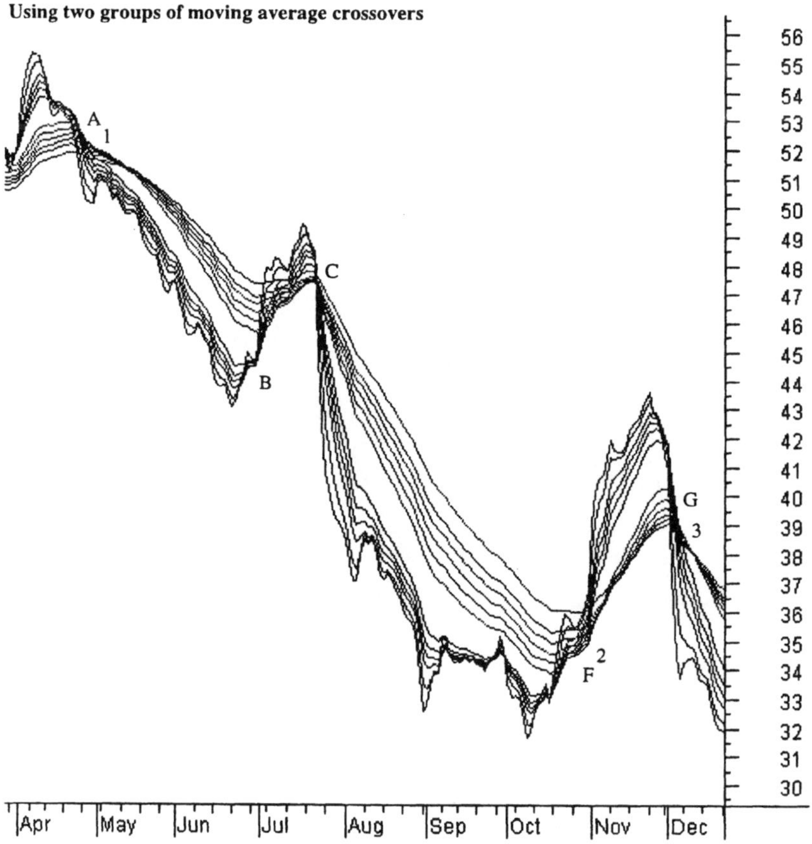

few days earlier as the short-term group of averages combined and drew the long-term group with them. Later we will look at rules to turn these areas into more precise signals.

Gold prospectors always have their samples, and we have perfect examples. By comparing a scrappy everyday chart with perfection we improve our use of trading tools. This combination takes place simultaneously in both time frames in Figure 10.5 when applied to Singapore-listed precision optics manufacturer Avimo. Here the major signals at points A and B were given in time for traders to jump into and out of the major price moves.

Figure 10.5 Guppy multiple moving averages
Avimo, Singapore
Daily

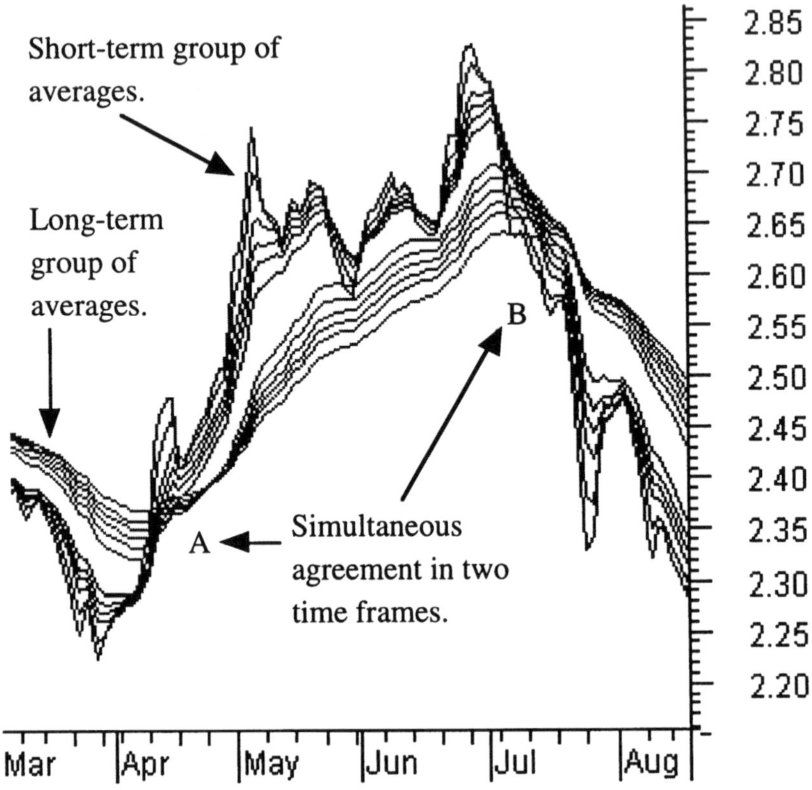

Real trading has to work with less than perfect examples, which is why we concentrate on Boeing. Figure 10.6 shows the daily bar chart with the MMA letters and numerals transferred from earlier charts. The confirming trading signals generated by the MMA indicator took traders out of a position in Boeing at point A before significant loss. The MMA assay test kept them out of the enticing potential, but disastrous, trade at point B. The MMA test put traders into a trade at point F in time to make a reasonable profit before getting out at point G. We look at trading rules in detail below.

Figure 10.6 Matching MMA signals with price activity
Boeing Co, USA
Daily bar chart

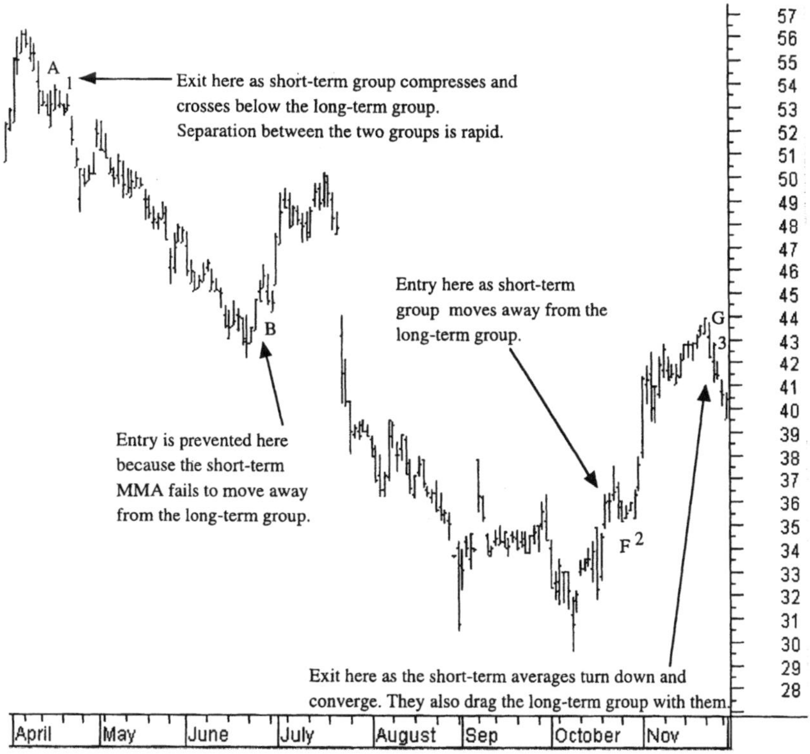

When these two groups of moving averages are combined and used in this way we call it a Guppy MMA indicator. The indicator does not signal a value, such as $12.00. Visually it highlights an agreement in valuation across multiple time frames. This is an agreement between both long-term and short-term stockholders. The agreement signals a greater than normal probability that the subsequent price action will be substantial.

When the market reaches agreement on the value of a security in both time frames explosive action often follows. Contrary to our intuitive understanding, the long-term averages do not lag so far behind the short-term averages that they provide no trading signal. At explosive market points the revaluation of stock, as reflected by price, is so fundamental that every calculation is effected. When each group comes into agreement and when both groups simultaneously cross within a single narrow window of time, we can be confident the balance of probability is very much on our side in this trade — it is going to move, and move soon.

We have searched our database with other indicators and they have already suggested the direction of the price move. The MMA indicator allows us to put this in a time frame narrowed by the balance of probability.

When we start to look more closely at our small list of trading opportunities this helps select those where action is imminent. The MMA gives a better understanding of how the market is viewing the value of the security. When agreement is high, disagreement is inevitable and we want to be in the market when it moves.

GUPPY MMA TRADING RULES

The MMA indicator develops seven main trading rules, but remember it is not a stand-alone indicator. It is most useful as a confirming entry signal, although it can assist with timing exits. The signals should be confirmed with the results of other indicators and price plots.

The trading rules for the Guppy MMA are:

- When the bands from both groups begin to narrow down and converge prepare for price action as the agreement on valuation collapses. For those using the MMA in a swing trading approach a combination of long and short positions straddle the potential price action. When prices do surge, the losing position is closed and traders ride the winner.
- Trade in the direction of the crossover. Go long if the crossover is on the upside. Go short or exit long positions with downside crossovers.
- Rapid separation of the two groups confirms the strength of the break-out.
- The long-term averages confirm the direction of the trend.

- The bubbles created by the short-term group of averages show the favorable exit points. This can be short-term rally trades. Judging the trend top is difficult so look for the leading two or three averages to converge or come together above a widely spread long-term group. Confirm this early signal with other indicator readings.
- False trend breaks are identified when the short-term averages strike upwards towards a well-spread group of long-term averages. Treat these as rally trades, not trend trades.
- Aggressive traders move in anticipation of MMA break-outs. Conservative traders wait for confirmation.

Each of these rules is applied to the exciting run-up in the London nickel price in Figure 10.7. Implementing these rules gives us a way to assay the quality of trading opportunities in this market sector.

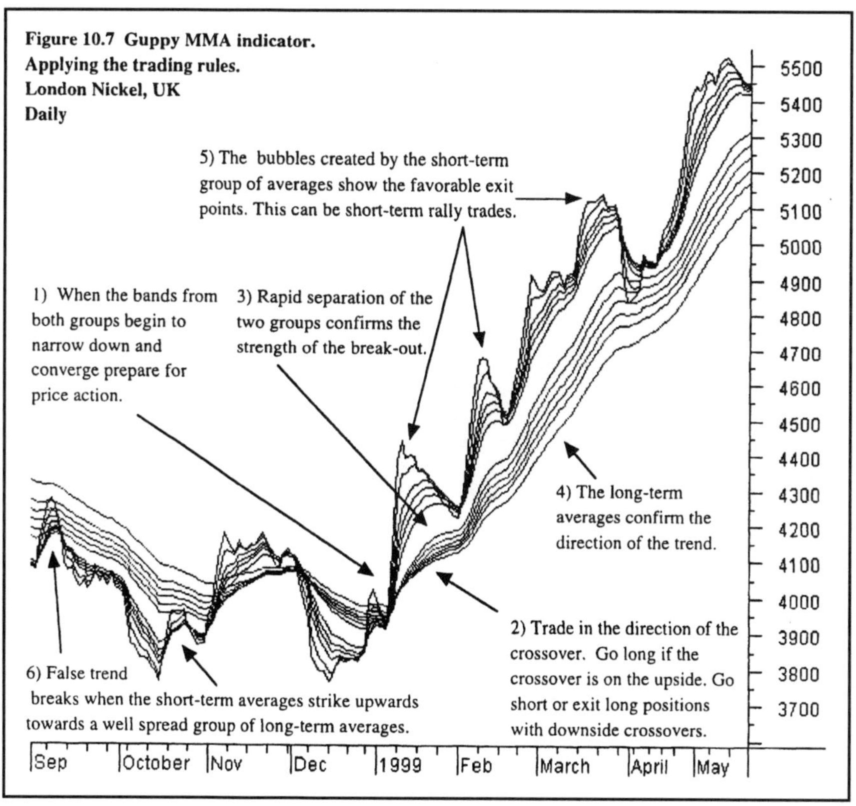

Figure 10.7 Guppy MMA indicator.
Applying the trading rules.
London Nickel, UK
Daily

This style of market analysis provides trading opportunities in all market conditions because each time frame is a fractual repetition of price activity. The structure of the market in large time frames is maintained and reflected in smaller time frames. When the Guppy MMA indicator is applied to tick charts sound trading signals are generated. The 10-minute S&P tick chart in Figure 10.8 reveals short-term intraday trading opportunities in the same way as the end-of-day charts help position traders. Here the time frames are measured in minutes, not days, with averages calculated in minutes.

Figure 10.8 Guppy MMA day trading signals
S&P 500, USA
10-minute tick chart

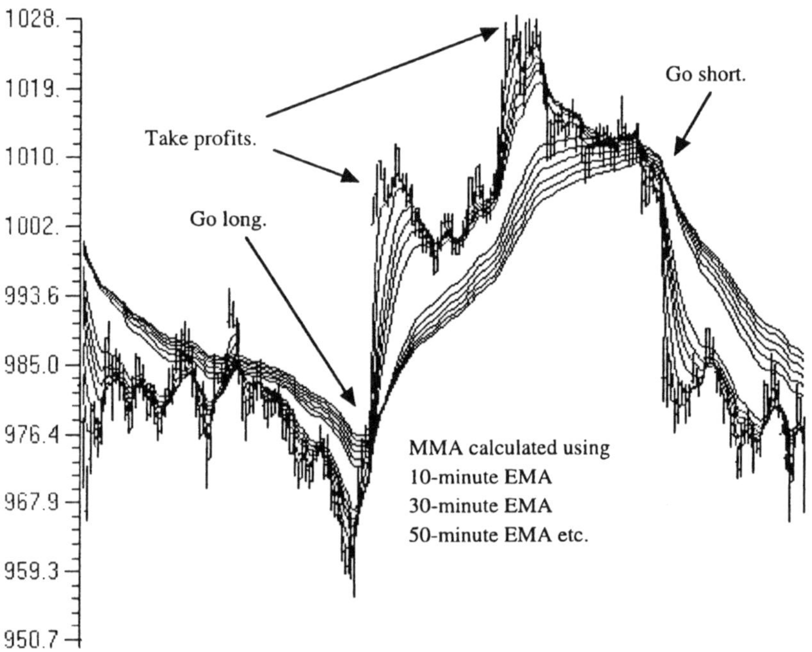

ASSAY RESULTS

The MMA is only used to fine-tune trading opportunities already selected by other processes. Like the merchant biting every proffered gold coin, we use the MMA to assay the candidates thrown up in early searches. The MMA is not easily defined as a search criteria because the mere crossover of one or two averages does not reveal the synergy displayed on the chart.

I use the MMA as one of the final steps in assessing trading opportunities identified as the result of other search methods. You may wish to use it as a prospecting tool applied to your entire database. A series of closely related custom formulas and subsequent Metastock Explorer search criteria for the MMA are shown in the annex below. This speeds up the database search by returning a 'yes' — 1 — response for securities. Charts from this list are inspected visually for the synergistic relationship. The significance and degree of the MMA constriction is a judgment call you make as a trader because no formula construction gives a definitive answer.

Synergy is one of those annoying terms that everybody uses knowledgeably, but that few people understand. In less pretentious days people used the term 'the sum is greater than its parts' to describe a synergistic situation. The MMA indicator does this by revealing additional information about the dynamics of the market system that cannot be obtained from any individual moving average.

There is no single calculated result — no single value, such as above 80 or below 20 — that reveals this dynamic. Stocks that pass the MMA test are alive and they get a tick because, on balance, the probability of a price explosion is greater. Stocks failing the MMA test are discarded.

By the end of this elimination round we want a short list of stocks meeting all of our conditions. The gilded lead coins go on the scrap heap and the real gold coins are sorted by value. Usually there are only one or two survivors that fit all these conditions. Sometimes there are none. We can do business with the survivors, but just like 18th century merchants working without a standard of currency exchange, we first need to make some decisions about the value of a Spanish piece-of-eight as measured against a Portuguese silver dollar. We must decide if our find is worth more smelted into bullion, or as a distinctive nugget. Our outlook on life colors this decision in important ways.

ANNEX

Creating a Guppy MMA display in Metastock requires several steps:

- Open a bar chart of a security with a long trading history.
- Delete the inner window showing volume. Click on the bar chart display to highlight it. Select Cut from the Edit menu. You will be advised that this action deletes the base security. This is OK. You now have a blank screen, but the underlying data is still intact.
- From the Indicator List select Moving Average. Add each of the short-term group of Exponential Moving Averages (EMAs) to the display by dragging down the indicator and changing the moving average value. Keep all these averages displayed in the same color. I use blue.
- Stay on the same screen display for the long-term group. From the Indicator List select Moving Average. Add each of the long-term group of EMAs to the display by dragging down the indicator and changing the moving average value. Keep all these averages displayed in a single different color. I use red.
- When the display is completed select Save As from the File menu. In the dialogue box next to Save As Type select the Template option. Give the template a name and click SAVE. This template can now be applied to any chart display.

To bring up the template just right click on the bar chart display and select Apply Template. Choose the MMA template from the dialogue box to see the new display.

Trader Bob Laidlaw has created a search that is similar to, but is not exactly the same as, the MMA indicator. He has added a layer of complexity to the MMA, but this is consistent with developing complex and subtle indicators based on simple concepts as discussed in previous chapters. Metastock users can add the custom indicator and formula to their indicator list and Explorer module.

The seven custom indicators used by Laidlaw are:

```
MMA 10/45
If(OscP(10,45,E,%)>0,+1,−1)

MMA 12/50
If(OscP(12,50,E,%)>0,+1,−1)

MMA 15/60
If(OscP(15,60,E,%)>0,+1,−1)

MMA 3/30
If(OscP(3,30,E,%)>0,+1,−1)

MMA 5/35
If(OscP(5,35,E,%)>0,+1,−1)

MMA 8/40
If(OscP(8,40,E,%)>0,+1,−1)

MMA TOTAL (Note space between MMA 3/30 must be
retained)
Fml("MMA 3/30")+Fml("MMA 5/35")+Fml("MMA 8/
40")+Fml("MMA 10/45")+Fml("MMA 12/50")+Fml("MMA
15/60")
```

The Exploration formula is:

```
Column A
Close
Column B
Ref(C,−1)
Column C
Ref(C,−2)
Column D
Fml("mma 3/30")+Fml("mma 5/35")+Fml("mma 8/40")+
Fml("mma 10/45")+Fml("mma 12/50")+Fml("mma 15/60")
Column E
Ref(Fml("MMA 3/30")+Fml("MMA 5/35")+Fml("MMA 8/
40")+Fml("MMA 10/45")+Fml("MMA 12/50")+Fml("MMA
15/60"),−1)

Filter source
Formula
When (colD,>,0) AND When(colE,<=,0)
```

This search formula will help you get to the right area, but you will still need to eyeball each of the results. We do not suggest that you use this as an initial search for trading candidates. Readers can cut, copy and paste this formula from *www.guppytraders.com* into Metastock.

11

Two Sides of the Same Coin

'Know your enemy' is the tactician's adage. Many traders believe the enemy is the person on the other side of the trade. Instead they need only to look in the mirror, not the computer screen, for the answer. The trader is often his own worst enemy, defeating himself before the trading battle starts.

The simple question: Are you a bull or a bear? tells us how this happens. With nuggets in hand we must answer this question every day: Do we buy or sell?

Intuitively we make a decision and intuitively bring our bias into action. Oblivious to this intuitive bias, we marshal a battery of indicators to support a decision already made subconsciously. It comes as no surprise that the initial good trading opportunities seem to get better — even when they start to lose money.

In selecting the way we mine our database for trading opportunities, in choosing the types of indicators we use, in looking for particular types of chart patterns, we act on our bias before we even glance at the day's price data. When the nugget is unearthed we do not thoroughly test for fools' gold. We believe we are good prospectors and often this belief trades us into trouble.

We get into trouble by confusing objective results with subjective conclusions. Every indicator, a stochastic, for example, consistently measures the same relationships in exactly the same way. The placement of the last data point is an objective calculated decision made according to the construction rules. Mathematics alone positions the line. Indicator results are arrived at objectively and this is often claimed as a technical analysis strength.

No such logic restrains the trader so we subjectively interpret the results. If the stochastic falls below the 20 percent line we believe the security is oversold. Above the 80 percent line we understand the market is overbought. The conclusions are valid because they concur with past behavior, but our interpretation of the potential for future price action is very subjective. We trade our interpretation so it doesn't pay to be blind to our bias and the ways it appears to shift the balance of probability.

If we do not recognize our bias then as trades fail it is easy to blame our indicators, or our technique. Instead of dealing with the real issue we chase after irrelevant solutions — buying more expensive software or trying different trading techniques. And the real problem remains unsolved.

The solution is in understanding our bias and using it to our advantage. For those with a bearish disposition, the process described below helps with the entry into long positions. For bulls it is particularly important in deciding exits, although it helps in assessing entries as well. This step fits into your personal trading process at the point you identify as your weakest. We have included it here because it plays a part in the entry decision for both bulls and bears.

THERE'S A BEAR IN THERE

Many traders believe it is sufficient just to acknowledge one's bullishness or bearishness about the current market in general or market segment in particular. This orientation does help to identify the better opportunities for trading with or against market feeling, and ways to use these market clues are discussed in the following chapter. This is a last process in a trading decision, all too often reached by taking a shortcut around our bias.

Understanding and using our bias involves two steps and determines, *a priori* — before the fact — how we look at a chart. In the first step we learn to recognize our bias. In the second we consistently take it into account when charts are being analyzed before a trade so that it does not unfavorably distort the entry or the exit decision.

The exit is no problem when we meet profit objectives. The exit becomes a problem when we think a falling price will stop and start to rise. We succumb to temptation and stay with the trade beyond our initial profit objectives. Or when prices falter before our objective is reached we hang on, ignoring the reversal signals and eventually riding with the trade into a loss.

In the best of all possible worlds these situations never arise. In the reality of the market they happen with alarming frequency and we cannot ignore them. We need to develop strategies and tactics to cope with these situations and retain profits. A trade that initially shows a profit but is later abandoned at a loss because you held on hoping it would return to old profit levels is a poor trade — even if the eventual loss is less than 2 percent of trading equity.

STEP 1 — GETTING AN ID ON BIAS

How do you decide if your bias lies with the bulls, or the bears? The two charts below give a simple test and show the impact of a bullish bias on trading analysis built around simple trend lines. In both cases we look for the best entry. In Figure 11.1 we want to continue a profitable trading band strategy. In Figure 11.2 we want the best possible entry for a long position, buying in anticipation of a price rise. These are two sides of the same coin so we see how a bullish bias gets us into trades early and out of them too late.

The security UKN in Figure 11.1 offers an entry opportunity in a rising trend as part of a long-term strategy based on trading bands. Let's explore the reasoning that encourages us to enter at point A and stay in the trade at point B.

- An established trend line is in place, line D, and the pullback at A is consistent with the price activity in December.
- A logical stop loss is around the support/resistance level shown at C. If the entry at A turns out to be incorrect then recent price action sets level C as a confirmation of the error and a good exit point.
- Pullbacks to the trend line, such as point B, provide additional buying opportunities. This trend is so well established that we can be fairly confident any spikes below it are very temporary.

- We set a series of conservative profit targets on the upper edge of the parallel trading channel trend line. Upper targets are set with reference to the upper trend line. Effective targets are also based on the general upper trend line shown in bold.

Trading summary

An entry at point A or B is consistent with a bullish trading strategy based on trading bands. An exit is not signalled at B. Good stop loss is provided by the trend line and nearby support levels.

Figure 11.1 Establishing bull points for a trade based on trading bands in a rising trend. UKN. Daily bar chart

In the second chart, ILM, Figure 11.2, we look for a bullish break-out to decide if taking a position at point A is worthwhile. Below we assemble all the points in favor of buying this break-out.

- The trend line, E, is validly drawn because it touches the maximum number of points. Shifting it further to the right, as shown by line F, ignores the September peak entirely. In its current position the January price action uses it as a support line.
- Conservative traders wait for a close to the right of trend line, F. Aggressive traders use the pullback to point B as confirmation of the up trend.
- Point B helps establish a new up trend and we tentatively plot this as line C. Any close below this signals our exit.
- The stop-loss conditions are set by the short-term resistance level shown as line D.

Figure 11.2 Establishing bull points for as trade based on a break-out from a falling trend.
ILM. Daily bar chart

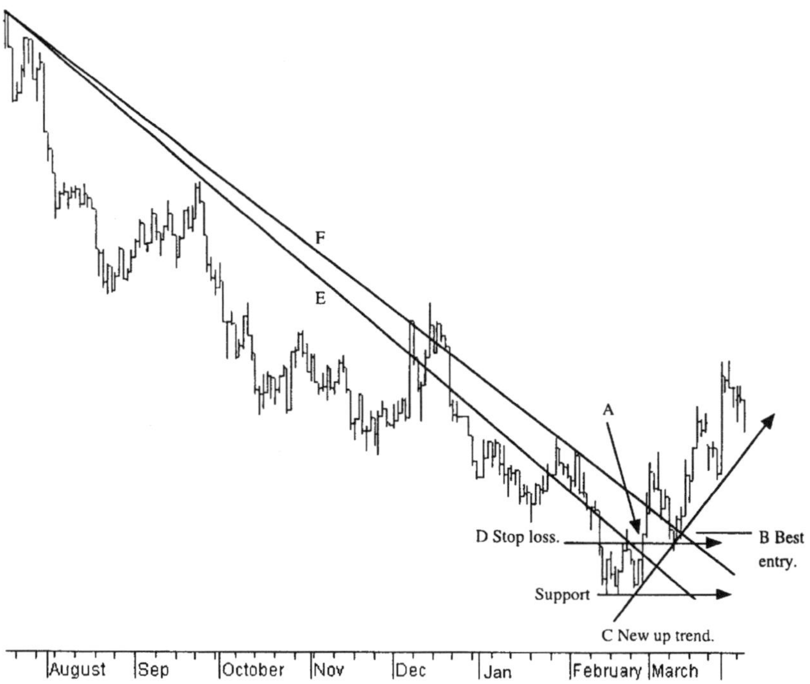

Trading summary

This is a bullish entry offering, as it turns out, a six-week trade. The entry is confirmed by the re-test of the new trend line and the stop loss is clearly set on old support levels just below our entry point.

BULLY FOR THE BEARS

In both cases we use a bullish bias to confirm the validity of the trend, to develop our trading tactics and to support our decision to take an early entry, or to stay with the position despite a temporary pullback. The analysis of these charts appears straightforward and is typical of the way we approach chart analysis with our eyes closed.

But there is one major problem.

Both charts are of the Australian All Ordinaries market index, but Figure 11.2 has been turned upside down using the Metastock Invert Scale function in the Y-Axis Properties menu. It has also been extended to show how market action did develop.

Bullish bias made us identify the best possible entry point, A or B, on the inverted chart in Figure 11.2 because we were psychologically prepared to act on the bullish signal.

When the chart is shown the correct way up, this bullish bias becomes a significant disadvantage because it gets us into, and keeps us in, a losing trade, particularly the one shown at point B in Figure 11.1. We suggested this pullback was an entry signal into the old trend, but when the chart is inverted, we suggested it was confirmation of a new trend. We can only have it both ways when we understand the role our bias plays in the way we see a chart.

In Figure 11.1 our bullish bias makes us reluctant to take the objective exit readings from our indicators. We don't draw a downtrend line from the high at E because it doesn't seem consistent with our overall bullish understanding of the previous long-term trend. Yet we draw this in Figure 11.2 as a new up-sloping trend line and use it to justify and confirm our entry.

Why the difference? In both cases we are look for evidence to support our bullish and biased belief in rising prices. We add a silver lining to every chart.

The result of our enthusiasm is often disastrous. We stay with established rising trends, delaying our exit and giving up a substantial part, sometimes all, of the profit. Yet, the bull enters early on downtrend break-outs. This maximizes the potential of the trade if only we were equipped to take advantage of it. We need to turn our strength into an advantage on both ends of the trade.

We cannot eliminate this bias. The glass tends to be consistently half full or half empty. The bias usually helps on one end of the trade — the long side entry if we are bullish, or the short side entry if we are bearish. Modern software gives us the means to turn the tables. This time, with our eyes open, we take the second step with a test for bias.

STEP 2 — THE BULL AND BEAR TEST

Consider the typical give-away signs of bullish behavior and look for a match with yourself. Bulls are surrounded by half-full coffee mugs. They know they are good at picking a break-out from a downtrend, or a price surge from resistance levels, or retracements. As a rule their entries are very good, made near the bottom, exactly on support, or just after the break-out has started. Most of their trades start out as winners. They like to think their judgment is superior, but hard reality would suggest it is their bias that puts a rosy glow on otherwise objective indicator results. This is their strength and they want to build on it.

Visit the bears for a moment. Of course the opposite applies to the group huddled around half-empty coffee mugs. Their entry on the long side tends to be their weak point because they are fearful the downtrend will continue proving the break-out is false.

Bulls are the last to leave the party. Their weakness is the exit. They wait too long, requiring too much confirmation that the trend has changed before selling. They give indicators every benefit of the doubt — on the upside. When the stochastic enters 80 percent every twitch down is ignored in favour of every twitch up. Their trades start with certainty and end with hope.

Bears, with their half-empty coffee mugs, have no such problems. Terrified of any bad news, they chop the trade immediately and protect profits.

Which are your give-away signs? It is hard to read them close up, so ask a friend to read them for you. You will never look at a half cup of coffee, or a chart, in quite the same way again.

The test answers are shown in Figure 11.3. The answers are read from the first column, using a standard chart, or from the second column if we start with an inverted chart. These answers use our bias in the most effective way at both ends of the trade.

Figure 11.3

READING INVERTED CHART TEST SIGNALS

TRADING SIGNALS **LONG** SIDE

Looking to →	**ENTER LONG**	confirmed by →	**EXIT LONG**	then →	**ENTER LONG**
Looking to →	**EXIT LONG**	confirmed by →	**ENTER LONG**	then →	**EXIT LONG**
Normal chart		**Inverted chart**		**Normal chart**	

TRADING SIGNALS **SHORT** SIDE

Looking to →	**ENTER SHORT**	confirmed by →	**EXIT SHORT**	then →	**ENTER SHORT**
Looking to →	**EXIT SHORT**	confirmed by →	**ENTER SHORT**	then →	**EXIT SHORT**
Normal chart		**Inverted chart**		**Normal chart**	

We want to use our bullish strength in entries to overcome our weakness in exits. We make a better exit by treating the exit as an entry. The mental gymnastics calls for a sleight of hand and this is assisted by a sleight of chart. The daily bar chart of American tobacco company, Philip Morris, Figure 11.4, has been inverted. We have one test question about this inverted chart: Is this a long side entry at point B?

The answer is 'yes'. The break past the current downtrend line at point A signaled a potential entry. The bounce at point B off this trend line confirms the entry and also hands the trader a better than expected entry price. This is a trading opportunity based on a clear trend break.

Remember, if the answer is 'yes' to a long side entry when the chart is shown inverted, then it signals a long side exit from any established open positions. This is consistent with the second rule

Figure 11.4 Philip Morris Co, USA. Daily bar chart. Inverted.

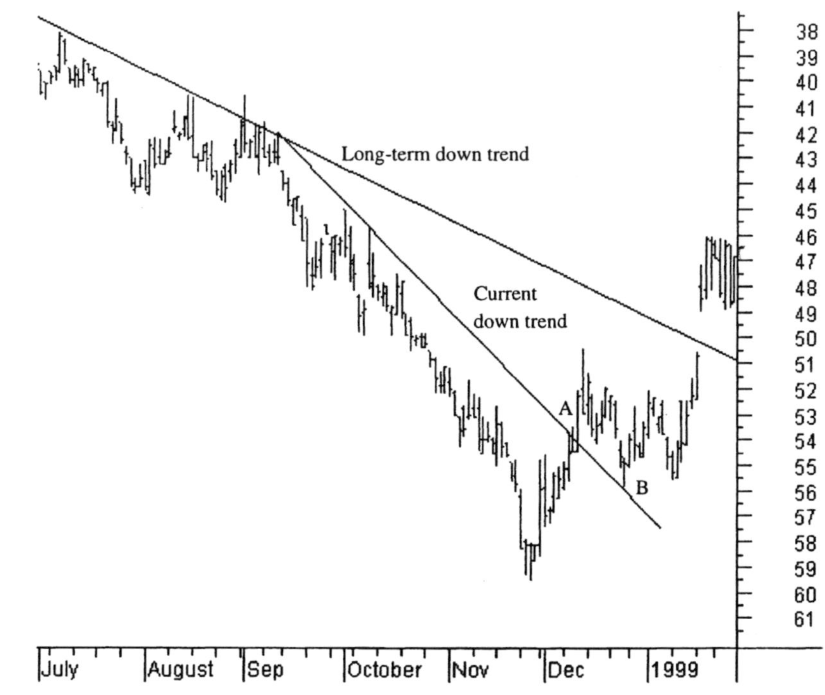

in the test answer matrix, Figure 11.3. This seems illogical, but closer inspection shows how it helps overcome our bullish bias.

APPLYING THE TEST

Inverted charts are difficult to work with at first so change the color of the bars using red for down and blue for up. Metastock users can save a template screen of the inverted display, making it easy to flip between the standard and inverted chart displays. Ignore the inverted scale and concentrate on the message delivered by the price bars and trend lines. If your charting software does not offer this facility then download the freeware program *Invert.exe* from the link on *www.guppytraders.com*. This temporarily inverts your screen display.

Our assumption in this Philip Morris test example is that we have entered the trade from the long side at around $45. To apply this bull and bear test we should try to forget our emotional involvement with the trade. If making money in a profitable trade clouds our judgment then losing money is a severe thunderstorm. We treat the inverted chart as a potential long position rather than an already open position.

With this in mind we ask one question: Does the inverted chart show a long-side entry?

Accepting our bullish bias, the answer is blindingly obvious. The price close at A is a break-out from the downtrend. Very bullish traders find this indication powerful enough to warrant an entry at $56 with a stop loss at $59.

This is confusing, so think of it in terms of chart lines. The stop loss is based on the trend pivot point low at $60. The exact trading decision based on this chart analysis using the trend line break is not as important as the bullish signals themselves. By many measures, this is a bullish break-out and gives an important test answer.

When the inverted chart passes the bullish entry test — enter long — then it signals an exit for any open long positions. Conversely, where an inverted chart gives a bearish signal — exit long — suggesting the downtrend will continue, then any open long positions should remain open. This simple test keeps bullish traders out of trouble by using the bias behind our interpretation of otherwise objective indicators.

The bull has problems believing in bears. When the bull looks at the Philip Morris chart with the scale placed correctly, Figure 11.5, the exit decision required at point A or B is more difficult to accept.

The bull too easily convinces himself the close at point A is an aberration and in any case he sees long-term support offered by the long-term trend line. Later he takes the close at point B as evidence of the continuation of the up trend where the short-term trend line now acts as a resistance level. He clicks through mental snapshots of other charts where trends developed in this way and gave

Figure 11.5 Philip Morris Co, USA
Daily bar chart

excellent long-term returns. He should not do this, but his bullish bias does it automatically for him, searching his memory for the most favorable gloss on a deteriorating situation.

Then he turns to the indicators, looking to support the decision he wants so desperately to make. When he made the original entry decision he recognized the time lag inherent in most indicators and he extrapolated their development in a favorable bullish direction. The stochastic wasn't really turning up, but it looked like it was about to, so he read this as a positive sign and put a tick against it on his checklist.

Unfortunately, he repeats this using the same indicators to manage the exit. Now the lag extends — it isn't really turning down. It is preparing to move up. He waits too long for confirmation of the bearish evidence. He becomes an expert in managing losses rather than profits.

Can we do this with Philip Morris? The bull has no difficulty in finding the silver lining. Although not shown here, the stochastic %K line temporarily crosses the %D line on the upside on the exact day shown as point A in Figure 11.5. The bull reasons this most recent crossover is true, so he gives price room to breathe.

The RSI turns up a few days later and the bull embraces the positive signals.

In making a decision not to close the trade at point A, he carefully and diligently lines up his favorite indicators, takes objective readings, and skews them towards his bullish bias. Do you do the same?

In this sample trade the bull's optimism defeats him, locking him into a deteriorating position.

PROFIT OR LOSS

By the time the exit signal is undeniably clear, even to the most convinced bull, the profit has often shrunk to a loss. Then the exit decision is grossly distorted by emotional quibbling where we convince ourselves that a loss at today's prices can be reduced if prices move up to yesterday's close. The lure of saving a few dollars is powerful and it paralyzes decision-making. In Chapter 18 we look at ways to minimize this emotional impact.

As soon as the answer to the exit question produces a loss our emotional reactions become much more severe. The loss may mean taking a lesser profit, or even a real loss on the trade. If fear of loss makes it difficult to decide what an indicator really signals, then exercising the discipline necessary to take a loss is even more difficult. The sooner we act, the smaller the loss and the better the chances of action being implemented.

Inverting the chart is only part of the solution in overcoming this reluctance to act. By taking positive action we make our bias work for us in all aspects of our trade management.

This is not just a problem for novice traders. Trading success does not eliminate it. Just ask Jim Paul, author of *What I Learned Losing a Million Dollars* or Nick Leeson, author of *Rogue Trader*. All traders are effected by their bias to a greater or lesser extent. It is very difficult to trade mechanically. There is no absolute solution so we make do with solutions that make us more aware of our trading strengths and weaknesses.

I have spent a lifetime developing my biases. I cannot reasonably expect to overturn them to accommodate just one aspect of my trading decisions — no matter how important. I must learn to live with them and turn them to my advantage. If something as simple as inverting a chart neutralizes my bias and makes it work in my favor on both sides of the trade, then I will use it. If you use a consistent method to identify and discount your biases when they adversely effect your ability to enter, or exit a trade, you will trade better.

We have applied this assay test early in the trading decision. You might find it more appropriately applied to the exit decision, but it is also a useful confirmation of every entry. The nuggets in our final list have been rigorously assayed, passing the inverted test, but before we trade, we look for the pulse of the market to make sure we are trading in the same direction. Although there are good trades available for cool heads in collapsing markets there is a difference between skilled traders and those who are oblivious to the collapse around them.

12

INDEX HUNTING

If you remain calm while those around you are losing their heads it may be that you haven't heard the news. In a falling market even the strongest stocks get battered, and rising stars, pulled back with the rest of the market, fail to rise as far or as fast. The nuggets we assayed so carefully may not suit the fashion of the market.

In a rising market, most stocks, even the weak and mediocre, rise in sympathy, so we profitably trade smaller nuggets in addition to the best of our finds. The general market index, or the sector index, tracks market activity in the same way a weather forecast tracks the weather.

Like a weather forecast, the Index sets the trading scene for the day, or for a period. The Index acts as a bell weather for general market behavior. This chapter looks at some ways to use information given by the general market or sector index to decide if our potential trade is consistent with market sentiment, and more importantly, if the trade stands a better probability of success. This assessment uses three steps:

1 Understanding the Index message.
2 Trading with index backing.
3 Assessing a security against the Index.

GET ME AN INDEX

What language does the index speak? The usefulness of an index is limited by the number of securities included. A broad index like the Australian All Ordinaries, which is taken as a proxy for the entire market, may at times be less representative than a sector index. The performance of a single stock, such as a bank may cause a significant movement in the Index. Some so-called broad indexes are composed of just a handful of stocks so the distorting effect is more dramatic.

The Dow Jones Industrial Average is the average of 30 stocks, weighted for splits, trading on the NYSE exchange. The S&P 500, not widely quoted internationally as a measure of US financial markets, is much broader, including 500 stocks weighted by capitalization. The composition of the S&P 500 Index changes intermittently to reflect market changes. The NASDAQ Composite Index is the most broadly based US index measuring the performance of over 5,000 listed NASDAQ stocks.

In contrast a sector index, such as the Finance index, includes all finance stocks listed on the Malaysian stock exchange. Obviously, the information drawn from this index is of a more precise nature than the broader indications given by the Malaysian Composite Index or the Dow.

With these caveats in mind, we look more closely at the role Indexes play in market decisions in the broader equity market. These conclusions are not relevant for those who trade the indexes directly on various futures exchanges. These derivative products are traded like any other security or futures contract. The conclusions reached by technical analysis apply equally to these derivatives as they do to any other individual security.

BILINGUAL INDEXES

Indexes provide us with two approaches to understanding broad market behavior. They use different languages to describe the same processes. The type of index you select determines the way you read the messages. The two index types are:

- **Representative approaches**

  Here the index represents a broad selection of available stocks. This includes the Dow, S&P 500, the Frankfurt DAX, Paris CAC 40, the Australian All Ordinaries and the Singapore Straits Times Index.

- **Absolute approaches**

  The index includes all of the relevant stocks in a sector, or nearly all. These are becoming more specific and include Dow Jones Utility, Engineering, Property, All Resources, Plantations, Hotels and Russell Small Growth, among others.

REPRESENTATIVE APPROACHES

These are the weather forecasts and this is the index message. The representative approach is a strange mixture of normal distribution theory and conservatism. The conservative aspect is present in the criteria for selection. The stocks included are the most active, the most prominent, and generally the better blue chips of the market. This elite selection is representative of the broader market — or so we are told.

It is claimed they are representative because their behavior will be reflected in the behavior of all other stocks, and understanding how this is true, or false, helps us to make better use of index messages. This belief is drawn from the theory of normal distribution, often shown as a Gaussian or bell curve, which is more fully discussed in *Against the Gods* by Bernstein. Our interest is in how the representative nature of an index translates into trading signals.

In 1877 the mathematician Galton used a simple experiment to graphically demonstrate the operation of normal distribution and the physical construction of a bell curve. This experiment also hinted at another useful trading concept, standard deviation, so it is worth taking a moment to examine this branch of mathematics from a trading perspective.

For his demonstration, Galton filled an hourglass-style device with shotgun pellets and let the small round lead balls fall through a narrow funnel onto a plate below. Small pins were stuck in the neck of the hourglass so the balls were dispersed randomly. The plate was covered with a grid of compartments so as each ball hit the plate it remained in place. The falling balls consistently built a three-dimensional bell curve, higher in the middle and sloping down to each side. The idealized result is illustrated in Figure 12.1. We return to the trading information in this shape a little later.

This bell curve shape suggests the normal distribution of, for instance, stocks, where they are sorted on the basis of performance. Most fall into the average category. How do we move from this to selecting a small sample as representative of a wider market?

Galton took another step that traders have been taking ever since. In his second demonstration, he drilled a hole in the bottom of each compartment on the first plate and placed another gridded and compartmentalized plate below it. Now the lead balls could cascade to another level. The extraordinary result was that each new and smaller pile of balls exactly duplicated the bell curve shape of the larger pile. Galton's theoretical objective was quite different from ours so we will leave him on the history shelves.

Traders, and exchanges, have been taking the next step ever since, using a small sample as representative of a wider market. We move from a single pile in the middle of the bottom plate — selected from the peak of the bell curve — and extrapolate the shape and distribution of the lead shot as it first hit the upper plate. We use a small sample to infer the shape and distribution of a larger sample.

Figure 12.1 A normal distribution curve (Gaussian curve)

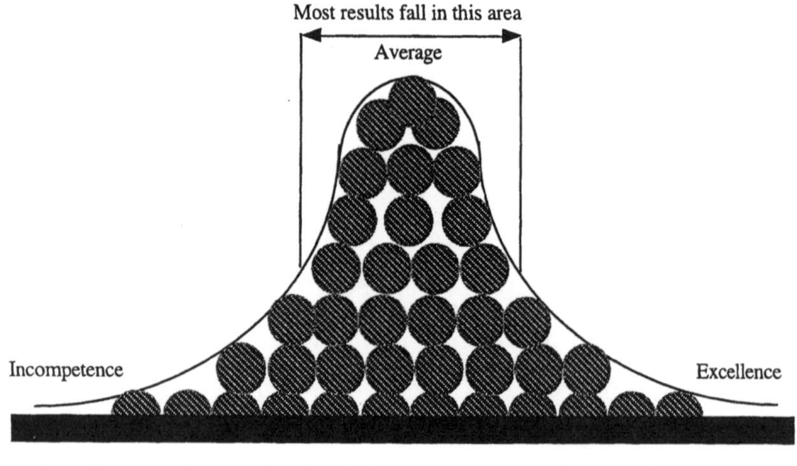

If the representative market index shows a bell curve normal distribution, and if each stock in the market index 'represents' a basket of stocks from various sectors of the market, then we expect the bell curve normal distribution pattern to be repeated at other levels. Going even further, we expect individual stocks will show similar patterns and if we select those we can duplicate the performance of the index, if not precisely, at least in a broad sense.

This understanding drives many funds and fund managers. Portfolios are weighted for exposure to market segments. Using the same principle, securities are selected from each segment. This compilation of averages not surprisingly most often delivers returns matching overall market performance. This is a good result in bull markets, but less desirable in bear markets.

Of course, the representative market index does not build a perfect bell curve, but the concept of distribution duplication at descending levels is usefully applied to trading strategies used by aggressive hedge funds. From here it is a short step to the extensive new trading road currently under construction. The Manderblot screen saver based on fractuals where each successively smaller level is a duplication of a larger pattern stands on the edge of chaos and reflects some aspects of market activity. This is distribution theory turned on itself and Deboeck and Peters deal with aspects of this in *Trading on the Edge* and *Fractual Market Analysis*.

We are not taking that short step onto the new road. Instead we will work further with the idea that the index is representative of the broader market as a consequence of normal distribution theory. In trading terms this suggests we search for stocks moving in the same way as the representative index. Our final choices are checked for consistency with the index behavior.

We have two important choices in considering how to use these broad indexes.

The first is to use the index as a guide to probable crowd and market reactions so we can trade with index backing.

The second is to use the index as a reference point for individual stocks placed on the left of the bell curve towards the incompetent end. This can be limited to securities that make up the index, or widened to include sector index groups, or more broadly still, individual stocks drawn from the entire market. All of these choices are similar in important ways and we discuss them as a group in the next section dealing with absolute approaches. Before doing this we will look at how the Index is commonly used to trade in the direction of the market trend.

MAKING FRIENDS WITH INDEX TRENDS

The first choice is a traditional way to incorporate representative index results in specific trading strategies by using them as weather forecasts and treating them with about the same level of reliability. This combines the last two assessment steps — trading with market index backing and assessing the security against the Index. The Dow is a broad indicator of past market directions and potential future directions.

In buoyant markets, chart patterns and indicators that suggest upwards movements for individual securities are more likely to be accurate because they are consistent with the market. The family of triangles is a good example of this process. The combination of these rules are illustrated in Figure 7.8, Chapter 7.

We visited the triangle family in Chapter 7, so briefly, an up-sloping triangle is an indicator of rising prices. The horizontal upper line of the triangle is formed by a resistance level, as shown at A in Figure 12.2, for the Dow daily bar chart. At the same time Caterpillar is building the first of two up-sloping triangles shown as B. The break-out builds another small up-sloping triangle at C. This is a powerful base for the move that follows the break-out of the Dow Jones from its triangle formation in April. Caterpillar acts in a bullish way in a bullish market, and takes further confirmation from the movement of the index.

It is the interaction of the up trend with a resistance level that is important, and markets do not always give perfect examples. The sloping up trend line creates the triangle in both cases and takes

Figure 12.2 Taking confirmation from market direction

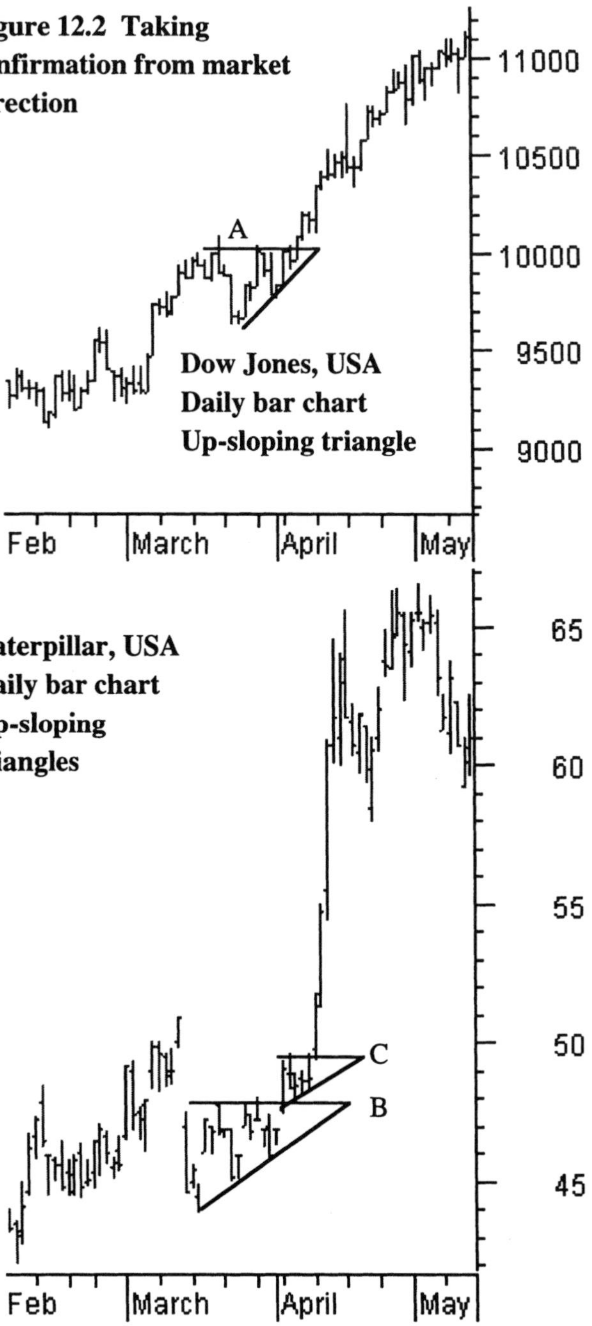

place in a generally rising, or bullish, trend. Prices pull back to these up-sloping trend line levels after hitting resistance. Buyers are so confident the stock is going to increase in value they refuse to let prices fall to old lows. Afraid of missing out, they bid slightly higher to get ahead of their competition.

Sellers see this action, and hold out, waiting for higher prices before putting their stock on the market. The result is an up-sloping trend line. As the tip of the triangle approaches, many sellers realize they can get even better prices and the supply of stock dries up. Bidders have to bid higher than the old resistance level and prices typically break out decisively and dramatically rocketing upwards in their search for new levels of stability.

Such, briefly, is the theory and the standard explanation. But remember it comes with no guarantees. The development of an up-sloping triangle strongly suggests further upwards price action. In reality the market shows some up-sloping triangles that react differently with prices moving sideways, or falling back below the trend once the pattern is completed.

However, in a buoyant market, as indicated by the market or sector index, break-outs from up-sloping triangles are more likely to be successful and sustained. Traders use this knowledge to trade in the direction of the market. When everybody is running for the elevator everything that looks like an elevator attracts a crowd.

In a bull market defined by a rising index even the most unlikely chart patterns look like elevators. As noted above, the equilateral triangle is a graphic representation of market indecision, but a rising market or sector index casts it in a different light. The weekly chart of the Aluminum Co of America in Figure 12.3 shows the way this indecision is bullied into a preferred direction by the market trend. This ship rises with the tide.

Nobody is fully convinced the security is undervalued, or overvalued. Some people think it is a bargain, and bid up to get the stock. Others think it is destined to fall, so they bail out at the best possible price taking a little less then yesterday's price because they are frightened the previous high will not be reached. The result is

Figure 12.3 Following the market

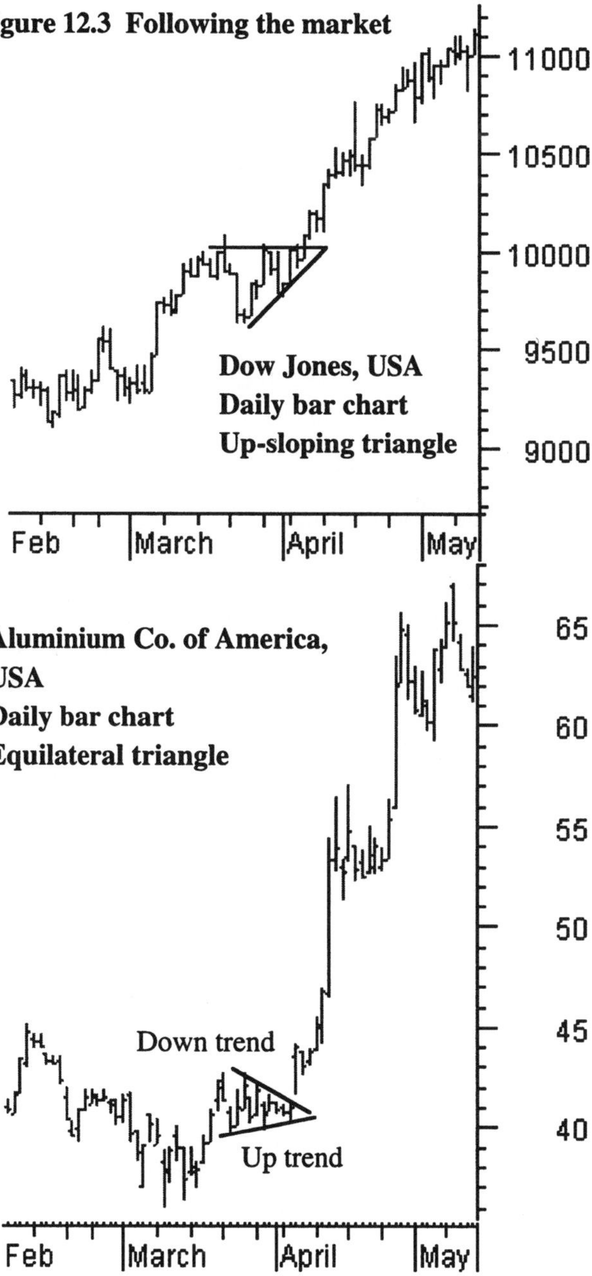

two sloping trend lines, one going up and one going down. They converge, building an equilateral triangle that once completed, is often followed by price action moving sideways for an extended period. In strong markets the break-out, as with the Aluminum Co of America, is in the direction of the index. As a creature of the index, reversals can be sudden and sustained, as shown, because the stock has no internal trading strength as would have been indicated by a stronger chart pattern.

In a buoyant market there is increased tendency for prices to break upwards. Using the index to identify the temporary or sustained direction of the market tells the trader if these weaker chart patterns have an increased probability of moving in a favorable direction.

Finally, the downward sloping triangle is the reverse of the up slope. The horizontal lower line is the support level as shown with the daily Kuala Lumpur Composite Index in Figure 12.4. Sellers offer stock, across the Index, at lower prices in an attempt to get rid of it quickly, but buyers snap up the bargains, so creating the support level. Buyers are relatively confident about the future of the sector and are hunting for a new break-out rally. As price action fails to develop, they lose confidence and are not prepared to bid as high above the support line. This index action is reflected in price activity for building supplier ACP Industries and other stocks. The chart shows a down-sloping trend line meeting the horizontal support line and suggests a further decline in prices once the tip of the triangle is reached. In a broad sense, down-sloping triangles are not good for trading from the long side — unless the bull roars. Traders usually wait until the price breaks down and new support levels are established.

Using an index in the standard way suggests the stronger sector index trends are more likely to carry the downside triangle upwards. A range of different trading approaches become possible by matching the chart direction with the index direction, or by understanding how the index direction shifts the balance of probability towards a specific outcome.

Figure 12.4 Tracking the index

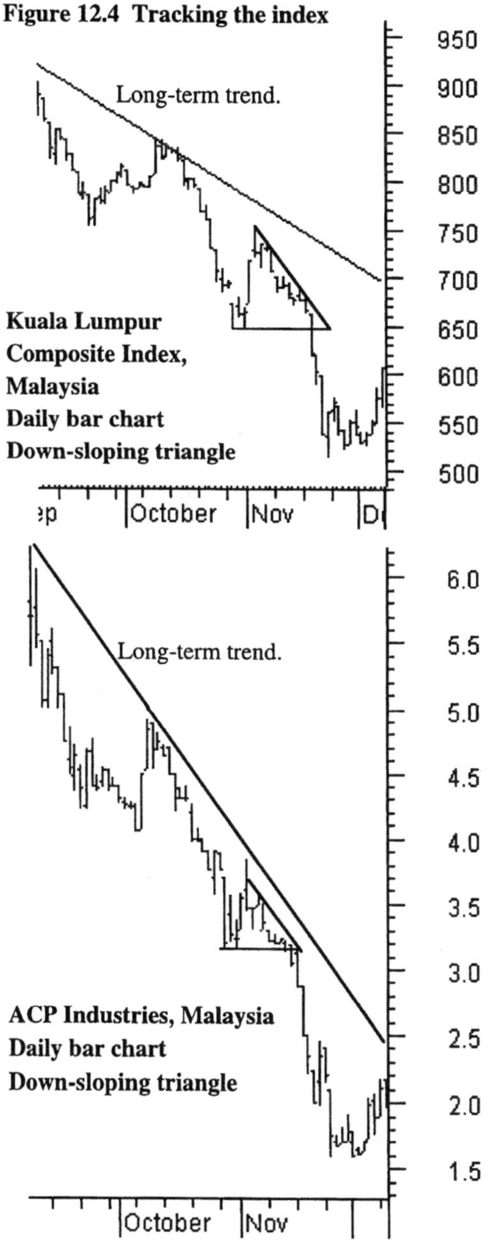

When the final list of trading candidates is complete we select the best possible opportunities. Generally, we will only want to add one, or perhaps, two new positions. Each trading opportunity is a valid one, but the probability of success is increased if the signals are consistent with the index weather forecast.

We used the group of triangles as an example, but the same applies to all chart patterns that are normally considered to be indicative of a bottom, or a top. Most of these reversal patterns are discussed in detail in Elder's *Trading for a Living*, or *Technical Analysis of Stock Trends* by Edwards and Magee. Books dealing with specialized charting methods, such as *Candlepower* by Greg Morris, *Point and Figure Charting* by Aby and *Martin Pring on Market Momentum* by Pring usually devote a section to reversal patterns. No matter which patterns you decide to use, the representative index both measures and helps to create or reinforce, market sentiment and can increase the probability of the pattern completing in its usual manner.

The penultimate step prior to committing money to a trade is to verify that the chart pattern, the current orientation of the security, is consistent with the market direction. This is the basis of many trading approaches and is an extension of the old market saying, 'The trend (of the index) is your friend.' But friends do not always point the way to better profits.

ABSOLUTELY MEAN

We talked of bilingual indexes — representative and absolute — and the way these dictate different approaches. The second approach uses the index as a reference point for individual stocks placed on the left of the bell curve. This involves assessing our trading nuggets against the sector index. This entails alternative ways of understanding the index message, trading with index backing and assessing the security against the index.

The absolute index message is subtly different because instead of using a small sample to generalize about the market, they use a small market segment to deliver messages about placement.

Absolute indexes include all stocks and are most commonly sector indexes. The Singaporean Hotels and Resorts index includes all the hotels. The Australian Gold index includes all gold producers. These are similar to the second plate Galton placed under his hourglass and we expect to see a bell curve of performance in each sector. We briefly return to the problem of normal distribution because it provides the core of a trading strategy for absolute indexes, and also a second way of using representative market index information.

A normal distribution curve, or bell curve, puts most result values in the middle, with fewer results at the extremes of excellence and incompetence. An absolute sector index most often shows this distribution — a few leaders, and a few laggards, and a substantial number of average also-rans.

This distribution can be based on many criteria, from rate of increase in security price, or capitalization, to earnings per share or net tangible assets. No matter which criteria are used, the distribution pattern tends to form a bell curve. But this is not a fixed constellation. It is a snapshot of a dynamic system. While the curve remains much the same shape, the relative position of each security changes over time. The leaders become laggards. This is how we understand this index message and the bell curve determines the signals we accept and reject.

Most traders are looking for superior performance and intuitively turn their attention to the securities on the right-hand side of the bell curve towards the end defined by excellence. This intuitive reaction is unthinking, and like many unthinking reactions in the market, not particularly profitable. We reason that what is good now will only get better — forever more.

This does not seem such a sound idea when stated baldly, but it forms the basis of thousands of investment decisions. The advice to buy strongly performing securities has a comfortable ring to it, but this bell curve has a crack called regression to the mean.

Once again we will sidestep the mathematics developed by Galton, Gauss and others and explained more fully in *Against the Gods*, and opt for a trader's application of the concept. It is illustrated by

Figure 12.5, which shows the normal distribution bell curve. We have inverted the traditional display, placing excellence on the right-hand side. From either extremity, incompetence or excellence, the tendency is to slide, or regress, towards the bottom of the curve, the mid-point or the mean.

This regression to the mean gives us a way of using information from absolute and also representative indexes, to confirm trading opportunities and know which nugget is best in current circumstances. It builds on the trading concept we used in Chapter 9 for a range of other indicator displays such as stochastics, and relative strength indicators.

FADING THE INDEX

Where do trading opportunities exist in a bell curve distribution under regression to the mean? In the assessment of the market, how can we trade with index backing? The mathematical rule tells us securities on the extremes will tend towards the middle. Visually this makes more sense on the inverted display in Figure 12.5 above. In some important ways this mirrors the bulge in probability used in Part I.

Figure 12.5 Using a normal distribution curve to fade the Index

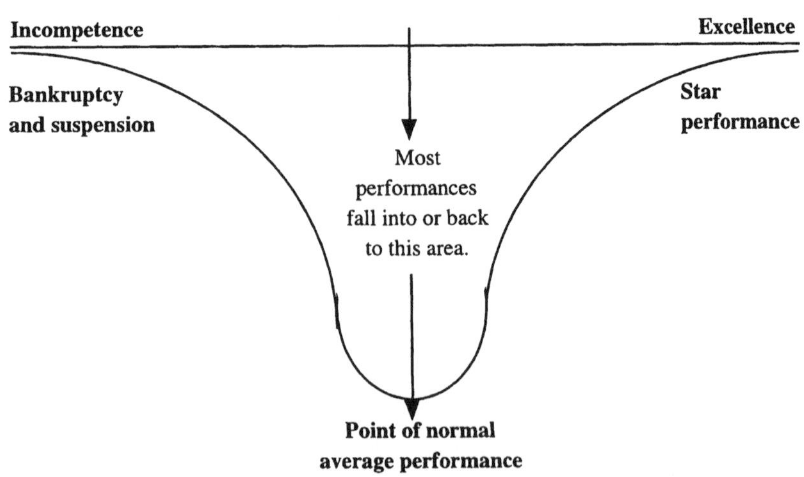

Those securities on the left — incompetence — will tend to move forward towards the middle. The high-performing securities on the right — excellence — will tend to move back towards the middle. In trading terms, the leaders of today's pack will be overtaken by today's unknowns launching themselves from the middle of the market group.

Obviously there are exceptions, and these provide excellent investment returns, although as the dramatic falls in Internet stocks in mid-1999 shows, good things do come to a sudden halt. These consistently high-performing exceptions are not exceptions to the rule. Consistent leadership only defers a reversion to the mean as the American computer giant IBM can attest.

Our prospecting search is for tomorrow's leaders and often it starts in the middle of the distribution. Candidates from here have an opportunity to move towards excellence. This is a conservative trading approach. They look for a trading opportunity developing in a security with average performance because it has more room to move towards excellence.

Aggressive traders look for securities on the left-hand side of the curve, the end defined by incompetence. These are catch-up stocks. On a chart they go down while most of their compatriots go up. When these laggards signal a break-out the aggressive trader looks for a swift move towards the middle level of performance — the mean. Enterprise Oil, listed in the United Kingdom, Figure 12.6, is an example of this process. Its sudden reversion to the mean was prompted by a rise in world oil prices, but it could just have easily, although less dramatically, been due to cost-cutting, a change in management, or a new product release.

The aggressive trader puts the balance of probability on his side because the laggard is moving towards the mean — towards the performance level enjoyed by most securities. The conservative trader is less well positioned because his security is moving away from the mean.

Figure 12.6 Regression to the mean
Enterprise Oil, UK
Weekly bar chart

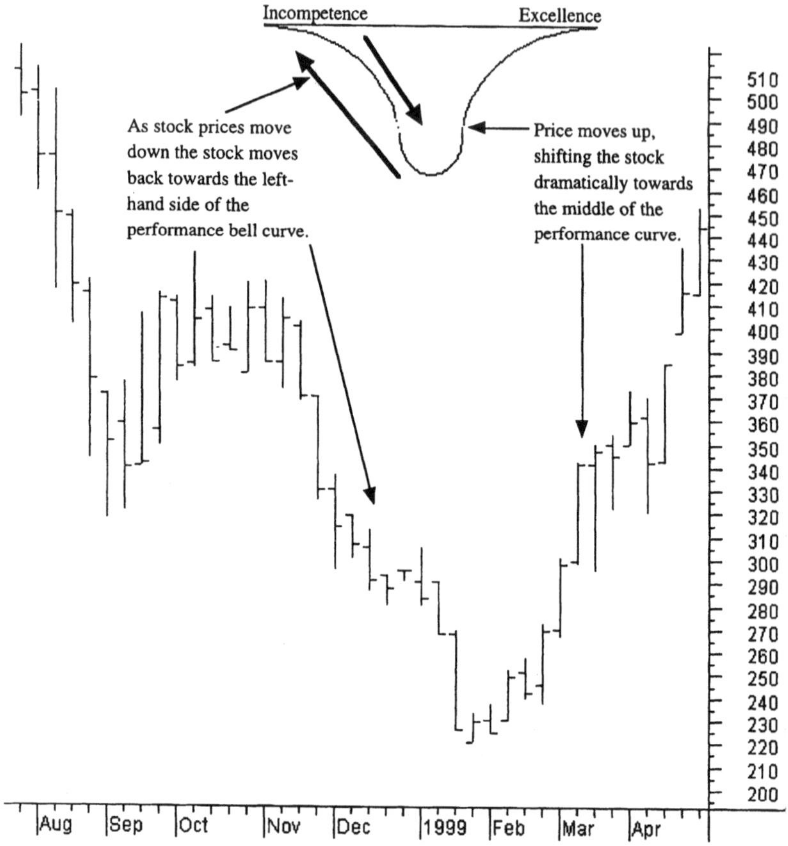

Let us be clear about how we use the bell curve to trade with index backing. Merely buying a security on the left-hand side of the bell curve does not guarantee success any more than taking a position in a stock towards the right-hand side implies a loss. We apply this analysis only to the nuggets exhaustively selected and assayed by other methods. These, by definition of our search, are the best trading opportunities available today. If the security is positioned towards the left of the bell curve we build profit expectations based on this. Stocks moving towards excellence have a harder task, and profit expectations from the trade may be reduced.

This style of index analysis is the first step towards building reasonable expectations that are consistent with our chart analysis. The next section explores these steps in detail. The trading opportunities we have selected by this stage of the process are all valid ones. The one that gets our money is the one that is consistent with our understanding of the probability of its future performance. Although we cannot see a bell curve on a chart, we can trade its inferred behavior.

TRADING THE BELL CURVE

We use the sector index to decide if our potential trade is consistent with market sentiment and we look for a better probability of success. The third step assesses the security against the absolute index.

The trader infers the relationship between the chosen security and the bell curve, aided by the knowledge that the value of the sector index, or representative index, can be taken as the mean. We build this plot by using the concepts of beta and standard deviation. These values provide an anchor point against which we compare the position of the security we have selected as our potential trade. If we use the day's closing price to build a single index reference line then we have a mobile 'mean' towards which other securities will regress.

In a perfect world our target, the mid-point, would stand still. In the market it keeps moving and is distorted by speed and direction so the bell curve is sometimes slanted to the right by bullishness, towards excellence — or to the left by bearishness, towards incompetence. A bullish bell curve is shown in Figure 12.7. This bias indicates and confirms the market trend, providing the base information used in common investment approaches. From our trading perspective it suggests stocks on the extreme left have been left well behind. These are candidates for bankruptcy, and financial oblivion. Make sure they don't take your trading capital with them. We look for stocks skewed to the right, matching the orientation of the index.

Fig. 12.7 A bullish distribution curve skewed towards better performance

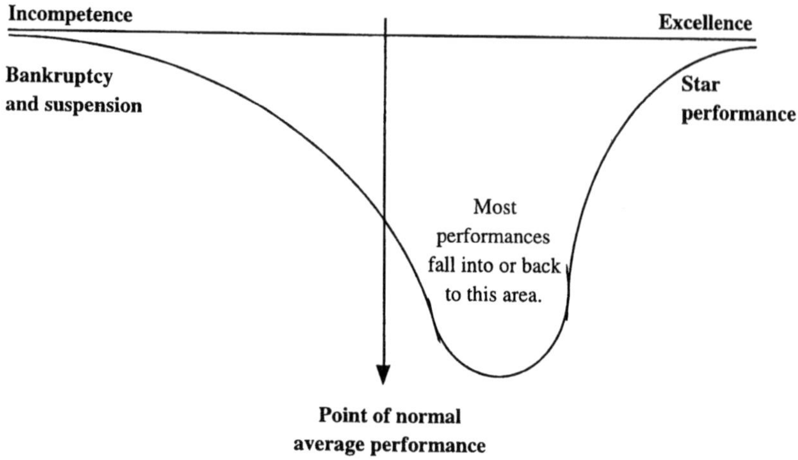

The single index line on a chart gives us the mid-point and two ways to confirm our trading opportunities:

- By plotting an individual security against the index to establish its position. This is the beta value. Beta is the amount a security moves in comparison to each move of the index it is compared to. A beta of 1 means for every 1 cent move in the index the stock also moves 1 cent. A beta less than 1 identifies the laggards and we put them on the left-hand side of the bell curve. A beta larger than 1 tags the leaders.

Figure 12.8 shows two Singapore electronic industry securities, Datacraft and CreativeT, placed parallel to and below the mean as defined by the Singapore Electronics Index close. This Metastock display plots the reference line, Electronics index in this example, and compares the performance of two other securities. Performance can also be smoothed using a 30-day exponential moving average.

Your trading approach — moving towards the mean, or moving towards an extremity from the mean — will determine which is the better position on the bell curve for each of your trading candidates.

Figure 12.8 Placing stocks relative to an index using a daily line plot. Singapore

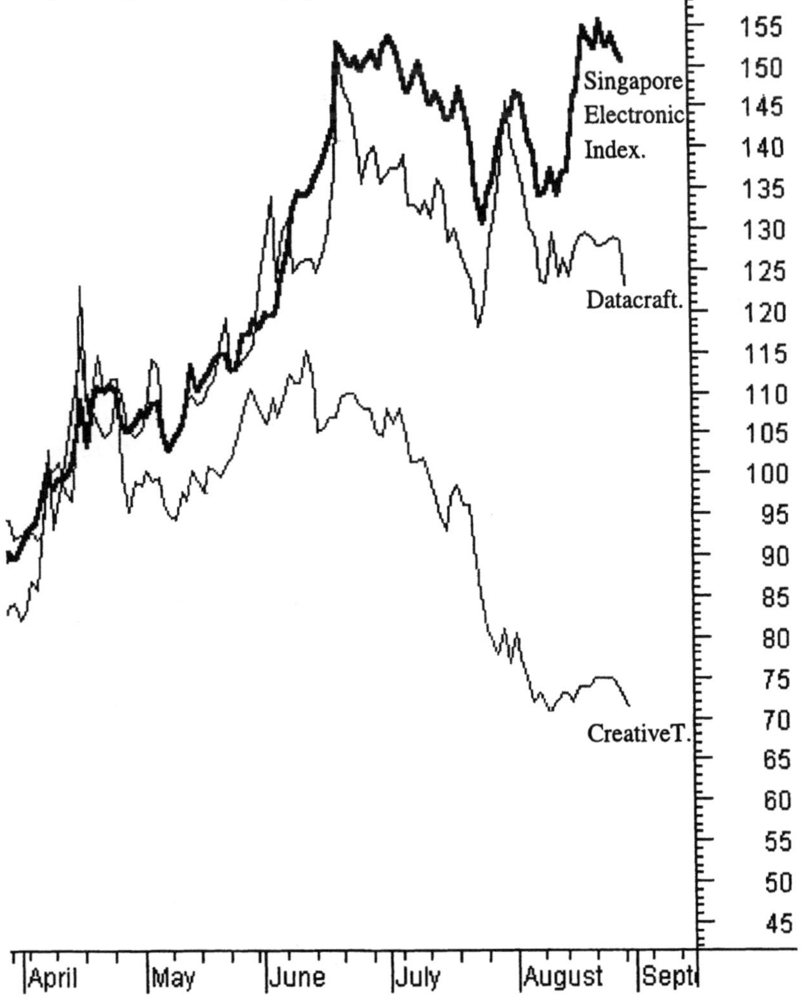

A trade taken in a security running below the index line is not guaranteed success. Although there is an increased probability that price will move upwards towards the mid-point, and if the mid-point is moving forward in a bullish bias, the upward pressures are much greater, but, it 'ain't necessarily so'. Other genuine fundamental factors may be responsible for the security appearing on the left-hand side of the bell curve. These include bankruptcy, expensive product liability litigation, mining a disappearing resource, or making hub caps for stagecoaches. It pays to check because not all laggards are potential winners. Many are potential losers so fading the trend from this end is a more aggressive strategy.

- By plotting an absolute index against the market sector index. The laggard sectors are bought in anticipation of a rise towards the general market mean. This is sometimes mistaken for a cyclical interpretation of the market, but in this case it fades the trend. Figure 12.9 compares several sector index examples with the Singapore Straits Times Index.

Traders looking to match the booming Singapore economy need only trade the finance sector. Those looking for an accelerated ride selected the construction index in early 1999 and enjoyed better than average gains.

TURNING SELECTED NUGGETS INTO PROFIT

The successful traders enter at the beginning of the move — either when the laggard starts to pick up speed, or when one of the pack breaks away to become a leader. Where we want to position our entry decides which trading candidate gets our money.

This is a weather forecast, not a trading signal. It helps establish the balance of probabilities by positioning the sector, or a particular security, in relation to its mid-point. If we accept that the security is more likely to move towards, or back to, the mid-point, then we are better equipped to decide the reasonable potential for our proposed trade.

In the final analysis, we are trading an individual security within an environment created by the market. Our initial selection of trading candidates is based on many factors. Our final selections are pruned by confirming the potential for explosive price action, by discounting our bias, and finally by verifying current performance against a representative or absolute index.

Figure 12.9 Placing a market index relative to sector indexes using a daily line plot. Singapore

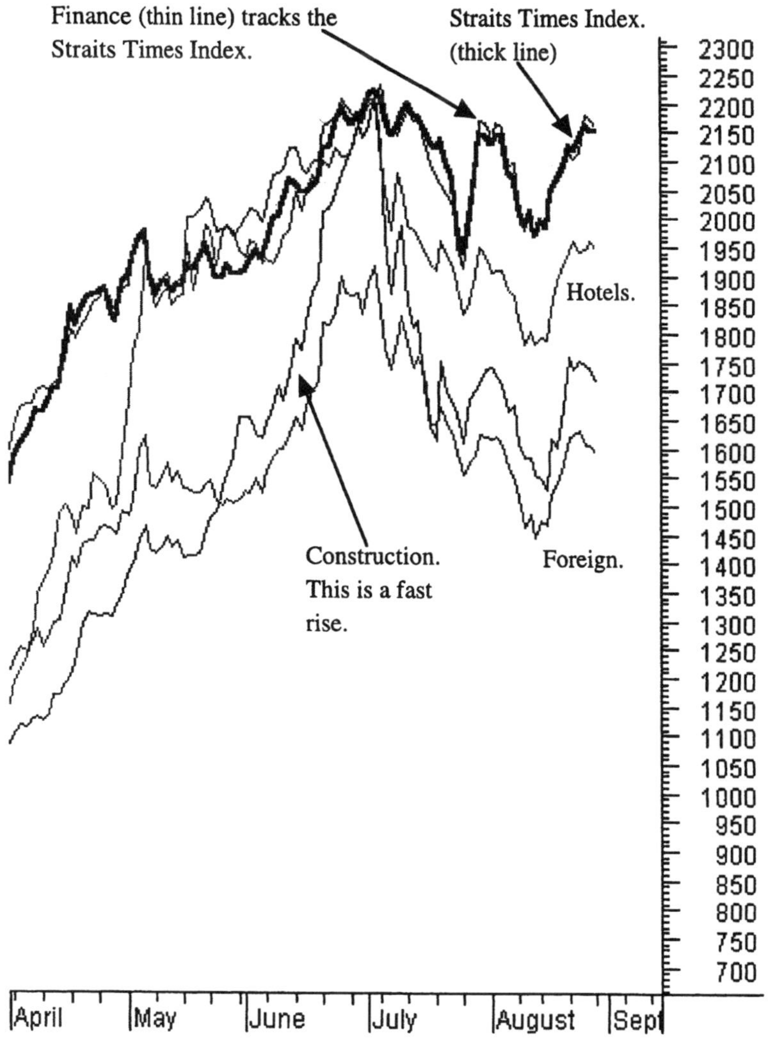

Now the trader turns the nuggets to a profit by using a spreadsheet and supplementary numbers from the trading screen to confirm our chart analysis, set our buying price, establish profit targets and to build a stop-loss safety net. This gold is ready to go to market.

Part III

SUPPLEMENTARY NUMBERS

13

THIS NUGGET GOES TO MARKET

Finding nuggets is one thing. Selling them is another and this chapter explores ways to identify the most willing buyers. If our market favors round nuggets rather than square ones, then we need ways to find this preference and shift the balance of probability in our favor. We do this by combining chart analysis and financial calculations.

At the beginning of the last section we stood on the edge of a financial escarpment. The track we used to get to the bottom, the methods we used to locate the best gold-bearing country and the way we assayed each potential trade were different from the methods used by those who chose the more traditional fundamental path. These two paths converge in this section and the steps we take to assess our trade will determine who is the more successful trader.

There are eight steps, too many to apply to every stock in our database. We reserve our judgment, taking these steps towards the end of the prospecting venture when the list is reduced to a very small number of opportunities. On many days there may be no opportunities at all. Later we look at ways to manage open positions.

Private traders have a luxury, and an advantage, not enjoyed by institutional traders. We have the time to make sure every trade is the best trade possible, but too often we squander this advantage. Many traders think once they have identified the trade and completed the basic analysis covered in *Share Trading* and other books that they can ring their broker and start trading. Sometimes this does work, but in the long run additional analysis is required. Spotting the probability is the starting point in the trading process. Calculating the potential for each trade provides supplementary numbers that make, or break, a trade.

Just identifying the trade through sound analysis does not mean we can financially afford to take it. Not all trades are created equal and separating the better winners further reduces the list of trading opportunities.

Our trading objective is to shift the balance of probability in our favor. This involves identifying a developing situation where the balance of probability suggests the market will reverse its current direction, giving us an entry on a break-out. Alternatively, we try to get on board an established trend, but only if the balance of probability suggests the trend will continue.

As discussed in Part I the basic bar chart is used to broadly identify these balance points, either as a starting point, as in the eyeball search, or as a finishing point after other analysis methods have been used. These include R-plot searches, performance searches using indicator results, or rankings based on accounting or fundamental analysis.

Immediately prior to entering a trade we return to the bar chart because it gives us a basic starting point. The supplementary figures required to confirm our analysis against our financial objectives for the trade are drawn from the bar chart. These financial objectives are more achievable if they are matched with the bulge of probability, both on the entry, and more importantly, on the exit.

This chapter explores these processes. There are eight steps in two groups of four. Each group weeds out the weaker opportunities, gradually reducing our initial extensive list to just a few candidates.

The first group includes steps to establish the break-even point. They are:

- assessing risk for this trade
- deciding position size

- including brokerage
- including tax.

The second group tests for time and risk. These include:

- setting realistic trade objectives
- estimating time in the market
- downside risk
- meeting money management objectives.

Chart patterns, or indicator readings, suggest when the balance is in our favor. We set exit targets based on the bar chart. The temptation is to take a position, hang on, and shoot for some vague notion of profit. This type of open-ended objective is built on hope rather than on good trade management.

To weed out the trades that are not worthwhile we test them with these two questions.

- Does the trade have enough meat on it — enough realistically potential profit — to be worthwhile? Some trading opportunities are so skinny that trading them is foolish because the potential returns are so small. To decide this we use a combination of chart and financial analysis to put some numbers on probability. The remainder of this chapter deals with this process.
- What are the financial objectives for this trade? Without objectives we are adrift in a sea of opportunity, constantly battered by fear and enticed by greed. By knowing our financial objectives in advance we steer a course with certainty and make a rational decision about when to end or extend the trade. The calculations involved are covered in the next chapter.

Of course, knowing when to make a rational decision and actually taking it are two different things. Many people fail the test because they cannot pull the trigger on a losing trade. Nor can they pull the trigger on a winning trade and we look at these problems, and some solutions, in the next section.

We use a bar chart to assess the validity of the trade after our research and before our entry. This has a significant impact on our overall trading success. It is not enough just to be confident the stock you have bought will go up. Nor is it good enough to believe, however sincerely, that the stock has good long-term prospects. The identification of a trading opportunity does not in itself mean the trade is worth taking. In Chapters 7 and 8 we looked at the way the concepts of support and resistance, or price projections and trading bands, help to establish trading targets. This chapter builds on those concepts.

GROUP ONE: HOW MUCH DO WE NEED TO BREAK EVEN?

The first group of four steps helps us decide how much we need from the trade to make it worthwhile. The steps are:

- assessing risk for this trade
- deciding position size
- including brokerage
- including tax.

Small nuggets are interesting curios so we discard them in favor of larger specimens. Four steps help decide the bare minimum return we are prepared to accept. Any trade not meeting these criteria must be discarded. A high probability of success does not compensate for a low return. It is no good being right if we cannot be profitable at the same time. The trader aims to match his capital with financial objectives and bring them together in a single trade. This defines the level of return you consider acceptable.

Step 1 Your assessment of the risk of this particular trade

How long will the trade take to complete? Is this a quick trade, measured in days, or is it a longer term trade that might take weeks or months to mature? The projected return must meet or beat benchmarks provided by other investment opportunities. The longer the trade is open, the greater the risk the trade will move in a way we have not anticipated because new events are, by definition, unknown.

Trading opportunity is matched with risk and volatility and assessed against time. Greater volatility applies equally to the downside as to the upside. Stable blue chip securities with low volatility, like American manufacturer 3M shown in Figure 13.1, can yield 15 percent to 21 percent between the trading bands over six weeks. The 40 percent return from the lower band at $70 with

Figure 13.1 3M, USA
Daily bar chart

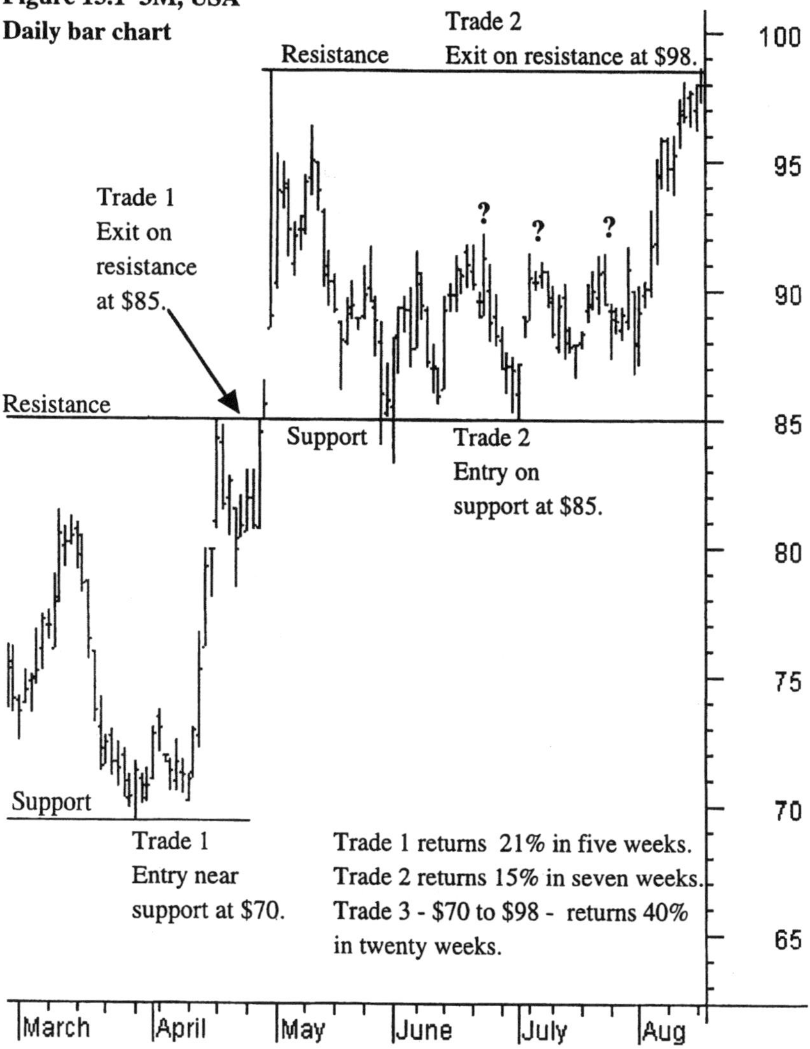

an exit on the upper band at $98 takes a minimum of 20 weeks. When this trade is compared with a similar security, Aluminum Co of America (ALCOA), the difference in return over time is a function of volatility. For ALCOA Figure 13.2 shows a 62 percent return in five weeks.

Fig. 13.2 Aluminium Co. of America, USA
Daily bar Chart

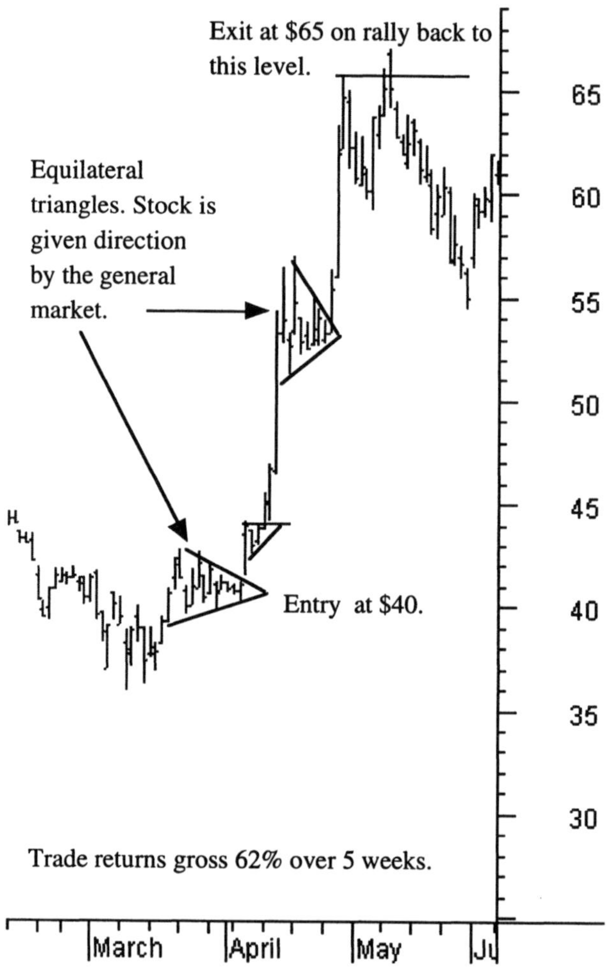

Both stocks are flagged in our search list as trading opportunities. Which is the better trade? The answer depends on your assessment of, and your tolerance for, risk, always remembering we approach the market from a trading perspective. However, as a general rule, when lower returns are matched with lengthy exposure to the market, the trade has increased risk. From an investing perspective this rule is less relevant because the objectives of the 'trade' are different. Steady returns over an extended period are desirable.

Which is a more difficult trade? The ALCOA trade requires better timing, but its signals are clear and consistent. Using an entry and exit technique based on anticipated triangle break-outs, or the Guppy MMA indicator, this trade is easily managed.

The second 3M trade is difficult, with several possible exit points indicated by the question marks in Figure 13.1. The possible early exit points return around 8 percent and do not offer additional enticing trades as the possible entry level rises. Unlike ALCOA, once an exit had been made from 3M it was not useful to enter the trade again looking for a return of similar size.

The trading opportunities turned up as a result of our prospecting process are unequal. The risk/return relationship varies. Past behavior shown on the charts helps to eliminate the weaker trades. Good chart analysis helps set profit targets, again weeding out the lesser trading opportunities. We look at volatility and using chart analysis in this way in more detail in the next chapter.

Step 2 How much trading capital do we commit to the trade?

The market may not let you spend as much as you would like, while at other times it absorbs your capital without a hiccup. This liquidity and depth of market eliminates some trading tactics and favors others.

All that follows in the next two chapters is based on what we pay for, or get for, a stock. While quotes in some markets are posted in eighths and sometimes smaller 'teenies' the impact on our trading equity is in dollars and cents. When you bid for a stock you might get it at twenty-three and a half, but you pay $23.50.

Most world markets now trade in decimals and US markets are joining this trend. Our concern here is with the impact of these decisions on your wallet so we stay with dollar calculations.

Depth describes the way orders are arrayed above and below the current bid and ask. A deep market where the last sale was at $40.50 will have sellers at $40.51, $40.52, $40.54, $40.55 and so on, all the way to $41.00 and beyond. Each higher level is only a cent, or tick, above the previous level. On the buying side, each lower level is only a cent or so below the previous level.

A shallow market might see a seller at $30 and the next seller at $30.60, then $30.70, followed by a gap to $40. Buyers and sellers are not required to neatly line up in one cent or one tick increments so it is not always possible to buy or sell stock at exactly the price we nominate. In markets dominated by market-makers the inside spread may be reserved for them and largely unobtainable by private traders. In these markets the spread is sometimes quite large and moves away from the trader even though no trades take place. This slippage and 'unables' make it difficult to get the price we nominate. Despite this we base all our trade planning starts with the assumption that we can get our nominated entry and exit price.

A liquid market describes the number of shares on offer at each price level. Highly liquid markets tend to have good depth, as in the $40.50 example quoted above. In addition, there are often three or four, or eight or ten, or more sellers at each level. The total number of shares on offer at each level is substantial. An illiquid market is most often associated with shallow markets. A single seller at $30 might only have 20,000 shares to sell. Buyers wanting to buy 60,000 shares must either wait, or bid higher to collect their preferred number of shares.

Some very liquid positions encourage scalping — large positions for small returns. With smaller stocks, large positions cannot be executed because there is just not enough stock available so smaller positions come with higher execution risk. These factors determine trading tactics, and in turn, decide which stocks will be retained in our trading list.

A highly liquid security like computer software giant, Microsoft, can be traded with confidence for scalping returns. With a significant number of buyers and sellers at almost every level there is enough depth in the market for Microsoft for traders to take large positions. Figure 13.3 shows an entry into the new trend rally at \$89 with an exit at \$94 and returns of 5.6 percent gross in 15 days. Under normal circumstances such position trading margins may be considered too thin.

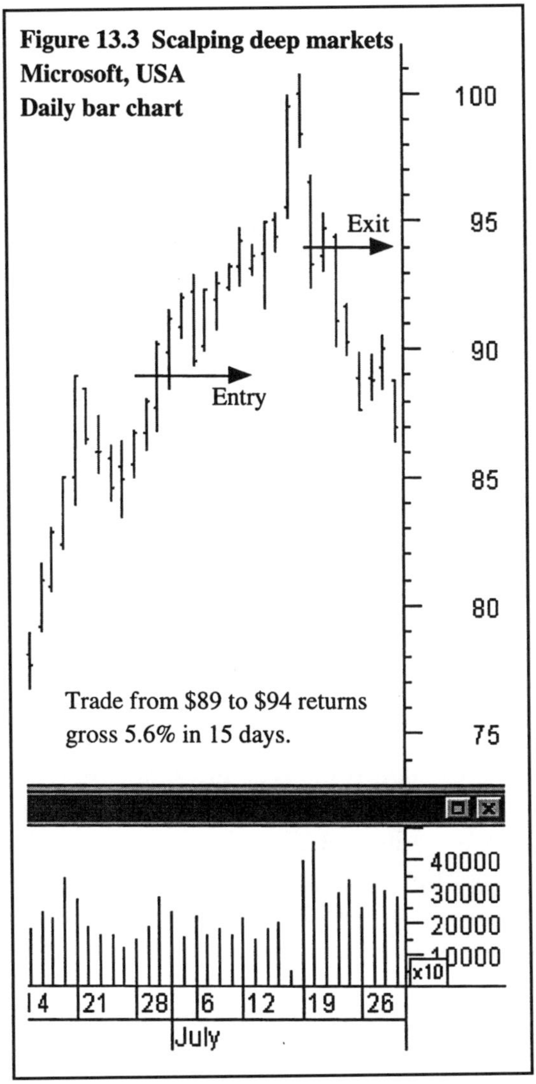

Figure 13.3 Scalping deep markets
Microsoft, USA
Daily bar chart

In this case the margin is profitable because we place large buy and sell orders confident they will be filled. Microsoft's daily turnover is measured in millions of shares. The market has depth and liquidity. A $50,000 buying order, or even $500,000 order does not stand out and is easily absorbed by the market.

With this liquidity the figures stack up attractively. Buying and selling 11,000 Microsoft shares goes almost unnoticed in the market of this depth. A trade of this size using the entry and exit points as shown in Figure 13.3 for $979,000 returns $55,000 gross profit. The net return depends on brokerage. Generally, we would want to do better from a trade, but it is still a handy dollar amount for 15 days of market exposure.

Position size does make a difference, but only if the market has sufficient depth to accept your order without a hiccup. Scalping opportunities are reduced with smaller stocks because the average order size is smaller and although the percentage returns are the same, the dollar value scarcely buys lunch. The average order size is easily obtained from the depth of market information discussed in Chapter 15. It can also be worked out by looking at average daily turnover. Your intended position size is unlikely to equal the average daily turnover of Microsoft, but with smaller stocks this can be a real concern. With $30,000 to commit to a trade in a small speculative stock we run the risk of becoming the market.

Step 3 The impact of brokerage

Brokerage is a cost of doing business. It is inevitable and, in most cases, unavoidable. The exceptions include friends and family offers, rights issues and take-over offers. Obviously, traders like to avoid paying unnecessarily high brokerage rates, but there are times when this is not possible. No matter what brokerage is paid, if the rate of brokerage makes a trade unprofitable, then the trade is not worth it. Do not blame the brokerage. A trade should be substantial enough to support the normal costs of doing business, and still return a healthy profit.

Factor in brokerage. Discount brokerage cuts out once you start trading large individual positions. This has a significant impact. If we are paying brokerage at 2.5 percent then effectively we need at least 5 percent return to break even — 2.5 percent on each side of the trade, the entry and the exit. Not all trades will offer this. If we are trading larger position sizes, and paying perhaps 0.5 percent brokerage, we still require a least a 1 percent price increase before we start making money.

Step 4 Tax

The structure of the taxation system encourages some traders to place undue emphasis on this factor. Tax is always an annoyance, but it should not be a major consideration in making a trade. The primary purpose of trading is to make money — not to reduce a taxation liability.

The full-time private trader uses his trading skills to generate his primary income stream. This is his strength and these trading skills are quite different from those skills practised by tax accountants and CPAs. In the same way that a businessman concentrates on improving his business rather than worrying about the tax effect of each transaction, the trader should do likewise.

From a trading perspective what is important is making a successful trade. If success leads to a tax liability then the appropriate person to deal with the problem is a CPA or tax accountant. Taxation advice will assist the trader to structure his business in a manner that is the most tax effective. Taxation advice should not be designed to structure each transaction, or trade, to be tax effective — at times this will be counter to the very objectives of trading. Such advice is more applicable to investment positions where ill-timed decisions can have major tax implications.

The best tax solution depends on many factors, including the annual turnover of positions, the contribution trading income makes to the total income stream and trading history. It is a complex field best left to the professional tax advisors and accountants. Consult with them but do not be driven by tax considerations alone. Trade well and be prepared to pay the price, or tax, of success.

The trader, by definition, is active in the market holding positions for short periods. Market timing is of the essence. If the trader falls victim to a preoccupation with tax, basing his business around taxation minimization rather than on making a profit, then trading activity is crippled by artificial restraints preventing timely exits based on market movements. When the market signals 'out' then the trader exits. The cost of ignoring the signal is often much greater than the taxation consequences of acting on it.

The way you take these first four steps sets an initial target for the minimum acceptable return from each trade — the break-even point. This is one of the important numbers in your trading universe. It tells you the break-even point for every trade.

If you need a minimum 5 percent from a trade to break even then potential trading opportunities are discarded if they do not meet these minimum requirements. If you do not have these minimum requirements you enter trades with your eyes closed. No matter how good your fundamental or chart analysis is, unless you know your break-even point, the trade has no starting point and no direction. The methods we use to create our list of trading candidates do not tell us anything about profitability until we assess them against our break-even point.

BREAK-EVEN

A spreadsheet calculation provides an example of how a break-even point is calculated. Figure 13.4 shows a sample trade with Microsoft at $89. With brokerage set at 2.5 percent, a level that is not unusual for some full-service brokers, the price must reach $93.51 before the trade starts to break even. Brokerage is a two-way charge. Brokerage on the purchase is $1,112.50. Brokerage on the sale depends on sale value. For convenience and ease of comparison between these two examples, we treat it here as the same on both entry and exit, incurring another $1,112.50 for total brokerage of $2,225.

For this trade to succeed the price must increase by nearly $7 ($6.79) just to remain in the game and not lose money.

In contrast, when brokerage is reduced to 1 percent, and every other factor left the same, the break-even point is reduced to $91.69 as shown in Figure 13.5. Now the same trade needs to add only $2.69 to break-even. This is 60 percent less than the break-even figure calculated with 2.5 percent brokerage. Switch to discount brokerage and the impact is even more dramatic.

Figure 13.4

BROKERAGE	
Av brokerage rate %	**2.500**
EQUITY DETAILS	
Equity name	**MICROSOFT**
Number of shares	**500**
Purchase price	**89.000**
Net cost	44,500.00
Av brokerage	2,225.00
Full cost	**46,725.00**
Break-even price	95.79

Figure 13.5

BROKERAGE	
Av brokerage rate %	**1.000**
EQUITY DETAILS	
Equity name	**MICROSOFT**
Number of shares	**500**
Purchase price	**89.000**
Net cost	44,500.00
Av brokerage	890.00
Full cost	**45,390.00**
Break-even price	91.69

Brokerage has been used as the variable in these examples. Position size — the amount you allocate to each trade — is a variable, as are any transfer taxes and the rate of riskless return in an at-call, market or CMA account. Make this calculation as complex as you wish, but one way or another, a calculation must be made. Establishing the break-even point in any trade is the first step in a business calculation of potential profit.

GROSS IS GOOD BUT NET IS BETTER

The first group of steps look confusing so many traders skip them — and so skip the next group. Traders do have a tremendous capacity for self-delusion. Profit is temptation so the danger in the first search pass is the bewitching attraction of gross returns rather than the lower net figures. It is so easy to see the entry on support and the exit at resistance. The calculations are completed on a scrap of paper — support at $40.00; resistance at $60.00. Profit equals 50 percent. The cash register rings obscuring rational thought.

These are initial calculations and do provide a further means of ranking the trading opportunities, but they need to be examined more carefully. We take Hong Kong-listed company Gold Face Holdings as an example. Using the start figures calculations shown in Figure 13.6 — entry $0.65, exit $0.80 — the gross returns of $2,250, or 23 percent are much more attractive figures than the net returns. We should avoid the temptation to dwell on these. Gross returns should be reduced to net figures and then ranked.

Getting net figures means:

- assessing risk for this trade
- deciding position size
- including brokerage
- including tax.

When each group of steps is completed we weed out the break-even and skinny trades. We move from good trades to better ones, and finally to the best trading opportunities on the day.

Before the better trades are selected they are assessed against the final group of four steps.

GROUP TWO: TIME AND RISK

The first group of steps gives us one number — the break-even point. Before we commit cash to a trade we take another four steps to calculate the potential profit based on and closely matched with chart analysis, and the stop-loss level, again based on and matched with chart analysis. The second group of steps builds a profit and loss statement by understanding the relationship between time and risk by:

- setting realistic trade objectives
- estimating time in the market
- downside risk
- meeting money management objectives.

Step 1 The ability to achieve the trade objectives

The size of the market for our selected security may make taking a large position impossible. If the stock is tightly held we might not be able to buy enough of it to make it worthwhile. When prices dip to our entry level we need to buy more than just a fraction out of our intended parcel of shares.

Gold Face Holdings has a profitable habit of bouncing from negative price dips to established resistance levels. The trading tactic is to buy at $0.65, just above the lowest level of the dipping spike, and to sell as it hits resistance at $0.80. The calculations are shown in Figure 13.6, on the left-hand side, Gold Face Planned. The proposed trade offered a 19.4 percent return and with 15,000 shares this translated into $1,924. Brokerage on the selling side is calculated at actual cost in this instance.

The trade was perfectly analyzed and prices behaved as anticipated. From these perspectives all trading targets were achieved, but only 1,000 shares are purchased.

Figure 13.6

BROKERAGE		
Av brokerage rate %	**1.500**	
EQUITY DETAILS		
Equity name	**Gold Face Planned**	**Gold Face Actual**
Number of shares	**15,000**	**1,000**
Purchase price	**0.650**	**0.650**
Net cost	9,750.00	650.00
Av brokerage	146.25	29.95
Full cost	**9,896.25**	**679.95**
REWARD PARAMETERS		
Sell price (inc. brokerage)	**0.800**	**0.800**
Gross return	12,000.00	800.00
Av Brokerage	180.000	29.95
Net return	11,820.00	770.05
Clear $$$$	**1,924**	**90**
%%% Return full cost/net return	**19.44**	**13.25**

These calculations collapse in the face of market reality. Gold Face Actual, the right-hand column in Figure 13.6 shows what happens when only 1,000 shares were available for purchase at this price. Faced with minimum discount brokerage on the purchase and the sale, return is reduced to 13.2 percent because brokerage is much higher as a proportion of total costs. In percentage terms the return is still acceptable, but when the dollars are counted out — all 90 of them — it seems barely enough to compensate for the potential risk.

The liquidity of the market may work against us so all spreadsheet calculations are compared with past market conditions and verified against the current market. The Gold Face trading example above was valid only if 15,000 shares were available for purchase. This assumption would be valid if average daily volume had been around these levels and the price spikes at the centre of the trading strategy had shown good volume in the past.

The trader should have verified these assumptions against recent market conditions when the order was executed. These supplementary numbers would have told him only a few shares were on offer at $0.65 and that the next parcel of shares was for sale nearly 1 cent higher at $0.70. A quick look at these numbers allows the trader to recalculate the financial viability of the trade and to abandon it if necessary. The use of these supplementary figures in this way is discussed in more detail in Chapter 15.

Step 2 Time in the market required to reach the profit target

In options trading time decay degrades the value of the option as the expiry date draws closer. The margin for hope is reduced. With only a few days to expiry the final option price is known and the market is not interested in bidding beyond this known value. When an option has months to run to expiry the market allows a larger margin for hope.

Equity trading does not include an expiry date, but time decay is a factor because longer market exposure increases risk. The relationship is shown in typical form in Figure 13.7.

Figure 13.7 Time/Risk/Reward

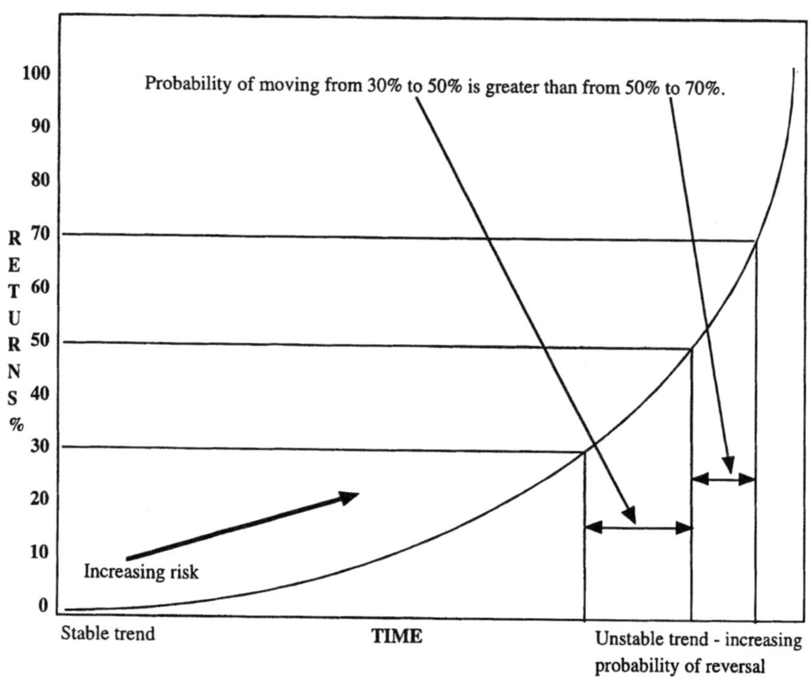

Risk increases with time. On a daily basis the probability of the market moving more than a few percentage points against us is small. Over several days, on a cumulative basis, this risk increases. The further we move along a price trend, logically, the closer we must be to the end of it. The longer we are in the market, the greater the probability the current trend will reverse, diminishing open profits with falling prices.

We find it difficult to tell when the trend will, or has, ended. We cannot put a time line on the curve, but we do know the typical shape of the curve. We use this information to protect current profits rather than by trading increased risk along the curve for incremental returns.

Although the left-hand scale caps returns at 100 percent this is not always the case. Returns may be well above this, but the shape of the time and risk curve remains the same. The risk of a trend reversal increases with time. Additionally, the pursuit of incrementally higher returns is inversely related to the probability of achieving them.

Putting precise figures on these relationships is easy in retrospect, but almost impossible in real time, since we cannot know in advance when a trend will end, or which level of return — 50 percent, 100 percent or 300 percent — will eventually determine the cap on the left-hand scale. Attempts to use Figure 13.7 in this way are inappropriate. However, two general trading conclusions are valid:

- The highest probability of return is matched to the shortest time exposure to the market. This suggests that spending a year in the market for a 10 percent return is a high-risk event and inconsistent with good trading.

  It also suggests if we do spend extended periods in the market that we must shoot for much higher returns to compensate for the increased risk.

  This is a fundamental time/risk/reward relationship we apply to several examples in the next chapter. There is no set formula for deciding this as each trader has a different capacity for risk. Some traders feel comfortable with a five-week market exposure for a 10 percent return while others are happy to leave the position open for five months. No matter where you set your benchmark starting point, the trade will still conform to the typical parameters shown in Figure 13.7. The time scale may change, but the relationships do not.

- When the profit targets are achieved, there is increasing risk attached to the pursuit of incrementally better returns. In Chapter 3 we showed how a bar chart is used to identify the balance of probability. When we make an entry these points set our profit targets. Using Figure 13.7 we may have set 50 percent return as consistent with our profit targets based on the balance of probability.

  When prices reach this level what should we do if they appear to be going higher? It is hard to take a profit and close your eyes to the growing pile of missed profit left on the table as prices continue to rise. If our initial analysis is correct, prices will pause at around our exit level. We are not shooting for the very top because we want to leave some potential profit for the person who buys from us. Chasing this additional profit gives an incremental return while dramatically increasing risk of a trend reversal. The probability of success is reduced because it requires prices to move beyond the level reflecting the balance of probability we identified before the trade was opened.

  Sometimes prices do move consistently above our profit targets. If our initial analysis was poor, or flawed, this is one consequence. The trader looks at the trade again, making perhaps a new entry, adjusting the time scale on Figure 13.7 as required. Alternatively, the trader can retire content with the achievement of his financial objectives in this trade.

  Time in a trade is balanced against the return and the estimated risk. Generally, more time exposure should be rewarded with better returns. In the final stages of analysis the time/risk/reward ratio is matched with all the previous analysis to identify the very best trading opportunity.

Step 3 Downside risk

If the trade fails, how much do we reasonably stand to lose and is this consistent with our stop-loss strategy? The interaction of this calculation with other factors is complex. For the moment we will note its importance. In the next chapter we look at how it is calculated in a way consistent with the balance of probability and incorporated into a full trading analysis.

Step 4 Matching your money management objectives

Does the trade and intended position size meet your capital allocation requirements? The consequences of this decision are often difficult. If taking the very best trading opportunity means your portfolio is overweighted in speculative stocks, the impact may be dramatically different from your expectations.

Establishing a portfolio balance and deciding how you will deal with profits and capital allocation between classes of stock has as much impact on trading success as the actual trade. Even the best trading opportunities are passed up if they distort money management objectives and outcomes. The money management models discussed in *Share Trading* and *Trade Your Way to Financial Freedom* explore these consequences in detail so here we only mention them in passing.

THIS LITTLE NUGGET GOES TO MARKET

We started this journey equipped with a pair of dice and a bulge in the balance of probability. From the top of the escarpment the path looked as if it finished at the point where we found trades that looked good on the chart. As we traveled down the path we looked for market confirmation of our analysis. Armed with this information, our trading list was reduced. Every twist in the path takes us to another checkpoint, reducing our list further because we want these trades to look good on the numbers. Not every nugget is good gold.

Many traders fail to complete this journey. Baffled by many checkpoints they launch into a trade before they reach the journey's end. For those who have traveled with us this far the prospects of success are enhanced, but not yet complete. Before trading we gather all this information together, setting precise financial objectives for the trade and matching them with market reality on the day.

14

PINNING A NUMBER ON RISK

At the very core of trading is the aggressive management of risk. It is too easy to forget this as the search for trading opportunities consumes our attention. The final selection is designed to tilt the balance of probability on our side but the advantage is squandered by poor risk management invariably accompanied by poor trading discipline. Improving both comes from planning.

Forget this core business and the market reminds you very quickly. Profit is not enough because loss is inevitable and loss is the generic risk in all trading activity. With certainty we can assign a number to some aspects of risk, but not to reward because it is always uncertain. Trading discipline is applied risk control. Without it, a string of winning trades is easily destroyed by a single losing position. Traders with the trading discipline to cut losers and ride winners avoid these losses by defining risk before the trade is opened.

Trading discipline supplies the answer to the question posed in the previous chapter: What are the financial objectives for this trade?

This discipline comes from sound trade planning constructed with reference to risk. Without planning we are adrift in a sea of opportunity, constantly battered by fear and enticed by greed. Pre-set financial objectives help us steer a course with greater certainty by pinning a number, by quantifying, trade risk. So armed we are better equipped to make rational decisions about when to end or extend the trade.

These calculated and inferred figures are vital supplementary numbers required to finish the search to identify and exploit trading opportunities. We use known numbers, drawn from the chart, to infer the value of other risk variables. The numbers selected define our trade risk and are a function of three elements:

- **The fear of loss**

  Good traders respect loss and use this fear to build sensible trading tactics based on specific financial calculations. Poor traders are terrified of loss. As a frightened child closes his eyes against the dangers of the night, so the poor trader skips these calculations, and pays a substantial penalty.

- **Profit objectives**

  Good traders chase carefully defined financial returns. We prefer to use charting techniques to establish these returns, but others use a range of benchmarks. Poor traders rely on satisfying a growing sense of greed. Sometimes they win, but often they ride from the top to the bottom always chasing the most recent high in the decline — promising whichever trading Deity they believe in that 'I will get out on the next rally.'

- **Timing financial objectives**

  Time is the third, and most difficult risk variable. Financial objectives bring together time and profit objectives. Good traders look for returns commensurate with the length of time exposure to the market. Poor traders become investors hoping to ride through the downturns and back into profitability by extending their time in the market. This is a valid approach in its place, but it is not a trading approach.

These elements come together in a single spreadsheet with three calculation groups. For clarity in this chapter we split the calculation groups into separate sheets. In examining these three elements we will select a plain trading example using a speculative stock. The substantial leverage in this style of trading effectively highlights the consequences of each of the three calculation groups. When you trade stocks priced at $9.50 or $95.00 the same consequences apply.

Establishing financial objectives involves building a trading plan. This does not have to be complex. Many plans look deceptively simple such as the summary of the DMR trading plan below.

Stop loss	—	$0.095 for $2,000 maximum
Entry conditions	—	on support
Exit conditions	—	at resistance or reassess after six weeks
Financial objectives	—	gross return 24 percent over four to six weeks

Determining the figures included in the plan requires more work than such simplicity suggests. Developing this plan, and others like it, is the subject of this chapter. This is an intensive process demanding time. When applied to a small number of trading opportunities we give planning the time it deserves. When applied to an even smaller number of open positions, we give them the trade management they demand.

The starting point is a weekly bar chart for the selected security. Diversified Mineral Resources (DMR) is a fairly unexciting miner with a well-established non-trending chart pattern. The DMR weekly bar chart, Figure 14.1, has been selected because the chart analysis is not complicated and the simple trading strategy is built around support and resistance — buy at $0.105 and sell at $0.13 for a 24 percent return. These levels provide two of the three base figures for every subsequent calculation.

The third figure is a function of long-term support, total trading equity and position size brought together in a stop-loss calculation.

We choose this stock because understanding its chart pattern does not add additional layers of complexity. It is easy to concentrate on the important factors of loss, profit and time. With more complex trading strategies and chart patterns the calculations do not grow substantially more difficult, although selecting the appropriate starting figures may be more time-consuming.

Additionally, DMR has an advantage of illustrating how simple chart concepts are profitable. The four indicated trades in

Figure 14.1 Using the chart to provide figures for financial calculations
Diversified Mineral Resources, Australia
Weekly bar chart

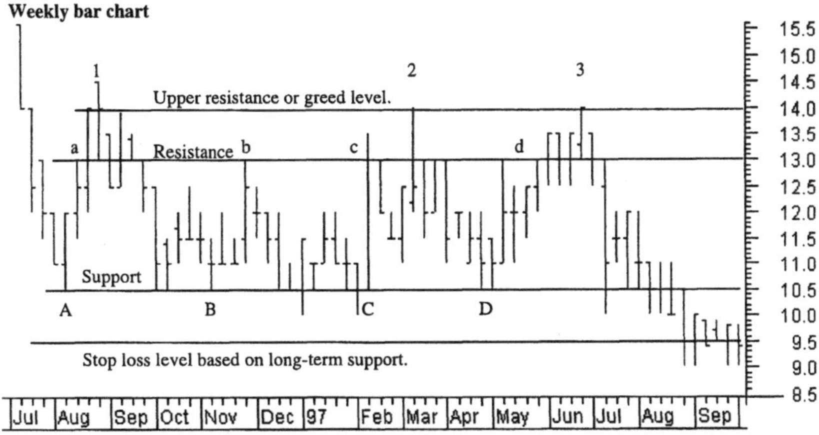

12 months, each returning 24 percent, are a handy consistent addition to any trading portfolio.

ELEMENT 1: FEAR OF LOSS

Taking a loss is difficult when you have a plan, but it is virtually impossible when you do not have any plan. Planning involves the entry, the potential exit to limit losses and the potential exit to realize profits. Private traders spend a lot of time on the entry, and too little time on the profitable exit. As for the stop loss, we tend to pick a fuzzy figure at random and call it a stop loss.

Trading is an emotional process, particularly when we are asked to take a loss, and we cannot eliminate this emotion. Successful trading requires us to sideline emotion in an open trade because rising prices galvanize us, while falling prices paralyze. As private traders we have to overcome these emotional responses ourselves because no one else will do it for us. There is no floor supervisor to step in and close a losing position. We beat this emotional blackmail by planning the trade ahead of time before the position is opened. We do this using the chart to set objectives, and to decide if those objectives match our money management requirements.

From this we develop a plan for taking small losses. The strategies employed to prevent losses from growing can be complex, or they can be simple, but the objective is always the same — to limit the loss. Good trading accepts the inevitably of a loss — not the inevitability of a profit. Using a spreadsheet to overcome the fear of loss is the first part of this process.

PLANNING FOR A PORTFOLIO BEREAVEMENT

The fattest spreadsheet trading opportunities are not always the healthiest. Although these initial calculations provide a means of ranking the trading opportunities, they need to be examined more carefully for defects on the downside. We do not know which way this security will move, and although we have taken care to shift the balance of probability to our side, we know this does not guarantee certainty.

If the stop-loss points do not match our criteria, then this nugget, no matter how good the potential upside, is no longer a trading candidate.

The first base figure is our intended entry price, in this case $0.105. As prices tumble towards our chosen entry level in the DMR example we must concentrate on the dreadful possibility we might be wrong in taking an entry at $0.105.

If we are wrong, and the price continues to fall, at what point do we recognize our error, or do we wait until it is totally beyond doubt? We need to build a big sign saying '*Wrong way go back!*' and the chart helps set the third base figure.

This is a central problem for every private trader. It is not enough just to trade well. The private trader must also know something about money management and trade risk. There are many options when it comes to money management. The one I prefer is the 2 percent rule. You may use something different, but you should go through a similar process of calculating the trade risk and setting your responses in a way consistent with your money management before you enter the trade.

MEASURING LOSS

How do we measure loss — against the cost of each position, or against the cost of the total portfolio? The 2 percent rule is one answer and it says no single trade should put at risk more than 2 percent of your total trading equity. Loss is measured against the total portfolio. This is not a complex rule and as it, or a rule like it, is central to any stop-loss strategy we will quickly refresh its main points.

First, trading equity. This is the total amount of capital we intend to use for trading. Active traders aim to have this entire amount exposed to the market in open positions most of the time. When we calculate 2 percent we use the total of our intended trading capital rather than the total currently committed to the market. When we add profits to our trading pile, then the 2 percent calculation changes. It also changes when we take losses.

The rule does not mean, if we have $100,000 in trading capital that we must allocate only $2,000 or 2 percent to each position.

It does mean when the position is 'marked to market' if loss is equal to $2,000 then we must exit the trade. This stop-loss strategy works best when the stop-loss point coincides with both the dollar value and a logical point indicated on the chart. The logical stop-loss level for this sample trade is shown in Figure 14.1 and at $0.095, is based on long-term support. Later our calculations match this level with other financial considerations. Most importantly, note that I do not exit when DMR shows a 2 percent loss from the entry point as price falls by 2 percent to $0.103.

By combining chart information with spreadsheet calculations, as shown in Figure 14.2, the trader sets the parameters of the trades. He has three known figures: the preferred entry price, the dollar value of 2 percent of equity and the price value of the stop-loss point. These figures allow him to infer the values of others to set appropriate financial objectives. Bringing these together in a single calculation includes three components: the chart, a spreadsheet and a matching process.

Figure 14.2

OVERCOMING FEAR OF LOSS		
Av brokerage rate %	**1.200**	
Total trade equity	**100,000**	
EQUITY DETAILS		
Equity name	**DMR PLANNED**	**DMR ACTUAL**
Number of shares	**180,000**	**100,000**
Purchase price	**0.105**	**0.105**
Net cost	18,900.00	10,500.00
Av brokerage	226.80	50.00
Full cost	**19,126.80**	**10,550.00**
RISK PARAMETERS		
Equity risk @ 2%	2,000.00	2,000.00
Risk on this trade	**2,000.00**	**1,100.00**
Stop-loss exit price based on full cost	0.095	0.095
Break-even price	0.108	0.107

Component 1: The chart

Basic chart analysis is used to establish support areas. The DMR bar chart indicates solid support at $0.105. The next nearest support level is at $0.095. Although not shown on this chart extract, this level acted as resistance in the previous three years. If prices do fall past $0.105 they are likely to pause around $0.095. This is a straightforward application of the trading approach discussed in earlier sections. These levels show where the balance of probability hides.

Component 2: The spreadsheet

We use this to calculate the dollar value of our total trading equity. To make calculations easy to follow we use $100,000 as Total trade equity with brokerage at 1.2 percent. Using the 2 percent rule this equals a maximum of $2,000 that we may risk on any single trade. This value is entered in the cell opposite the label: Equity risk @ 2%. This value changes as our trading equity increases when profits are added, or as equity decreases when losses are taken.

Component 3: The challenge — match position size with risk

Here we bring together long-term support and total trading equity to calculate position size consistent with stop-loss conditions.

The 2 percent rule puts a figure on risk — $2,000 — and a price value on support — $0.095. The price value is calculated from the chart based on the support level. These two known figures are the reference point for all further calculations. Here we choose to limit the dollar risk to $2,000 and this is entered into the cell Risk on this trade. We could select a different figure but we will obey the 2 percent rule for this example.

Our task is to get the cell Stop-loss exit price based on full cost to read $0.095. For traders who use a spreadsheet to compensate for a lack of mathematical dexterity this process is based on a juggling act where position size — Number of shares — is manipulated until the $0.095 target is achieved.

We skip the juggling and show the solution. The maximum position size is 180,000 shares for a total cost, including brokerage of $18,900 as the column DMR PLANNED shows in Figure 14.2. These results are always the starting point for further calculations.

However, risk is a function of position size. It is further reduced when position size is reduced. This is sometimes deliberately manipulated to suit our current circumstances. The maximum position size, for instance, might be inconsistent with our portfolio allocation strategy creating a mismatch between time and risk as discussed below. More frequently, traders do not always have access to the maximum cash amount. Not having enough cash exactly when you need it is a trading reality.

By reducing the position size as shown in the last column of 14.2, DMR ACTUAL, the overall risk is reduced. This is why the spreadsheet shows two cells. The upper cell Equity Risk @ 2 percent is calculated automatically from total equity size. The lower cell forces the trader to make a conscious decision to accept, or lower this risk factor.

With 100,000 shares costing $10,500, the calculation reveals prices could fall to $0.086 before $2,000 of trading equity is lost. This does not mean we now exit at $0.086. The stop-loss figure derived from the chart and based on support is still valid. Using it, the dollar risk on this trade is reduced to $1,100 making this a safer trade by reducing the impact of failure on our total trading equity. We do not expand our risk level beyond the logical stop-loss points indicated on the chart.

These calculations acknowledge we have very little real control in the market — the odds are against us. All we control is the entry, the exit and our position size, and we use the balance of probability to match these events with market conditions. The market controls every other aspect of the trade. Of the three we do control, it is the exit that allows us to manhandle risk.

ELEMENT 2: PROFIT OBJECTIVES

Calculating profit objectives is a pleasant task and as most traders are familiar with it we only cover this briefly. Calculating profit is independent of setting financial objectives although the novice trader usually confuses the two. Financial objectives determine how the profit contributes to overall portfolio risk. Calculating back-of-the-envelope profits is a dangerous task if not balanced against more structured calculations.

The question 'How much profit is enough?' has a definite answer. In the same way that the chart, and associated spreadsheet calculations, help to set a stop loss they are also used to set profit objectives based on past price action.

The DMR PLANNED column in Figure 14.3 outlines the process using the chart in Figure 14.1 as the starting point. The trading strategy provides the price figures for profit calculations. In this case an exit at $0.13 based on resistance returns 21 percent. Greed beckons at $0.14 and the results are shown in the last column DMR GREED. The 30 percent return looks enticing but at what additional risk? Ways to make this judgment call are considered below.

Figure 14.3

BROKERAGE		
Av brokerage rate %	**1.20**	
Total trade equity	**100,000**	
EQUITY DETAILS		
Equity name	**DMR PLANNED**	**DMR GREED**
Number of shares	**180,000**	**100,000**
Purchase price	**0.105**	**0.105**
Net cost	18,900.00	10,500.00
Av brokerage	226.80	50.00
Full cost	**19,126.80**	**10,550.00**
REWARD PARAMETERS		
Sell price (inc. brokerage)	**0.13**	**0.140**
Gross return	23,400.00	14,000.00
Av brokerage	281.00	168.00
Net return	23,119.00	13,823.00
Clear $$$$	**3,992**	**3,282**
%%% Return full cost/net return	**20.87**	**31.11**
%%% Impact on total trading equity	**3.99**	**3.28**

There are other ways of establishing profit objectives based on exit prices. These might range from using a set of moving average crossovers, or when the stochastic turns above 85 percent, to exiting on a 10 percent return or when the current close is below the previous day's low. Had this trade been based on any of these other strategies the figure entered in the cell opposite Sell price (inc. brokerage) would be different. It may be more difficult to calculate or estimate but this is not an excuse for not having a figure. No matter which exit conditions you choose, you should add, and later adjust if necessary, the exit price. This is the final base figure required to manhandle trading risk. Without it you are fully exposed to the emotional turbulence of the market.

It does matter how you decide on this profit figure. The one indicator measure to avoid is Higher Opening Prices Everyday, or HOPE. The market leaves no room for wishful thinking. The profit objective must be realistic.

Realism comes from chart information, either past price action or anticipated price action based on a consistent analysis of current price behavior. Realism requires, and good trading demands, a clearly defined set of exit conditions preferably defined with a figure.

The gross figures we jotted down, after deciding all trades are not created equal, provide an intuitive ranking. It is natural to lust after bigger profits and unless we are careful, these trades will always receive the benefit of the doubt. Traders must be particularly vigilant in realistically assessing the upside potential because this impacts on the achievement of our financial objectives.

In ranking these outcomes, and in making decisions about financial objectives for the DMR example, the 21 percent figure is preferred. It is realistically consistent with the third variable — time.

ELEMENT 3: TIMING FINANCIAL OBJECTIVES

Selecting profit objectives is a process combined with estimating the reality of time in the market. For clarity we have separated these processes to consider more carefully the impact of time, as measured by volatility, in the final ranking and selection of trades.

A good trade meets its financial objectives. The worst objective of all is to maximize profit. Riding the price rise to the very top involves increasing risk as discussed at the end of the last chapter. Good traders understand the relationship between time and risk so they balance reward in a way designed to achieve their preferred financial objectives.

Profit plays a vital role in these calculations. The primary obstacle to sound financial planning in a trade is unrealistic profit expectations, either because we think the stock will give us more than it is able, or because we feel if it continues to make a profit this is enough without having to calculate it. Either way is fatal because without a better way to measure achievement the trades start to manage us.

Taking a loss is easy when compared to turning your back on a profit. Watching a stock go onto new highs after your exit is the hardest aspect of trading. Nevertheless we must put a cap on greed because greed keeps us in excellent positions that turn into losers. The price goes up and we hold on, giddy with excitement and unrealized profits. When it turns, we cannot believe it, and we refuse to sell, hoping to regain our lost profit. We hang on because we have no realistic financial objectives.

VOLATILITY

The first step in developing financial objectives for the trade is to eliminate unrealistic expectations. Trading volatility provides the measure. This is obvious when you pause to think. There is no point in trying to take a 100 percent return from a staid blue-chip like Pearson, Merck and Co, or Chevron because it is unlikely to happen. With a skyrocketing chart of a speculative Internet company why take a 10 percent return when a lot more is on offer? On the other hand, there is no point in buying a stock at $7, and refusing to sell it at $20 because 'This is going to be a $100 stock.'

Unrealistic expectations disappear when we identify the trading volatility of the stock we are dealing with. Essentially, we identify three groups or classes of stock, based on trading volatility. We use the term in a specific way, defining it as the distance between the year high and the year low combined with the frequency and ease of movement between these extremes.

Volatility is usually associated with daily price ranges and has two more common understandings in the market so it is important to explain the differences.

The first compares daily ranges to select those with increasing or decreasing volatility. In addition to the indicators discussed in Part II, the Chaikin volatility indicator compares the spread between the high and low prices using two moving averages. The first plots the difference between the daily high and low prices, and calculates the rate of change in the average as a percentage. This indicator is standard with Metastock and the default uses ten periods for each calculation.

It does not serve our purpose of defining trading volatility because the indicator measures volatility as a function of wider price swings during the day rather than total behavior over a year or more.

The second is implied volatility, a concept used in pricing options and other derivatives. It is an inferred figure derived from the actual option price and the actual security price. Essentially, implied volatility arises when two different financial products are compared. Sheldon Natenberg covers these issues in *Option Volatility and Pricing Strategies*. Metastock users have the opportunity to play with the calculations in the OptionScope module.

For our purposes, implied volatility is not useful. Later we want to compare and rank several trading candidates but they are not related in the same way as a security and its option. Implied volatility does not give us a way to measure the internal historical ranging behavior of a single stock. Chaikin concentrates on a single stock, but the time frame is too short and cannot be meaningfully extended to encompass the variety of ranging activities in a year.

TRADING VOLATILITY

Trading volatility is a long-term estimated figure used in the calculation of risk by defining profit. It establishes the range of reasonable return and allows us to draw comparative conclusions about the frequency of these returns. Trading volatility is the return realistically achievable, given the trader is likely to enter late, above the absolute low, and exit early, below the absolute top.

The concept is simple, but its application is inelegant. It requires judgment rather than mathematical precision so it is difficult to program as search criteria. It is a time-consuming process and impractical to apply on a daily basis to every chart in the database. Because trading volatility supplies the vital 'estimated' figures used in final trading calculations it is more efficient to apply it only to the very last candidates examined as trading opportunities.

In classifying these stocks we use low trading volatility, mid-range trading volatility and high trading volatility. Trading volatility is determined by the annual trading range, from peak to trough, and by the frequency of these moves. Some equities give multiple trading opportunities of about the same range many times a year. DMR is an example. Others offer these opportunities infrequently and this is an important time factor in the risk calculation.

Low trading volatility describes those stocks consistently yielding realistic trading returns around 10 per cent. The range of reasonable returns varies from sector to sector. It is difficult, for instance, to find a bank with high trading volatility but in the Internet sector these are reasonably expected returns. These volatility returns are grouped as shown:

Low trading volatility — 10 percent — usually includes most blue chips
Mid-range trading volatility — 20 to 50 percent — often stocks in the mid-cap grouping, the so-called green chips
High trading volatility — 50 to 100 percent plus — usually stocks with low capitalization

The actual tradeable moves may be greater, but on average these classes of stock, based on trading volatility, offer price movements in these ranges.

Deciding which class of stock each of the selected trading opportunities belongs to determines if our profit levels are within reasonable expectations. Without this decision it is impossible to set financial objectives and the trading plan is incomplete.

Setting financial objectives is based on the spreadsheet calculations and chart analysis, but ultimately it is a judgment call. Judgment does not mean we make a decision on the day when profits look good. This is a perfectly sound plan in theory, but in practice we rationalize, quibble, hang on and ultimately, all too often, hand back substantial chunks of the profit. When we reach judgment day we often discover we do not really have a plan beyond avarice.

PLOTTING TRADING VOLATILITY

Judgment calls are made before the trade is opened and are based on chart analysis. The first set of estimated figures is drawn from here. The upper parameters of the judgment call with DMR are set by the resistance level at $0.13. This offers a gross 24 percent return. The profit calculations in Figure 14.3 brought this closer to reality by including brokerage, indicating a 21 percent return.

The final judgment is based on the weekly bar chart. Our example is chosen for charting simplicity so the placement of the trading band using support and resistance is clear cut. Similar bands are drawn on every chart of our trading candidates. Like a trend line, the lines are placed to encompass a significant section of the price extremes. Unlike a trend line, our objective is to identify those areas where a trade entry or exit is most realistically possible. This is rarely at the extremities.

The weekly bar chart in Figure 14.4 from the United Kingdom lists the material-handling company FKI Plc. It shows the difference in the two plots. The upper and lower thick lines are correctly plotted trend lines defining the trading band. They touch the maximum number of extreme price moves defining the limits of trending activity. The arrows show the best fit to identify the five realistically achievable trades each returning about 10 percent. The thinner outer lines define trading volatility. In contrast, only a single trade based on the trend line extremities was possible in the same period. This is shown as X–X.

How many times in a year is it reasonably possible to take a trade between the lower and upper sections of the trading band? Only once in this extract, but a better measure of volatility is derived from the activity between the two thick trend lines. Here five good trades are possible in this low trading volatility candidate. The answers not only show the trading opportunities, but also the trading volatility.

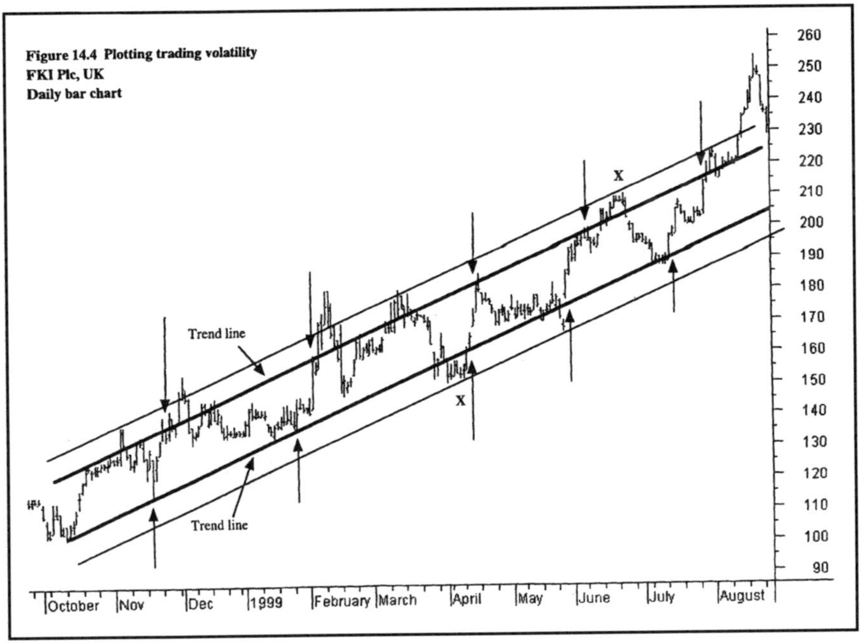

Figure 14.4 Plotting trading volatility
FKI Plc, UK
Daily bar chart

The DMR chart in Figure 14.1 shows how these comparison figures are obtained for DMR PLANNED. The entry is at \$0.105 and exit at \$0.13. The first trading opportunity marked by A–a developed over three weeks. These are 'at best' estimates derived from the latest possible entry and the earliest possible exit. The second, B–b, at best, took four weeks. The third and fourth, C–c and D–d, again at best, took two weeks. These trades potentially return 21 percent over an average 2.75-week period. For our example we stay with this average, but understand this is deceptively clear-cut.

The time spans must match reality. The time of exit is accurate on the chart and in trading terms when advance sell orders are placed at the target level. Timing the entry is not as precise, so additional time is added to reflect the reality of market timing. On average if you were taking these trades, would you have entered one day, several days, or weeks, before the 'up-leg' began? The answer depends on your trading style. Applied consistently it lengthens the average time span for the trade.

Using the 'at best' solution for each trade the calculations provide a measure of comparison. It does not tell us how long each trade will take in the real market.

The time in the market for DMR PLANNED compares sharply with the DMR GREED calculations that beckon with a 30 percent profit. These are shown as A–1, C–2 and D–3. The chart puts these better returns into perspective. Although the first 'greed' trade was initially achievable in a three-week period, the next best was six weeks, followed by nine weeks. This is an average of six weeks required to attain a 30 percent return, or more than double the average time exposure for DMR PLANNED.

In other words, for an additional 9 percent the trader is exposed to the market for 3.25 additional weeks. In actual trading terms the result is less favorable. Using 180,000 shares at $0.105 for each of the four trades, DMR PLANNED clears $15,968. Again, using 180,000 shares at $0.105 for each of three trades, DMR GREED clears $17,313 or 8.4 percent more after brokerage is included. This type of information is easily plotted on the typical time/risk/reward curve discussed in the previous chapter and shown in Figure 13.7. These types of comparisons are a useful way of ranking candidates based on trading volatility and they should only be used for this purpose.

Support and resistance levels lend themselves to precise numbering, as does the dollar value of the 2 percent rule. Putting an absolute figure on trading volatility in the past is achievable, although the precision belies the imprecision of the market. Putting an absolute figure on trading volatility in the future has no better status than an informed guess. The inferred figure is only useful in our calculation of risk because it facilitates comparison and ranking. It does not imply precision.

HARD NUMBERS

In this final sequence of calculations the inferred risk is a product of time and trading volatility. We will build a spreadsheet formula to deliver a hard reward/time number, but ultimately this is a judgment call.

Trading volatility is a function of reward and time. Dividing reward by time, expressed as weeks, produces a single figure used for ranking purposes. The DMR PLANNED reward/time number is 2.75 (11/4). The DMR GREED number is 6 (18/3). The DMR PLANNED gives a smaller and better reward/time result suggesting this is a better trading strategy based on a more realistic estimation of profit objectives.

Referring back to the FKI Plc chart, Figure 14.4, the same calculations also provide hard numbers. Only one trade was possible based on the trading band extremities — X to X. It took 53 days for a 37 percent return. This gives a reward/time number of 1.43. Trades made using the trading volatility plots shown as thick trend lines, produced five trades lasting on average 6.75 days. Each returned around 16 per cent. The reward/time result is 0.42 (6.75/16). The lower the reward/time number the lower the market risk in the trade.

These are hard numbers but they are based on estimated figures derived from subjective judgment about when you would enter and exit an historical trade based on chart plots. The objective is to maximize profits in a way consistent with risk as measured by time exposed to the market. Obviously, by narrowing the trading volatility bands we reduce the time — but we also reduce the percentage profit to a meaningless level.

The basis of estimation must be consistent across all examples. When comparing two securities as potential trading candidates do not mix weekly with daily charts. The results do provide a basis for ranking trade opportunities, but do not confuse this with trading reality. Ultimately this is a judgment call and your trading discipline determines if the call heralds your trading apocalypse.

As a trader you must decide if exposure to the market for more than three times the time — ten vs three weeks with DMR — for this difference in return represents an adequate balance between risk and reward. Your judgment as a trader balances the return against the time and the probability of achieving it considering the class of stock. Trading takes skill as well as sound analysis.

The DMR trade is on the lower end of mid-range trading volatility, but the short time factor reduces risk and makes it attractive. Our profit objective — 21 percent — is reasonably achievable in a four- to six-week period. Although the averages said three weeks we suspect a longer period is closer to market reality. This mix sets our financial objective for this trade.

The DMR sell order placed at $0.13, point D on the chart, was filled, satisfying the financial objectives within two weeks. You might think the objectives were too limited. That is OK. This example shows how to set precise exit conditions. Your challenge is to develop exit conditions compatible with your trading style and that lock in consistent profits.

TRADING PLAN SUMMARY

Good trading is the achievement of financial objectives. These objectives might be limited or extensive, but any trade meeting those objectives is a good trade.

Prices may continue to rise after our exit, but by taking profits at a predefined level in accordance with financial objectives we manage the trade without emotional interference. We are not managed by this trade because we know the objectives before we open the position. Under certain conditions using depth of market information discussed in the next chapter, we might stay with the trade beyond our initial exit point.

Staying with the trade calls for a repeat of the trading calculation to set new financial objectives as rigorous as the first because the only market 'gimme' is a loss. Trading plans do not need to be complex. Four or five lines written on the chart gives more detail than the plans used, or unused, by many traders. When I open a position I print out the chart and write these details on it. The chart and notes are pinned next to my computer for daily reference.

The trading plan for DMR fits easily into a chart margin. As shown at the start of the chapter, it looks like this:

Stop loss	— $0.095 for $2,000 maximum
Entry conditions	— on support
Exit conditions	— at resistance or reassess after six weeks
Financial objectives	— gross return 24 percent over four to six weeks.

Each figure, calculated and inferred, provides a ready reference for risk. When each open position is monitored daily these are the figures that count. The full trading calculations combined in a single spreadsheet to show entry, risk and reward are contained in Figure 14.5. Using this information we are prepared to take action at specific levels. By taking control of our entry and exit we manhandle risk.

Figure 14.5

BROKERAGE	
Av brokerage rate %	**1.20**
Total trade equity	**100,000**
EQUITY DETAILS	
Equity name	**DMR**
Number of shares	**180,000**
Purchase price	**0.105**
Net cost	18,900.00
Av brokerage	226.80
Full cost	**19,126.80**
RISK PARAMETERS	
Equity risk @ 2%	2,000.00
Risk on this trade	**2,000.00**
Stop-loss exit price based on full cost	0.095
Break-even price	0.108
REWARD PARAMETERS	
Sell price (inc. brokerage)	**0.13**
Gross return	23,400.00
Av brokerage	281.00
Net return	23,119.00
Clear $$$$	**3,992**
%%% Return full cost/net return	**20.87**
%%% Impact on total trading equity	**3.99**

LAST STANDING, BEST DRESSED

Trading is the active management of risk and our calculations give us a way to rank risk, even if in the final analysis some judgment is involved. When risk inflicts damage on our open position we are better equipped to manhandle it, keeping it at bay and giving us time to make a dignified exit.

Which trading opportunity gets our money? In selecting, it is useful to compare the summary trading plans developed for each identified stock. The final selection depends on many factors, but having followed this process in this book the one factor not lacking is adequate planning and analysis.

By applying this rigorous set of financial criteria to the final candidates on our list we further reduce the nuggets to just a few. Whether we take the trading opportunity or not will depend on our cash position. Not every day will turn up a trading opportunity meeting all of our criteria. Not every opportunity will be traded, but by the end of this process the trader knows which ones are most probable and financially rewarding, and he has a clear plan of action for all eventualities.

A well-planned trade does not manage itself. The open position must be monitored each day and the next chapter looks at how depth of market information helps make the entry and the exit more effective.

15

USING THE INTERNET AND ELECTRONIC DEPTH OF MARKET

Setting financial targets and objectives is a wasted exercise unless matched with financial reality on the day. Many times the match is perfect. When the match is imperfect our previous analysis allows us to assess the best fit. Based on previous calculations — the trading plan notes — we know immediately how far we can afford to chase our preferred price. Depth of market information hands the private trader tools to hone this trading edge.

Depth of market gives a glimpse of future intentions by permitting us to verify conclusions based on our chart analysis. It is a link with market reality, both prior to the entry and at the exit. Using depth of market effectively depends on the structure of the market and the mechanics of trading. We take time here to consider these differences because they have a dramatic impact on how we use this market information.

Market structure is divided into two quite distinct camps. Some, like the United States, are quote-driven markets. Others, like Australia, are order-driven markets. A few, like the United Kingdom, use a mixture of order-driven for the top FTSE listings and quote-driven for the remainder of the market and smaller orders.

The quote-driven market uses market-makers or specialists as middlemen. They quote prices at which they will buy or sell shares. These are displayed on Electronic Communication Network (ECN) screens. These ECNs are operated by the exchange; NASDAQ and the NYSE SuperDot system are examples. Additionally, third-party providers including InstiNet, Island, Archipelago, RediBook and Attain provide quote information.

An order-driven market matches buyers with sellers without the intervention of a middleman. Orders are displayed usually on the equivalent of a single ECN system for all market participants to see. Trades are automatically executed when prices are matched. These systems include the Australian SEATS, the United Kingdom SETS, and several Asian exchanges. A schematic outline of an order-driven market is shown in Figure 15.1. Compare this with the typical quote-driven market shown in Figure 15.2.

Figure 15.1 Mechanics of a trade. Order-driven market

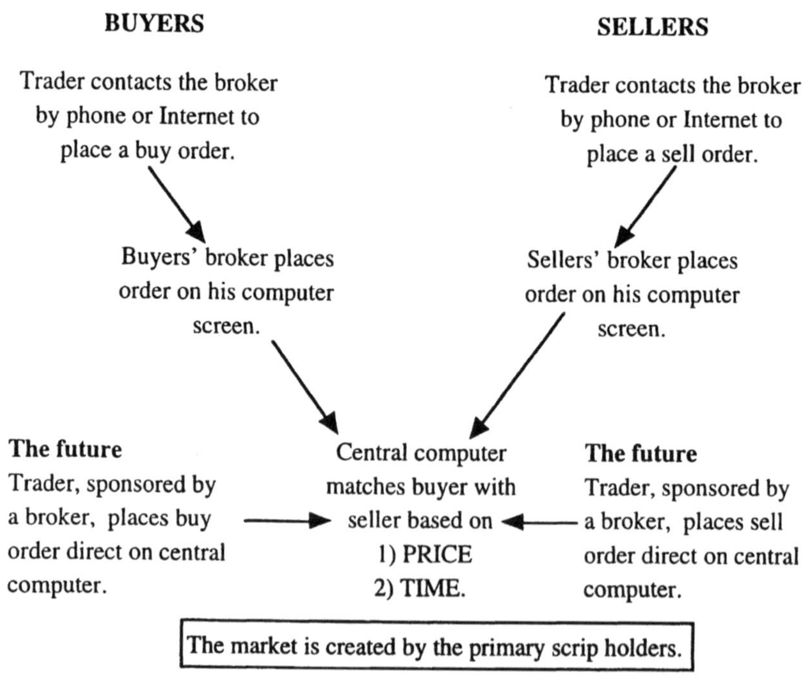

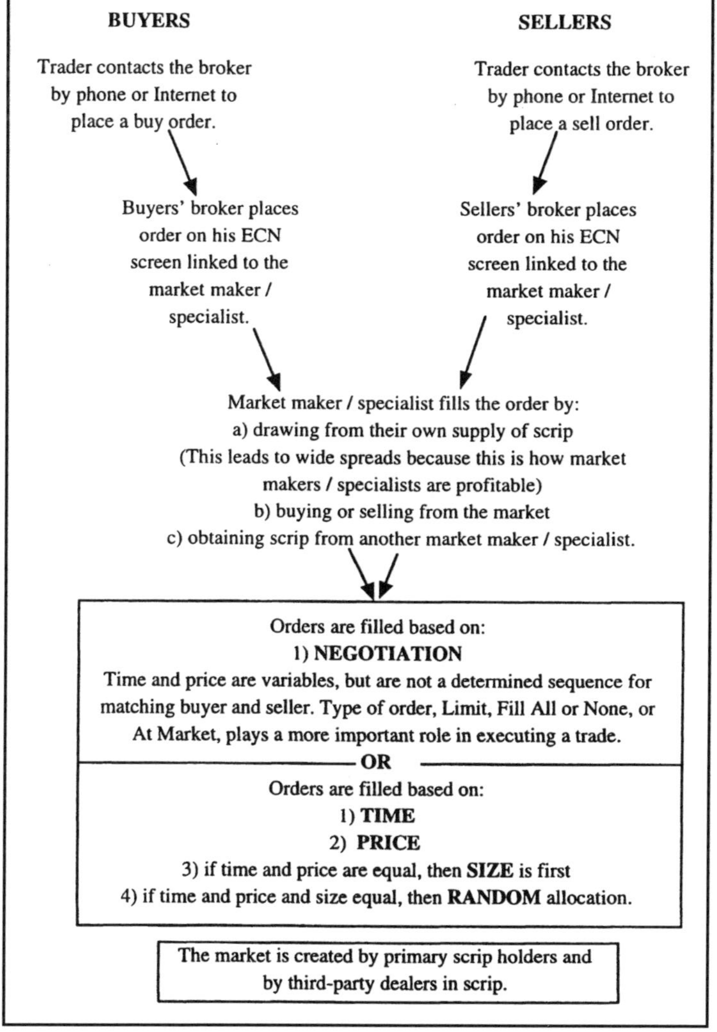

Figure 15.2 Mechanics of a trade. Quote-driven market

It is not just traders who want to make money from the market. In quote-driven systems there are many others who also want to take a cut from the trading traffic and this adds unexpected value to information about buyers and sellers. Quote-driven systems place a high value on this information and restrict access to it. Order-driven markets are built on trading transparency so information is more freely available.

LEVELS OF INFORMATION

In the best of all possible trading worlds every private trader would have access to five levels of market information. This would provide total transparency, make for efficient trading, speed the flow and allocation of capital, and enrich all traders who are prepared to carry and manage risk. Every market includes some of these characteristics and it is useful to assess your market against what is possible. We start with NASDAQ levels of access, and add two additional levels.

LEVEL 1

Level 1 data display what NASDAQ calls the inside market. This is the highest bid and the lowest ask. This information is typically available from many Internet sites. Live Level 1 data attracts an exchange fee, while delayed 'live' data is free. It is useful, but serious traders need more. The market fluctuates so the Level 1 quote is not always accurate and no broker or registered representative can guarantee a Level 1 price to a client.

We use Level 1 to monitor open positions.

LEVEL 2

Level 2 data shows consolidated orders, or quotes. Only recently has NASDAQ allowed the public to access this data and this has fueled the Internet and day trading boom. As expected, Level 2 data means different things in quote- and order-driven markets.

In a quote-driven market a Level 2 screen provides current quotes and the size of those quotes are available from each market-maker in a particular security. An example of the display is shown in Figure 15.3. This is a consolidated display because the 10-lot order at the top of the bid screen does not tell how many buyers are represented. It could be one large order for 10 lots, or five orders of two lots each. It is always useful to know if you are standing in front of an institutional order, or many small orders.

Figure 15.3 Level 2 Market maker screen

XXXX, INC								
	XXXX	1000		64 1/2		1000	*	+2 7/8
C	61 5/8		B	62 1/2	A	64 9/16	R	1 @ 2
O	61 5/8	V	H	64 13/16	L	61 1/8	V	3228900

Name	Bid	Size	#Best	Name	Bid	Size	#Best
MADF	64 1/2	10	10	MONT	64 9/16	10	13
PWJC	64 3/8	10	3	SNDV	64 9/16	5	10
NFSC	64 3/8	10	7	SBSH	64 5/8	10	72
SHWD	64 3/8	3	6	MASH	64 5/8	10	3
OLDE	64 3/8	5	4	MLCO	64 5/8	10	6
SBSH	64 3/8	10	2	LEHM	64 5/8	5	7
DEAN	64 1/4	2	5	INCA	64 5/8	5	100
HRZG	64 1/4	5	1	PRUS	64 3/4	3	5
GSCO	64 1/4	10	3	CHGO	64 3/4	5	8
MLCO	64 1/4	5	7	NITE	64 3/4	3	9
JPMS	64 1/4	3	0	DEAN	64 3/4	8	3
RSSF	64 1/4	5	8	COWN	64 3/4	10	6
TSCO	64 1/4	10	3	ISLD	64 3/4	10	0
SNDV	64 1/8	8	0	DMGL	64 3/4	10	7
PERT	64 1/8	2	0	HRZG	64 7/8	3	3
LEHM	64 1/8	10	3	RSSF	64 7/8	10	8
HMQT	64 1/8	4	3	PERT	64 7/8	10	3
DMGL	64	5	1	ABSB	64 7/8	10	5

Quote-driven Level 2 screens tell us how many market makers are offering stock. In the US market there is no obligation for market makers to honor these quotes. The exception is the NASDAQ Small Order Execution System (SOES). Despite the indicative nature of these Level 2 quotes, this information allows the trader to develop a range of specific trading tactics designed to exploit the differences between market makers. These include better use of the SOES to get the best price. The tactics of the SOES 'bandits' and day traders are discussed more fully in *Secrets of the SOES Bandit* and *Internet Day Trading*.

Order-driven Level 2 screens provide consolidated information for many price levels. Rather than each price level being represented by three or four market makers each price level shows the total number of buyers or sellers from all sources. This provides greater depth to the display as shown in Figure 15.4. The display suffers from the same limitations because we do not know how large the individual orders are at each price level.

Figure 15.4 Level 2 consolidated information
Lend Lease, Australia
William Noalls trading screen

Market Depth Summary for LLC ASX

Total	Qty	Bid	Ask	Qty	Total
2	4209	1962	1967	5379	2
2	2255	1960	1968	1698	1
1	2000	1955	1970	905	2
1	150	1950	1972	500	1
2	900	1945	1975	4000	3
5	11655	1940	1980	12723	4
2	580	1935	1981	510	1
6	2614	1930	1985	7900	1
1	100	1927	1990	11648	5
7	10700	1925	1991	550	1

These Level 2 screens quickly tell us the total number of buyers and sellers at each level. In an order-driven market displayed orders must be filled if matched. What you see is what you can get — every time. Here the trader fine-tunes trading tactics to get ahead of buying or selling pressure. Order-driven markets execute trades on strict time and price priority. If you are first to meet the displayed price then your trade is executed. It does not matter if it is for just a handful of shares, or for thousands.

LEVEL 3

NASDQ Level 3 allows registered market makers to update their quotes on any security in which they make a market. This information is not available to the general public. In order-driven systems the ability to place new orders into the order line is often restricted to brokers. The broker enters the order directly into the SEATS or SET terminal. They may directly enter an order for any listed stock. In order-driven markets there is increasing pressure for straight-through processing, which gives individual traders the ability to enter orders directly into the market order system. Here they are sponsored by a broker, but do the work themselves.

Access to Level 3 data is not critical for most trading strategies and we list it only because it defines the end of the well-known NASDAQ structure.

LEVEL 4

We are dealing with a trading structure available in the best of all possible trading worlds so we add two new levels of transparency. Level 4 data shows the trader every individual order, including his own. In an order-driven system the screen display is shown in Figure 15.5. It is a level below the screen shot used in Figure 15.4. Here the trader sees all of the orders that make up the bidding at each price level. Of the two buyers at $19.62 he knows the mix of large and small orders.

Figure 15.5 Level 4 full depth of market information
Lend Lease, Australia
William Noalls trading screen

Market Depth Detail for LLC A...

Qty	Bid	Ask	Qty
2209	1962	1967	379
2000	1962	1967	5000
2001	1960	1968	1698
255	1960	1970	500
2000	1955	1970	405
150	1950	1972	500
400	1945	1975	2000
500	1945	1975	1000
300	1940	1975	1000
255	1940	1980	10000
100	1940	1980	200
6000	1940	1980	523
5000	1940	1980	2000
380	1935	1981	510
200	1935	1985	7900
100	1930	1990	1200
260	1930	1990	1300
300	1930	1990	2500
234	1930	1990	300
1200	1930	1990	6348
520	1930	1991	550

Our buy order.

He knows the status of his own order in the order line at $19.60. It is further identified by the odd lot size. In order-driven electronic markets where paper share certificates are replaced with electronic statements, the concept of odd lots inevitably disappears. It is just as easy to complete settlement for 100 shares as it is for 101.

This is incredibly useful information and we show how it is applied in the sections that follow. Now the trader can surf ahead of buying pressure, bidding just a tick ahead of the current bid. In quote-driven markets this is an 'inside bid' reserved for market makers. In order-driven markets the 'inside bid' is reserved for the smartest traders no matter who they may be.

Level 4 information is available for private traders using the Australian SEATS system.

LEVEL 5

This level applies only to order-driven markets. The screen display shows which brokers have placed each order. In this sense it resembles the information available with Level 3 market-maker information. It is not vital for the private trader. We include it only to show the levels required for total market transparency.

A summary of these differences is shown in Figure 15.6. No market has this absolute transparency but it is coming. Better trading requires better information. Electronic and Internet market access exert increasing pressure on exchanges to operate efficiently and transparently. You may not have them just yet, but all these levels will come to a screen near you. All it takes is a mouse click.

READY, SET, TRADE

In the last chapter we were able to pin a number on risk. For the rest of this chapter we examine how depth of market information is used to turn trade planning into reality.

Depth of market information is different from the current bid and offer or inside market provided in the newspapers and by some Internet providers. This shows the price at which the last trade was

Figure 15.6 Levels of market transparency

LEVEL 1
Current bid and offer or ask.

LEVEL 2
Prices above and below the current bid and offer.
Shows the market maker quotes in lots
or
shows consolidated orders for each price level.

LEVEL 3
Gives market makers the ability to update quotes.

LEVEL 4
Shows all individual orders at all price levels.
market maker's quotes shown in detail of order placed.
Screen display usually limited to 50 levels above and below the last traded price.
Buyers and sellers are anonymous.

LEVEL 5
Shows the sponsoring broker used for each order.

completed and the current bid and offer above and below the traded price. The bid is the amount the current buyer is prepared to pay. The offer is the amount the seller is asking for his stock. In some markets this is called the ask. A trade takes place when the buyer and the seller agree on price.

This Level 1 bid and offer information is basic to understanding the current state of the market for the security you are trading. Many Internet providers service supply this basic information and the examples below are based on a typical format. The screen display you use will differ in layout, but generally they all show much the same base information. The information is also available from your broker and it is very useful because it gives us immediate clues about the enthusiasm of the market.

The bid and offer Level 1 details for a sample security, YDN, Figure 15.7, show an active market. The buyer's bid is the same as the last traded price, and the seller's offer is only one tick above it. Six buyers are chasing one seller. The spread is 1 cent. Compared to the previous close, prices are up by 4 cents.

Figure 15.7 Using the bid and offer to track buying pressure

Code	**YDN**	
Last sale	19 -Aug 11.45	
Last sale @	**1.62**	
Change since close	**0.04**	
Today	Buyers	6@1.62
	Sellers	1@1.63
	Open	1.59
	High	1.62
	Low	1.59
	Volume	1,187,846
Yesterday	Close	1.58
	Volume	2,976,119

Compare this quickly with the same screen for GDC in Figure 15.8. Here five sellers are offering stock at the same price as the last trade, but the single buyer will only pay 2 cents below the last traded price. The spread between the bid and offer is 2 cents on a stock that has already fallen 5 cents from the previous close.

With just this basic analysis we know many buyers are chasing YDN, pushing the price up as sellers hold out for better prices. This is upward-buying pressure. In contrast, GDC has lots of sellers and very few buyers creating downward-selling pressure. This information alone has an impact on our trading decision.

If we hold stock it is a good day to sell YDN as prices move towards our sell point. If we want stock, then GDC offers better opportunities. With so many sellers of GDC stock it is better to wait for even lower prices if we are a buyer. On the other side of the transaction, if we want YDN stock, and the price is within our target calculations, then it is advisable to bid a cent higher to meet the offer. As a seller of GDC it would be wise to meet the bid if we were protecting a stop-loss position.

Figure 15.8 Using the bid and offer to track selling pressure

Code	**GDC**	
Last sale	19 -Aug 11.45	
Last sale @	**0.27**	
Change since close	**-0.05**	
Today	Buyers	1@0.25
	Sellers	5@0.27
	Open	0.27
	High	0.27
	Low	0.27
	Volume	1,000
Yesterday	Close	0.32
	Volume	70,000

We will move beyond these simple conclusions to more complex ones built on this base information. These two examples tell us more than just how much we would have to pay to obtain either of these stocks. We could meet the offer in each example, but the consequences would be different. From a trading perspective this helps us to fine-tune our entry, or exit, positions. Before moving on to consider the way traders use full depth of market information we look at ways to make better use of bid and offer screens.

Part-time traders find it difficult to access these screens during the day so ask your broker to provide the same information over the phone. Understanding how to read it and use it will improve your trading.

READING THE SCREEN

Returning to Figure 15.7 we note there are six buyers but only one seller. This tells us there is more buying pressure than selling pressure. More buyers are chasing fewer sellers.

As this is a snapshot screen it shows the balance of the market orders at just one time — 11.45 a.m. on 19 August. Orders meeting the offer — those entered at market — are instantly matched and traded and do not appear in the order line. If we placed a new order to buy the offer at $1.63 this screen would not show Buyer 1@1.63 and Seller 1@1.63. The screen would show the last sale @ 1.63. The six buyers at 1.62 would remain in place and the next seller, perhaps at 1.64, would be added.

This screen does not show the sequence of trades, but this information about the unexecuted bid and ask orders is useful. With only one seller at $1.63 we know we can get stock by raising our bid by 1 cent from $1.62. We know that if we take all the stock on offer at $1.63 the next seller is likely to be at the same price, or a few cents higher.

This buying decision is driven by fear. If nobody is offering stock at lower prices, then an entry at $1.63 is cheap compared with the other offer prices in the market above $1.63. In this type of market it is almost certain one of the six buyers, afraid of missing out, will bid higher to be sure of getting stock. He may be beaten to it by another trader who meets the offer. The fear of missing out in a rising stock encourages traders to jump the line and bid up.

Potential sellers are also driven by greed. After checking the market price they are more likely to hold out for higher prices at $1.63 or above knowing that if the worst happened they could always sell to any of the six buyers at $1.62.

This is the logic of the market. Buyer and seller must agree on price and when all the stock available at a particular price level has been purchased the price will move in the direction of the most frightened participant. With YDN fear rides beside the buyers. After all, if you had YDN would you sell it at $1.63 knowing there are six buyers chasing you and the price has already increased 4 cents since yesterday's close. Often we do not have to sell, so surfing ahead of buying pressure is very profitable.

Of course, the logic applies in reverse, as shown with the GDC screen in Figure 15.8. Here five sellers chase one buyer for a stock that gapped down 5 cents on the open. The potential buyer waits, confident a seller will weaken, lowering his price just to get rid of the stock. This selling decision is driven by fear. Many of the sellers are worried the buying will dry up, and if it does, they will be left holding stock. In this situation, somebody gets frightened first, and they lower their offer price to meet the bid.

For buyers, patience is likely to be rewarded as sellers become increasingly desperate. The difference in the spread, 2 cents, as well as the uneven number of orders on each side of the bid and ask, provides the information to support this conclusion.

Unfortunately this Level 1 snapshot of the emotional balance of the market at this single point in time can be misleading. The battle between those closest to the last traded price might not necessarily be representative of the overall campaign. For the position trader, the battle is interesting, but we really look for a wider campaign perspective.

What is particularly useful is not just the number of buyers and sellers at the level nearest to the last traded price, but the number of buyers and sellers and levels below and above the last traded price. This is Level 2 information. When this is supplied with full and detailed volume information we have a gold mine of market advantage. Not only do we make better judgments about the potential course of trades today, but we also use this information to confirm our chart analysis.

MINING MARKETS

Armed with financial calculations and a clear knowledge of how much we are prepared to pay, or sell for, we do battle with the market. The bid information about GDC is useful, but what is below and above the current bid and ask? Are these orders a temporary phenomenon, or are they indicative of a wider selling campaign? To find the answer we need Level 2 depth of market information. The most obvious advantage of this information is that it prevents us buying at $0.25 when the next buyer is at $0.23 or less. Depth of market allows us to fine-tune our trading — and also to occasionally outsmart ourselves.

This information is shown in Figure 15.9 and uses consolidated order volume available from one of the Internet providers. This is the screen behind the market information shown in Figures 15.7 and 15.8. The display on a NASDAQ, Malaysian or Singaporean screen would show this as lots or parcels. This type of information is available from many ECNs, brokerage services and some Internet-based providers. The same information is available on any broker's screen and your broker should be able to read it to you, or fax a copy on request.

Many of the trading tactics made possible by this information are also applied to Level 4 information. Rather than repeat ourselves we will move to a more detailed discussion of this example based on Level 4 access remembering that much of it applies to Level 2 as well. In all that follows, the assumption is that what we see on the screen we can get. In quote-driven markets, particularly in the United States, this assumption is flawed. We believe this will change as Internet trading efficiency, execution and settlement demands that posted quotes be honored.

What follows is an introduction to the world of electronic trading as it is likely to become. Exchanges are realizing that electronic share scrip speeds settlement so that old restrictions on lot and parcel size are no longer relevant. The examples below routinely

Figure 15.9 Level 2 depth of market. Buying pressure, typical example

YDN Last sale 1.62			
Qty	BUY	SELL	Qty
317,091	1.62	1.63	3,097
100,000	1.61	1.64	46,900
200,000	1.60	1.65	25,000
200,000	1.59	1.67	62,000
107,900	1.58	1.68	30,500
126,111	1.56	1.71	170,686
6,000	1.55	1.72	3,100
4,000	1.54	1.73	2,500
2,000	1.52	1.75	3,500
26,000	1.51		

show odd lot bids for 101 shares. Traders use this as a way to identify their personal orders. All prices are shown in decimals, again reflecting the force of progress pressing on all exchanges.

The future is here. The Level 4 structure comes directly from the trading screens that I use to trade the Australian market.

MINING DEEP MARKETS

The full Level 4 market information is shown in Figures 15.10 and 15.11. The depth of market information gives details of each

Figure 15.10 Level 4 depth of market.
Buying pressure, typical example

YDN Last sale 1.62							
		Qty	BUY	SELL	Qty		
6,300	3,050	250,000	1.62	1.63	3,097		
*0	30,000	27,741		1.64	16,900	30,000	
		100,000	1.61	1.65	25,000		
	100,000	100,000	1.60	1.67	12,000	50,000	
		200,000	1.59	1.68	2,200	25,000	3,300
100,000	1,900	5,000	1.58	1.71	2,537	8,520	10,000
		1,000			5,000	2,000	5,000
23,111	100,000	3,000	1.56		19,000	10,000	2,000
	*0	6,000	1.55		13,500	5,000	25,000
		4,000	1.54		4,000	10,329	7,300
		2,000	1.52		5,000	3,500	4,500
4,000	20,000	2,000	1.51		10,000	4,500	3,300
					4,000	6,000	700
				1.72	25,000	6,000	
				1.73	25,000		
				1.75	5,000	10,000	20,000

Figure 15.11 Level 4 depth of market.
Selling pressure, typical example

GDC Last sale 0.27							
		Qty	BUY	SELL	Qty		
		30,000	0.25	0.27	15,000	16,000	10,000
		15,000	0.23		19,143	4,000	
		48,626	0.20	0.28	4,000	19,885	144
15,000	19,885	10,000	0.17		3,000	6,970	1,620
	10,000	30,000		0.29	10,000	4,000	1,080

bid and offer at each price level. It also lists the number, the size and position of orders in line at each level. The buy orders closest to the Buy column are the first orders in line at each level and will be executed in this exact sequence. Orders remain in place until filled or withdrawn. Sell orders closest to the Sell column are the first executed.

This new information represents only the potential for price action because not all these orders will be filled during the day. As prices move in one direction or another, the gaps in price levels may be filled with new orders. Someone may choose to place a new buy order for YDN at $1.57, for instance. During the day the number of orders at any level may swell as people join the rush. They also fall away as traders cancel their market orders, placing them at new levels, or leave the market entirely.

And of course, the most important caveat of all, what you see here is not what you will see in one hour's time, or in two days' time. But all this said, these figures provide a remarkably useful guide for trading activity, and they support chart analysis in some very interesting ways considered below. This is our focus as position traders. The day trader uses this information to identify momentum. We do not explore these tactics here.

Some exchanges clear all unfilled orders at the end of the day. Others allow good-till-canceled orders to remain in place. Where this happens it gives a specific characteristic to the market. Orders at specific price levels are lodged early and remain in place for extended periods. Unless instructed otherwise, many brokers leave orders in place for three days before they automatically expire. These semi-permanent orders provide an outline of the structure of the market and help us to identify the bulges in the balance of probability.

GOING UP

In mining this depth of market information the first nugget is the number of buyers and sellers. The second nugget is the order volume. It is all very well to know there are six buyers and one seller for YDN, but having decided our trading opportunity lies in an entry with YDN, additional volume information helps fine-tune the entry.

The six buyers want at least 317,091 shares. The order marked *0 is for an undisclosed quantity. The seller has only 3,097 to sell. Unless many more sellers come into the market at current prices, buyers will not be satisfied at this current level. Most will miss out on stock. This in itself suggests rising prices as buyers outbid each other to chase scarce stock.

Moving down the Level 4 depth of market screen gives additional advantages by showing the buyers and sellers at each level. Traders looking to buy YDN draw seven conclusions from Figure 15.10. The first five also apply to traders with access only to Level 2 screens.

- There are consistently large orders at every level below $1.62 down to $1.51.
- Some of these buyers are certain to become fearful and move their bid prices up towards the last traded price. This will swell the buying orders at higher levels.
- Only two price slots — $1.57 and $1.53 — do not have buy orders. An order placed in either of these gaps would be first in line and first filled if prices fell to this level.
- To get to the front of the order line we need to meet the offer at $1.63.
- If we want more than 3,097 shares, we may have to bid to $1.64 or higher to get our entire order filled.
- Placing a new order at $1.61, or $1.59, puts us second in line. This is only useful should prices fall to this level.
- The selling activity at $1.71 comes from many small orders. This suggests small traders rather than institutions. The larger order size on the buying side suggests large traders and experienced market participants. This conclusion is based on the assumption that size tends to equal experience. As Elder writes in *Trading for a Living,* 'Big money didn't get big by being stupid.'

Let's take a closer look at how this works to give traders an advantage. Assume the first buyer in line at $1.62 desperately wants

250,000 shares, for whatever the reason. It may be that 250,000 rounds out his existing portfolio, or it may represent a dollar value he is prepared to commit to the market. If this is the case, the size of his order, 250,000 shares, will decrease as the price increases.

To fill his order in this market on current figures he must pay at least $1.64. A more likely outcome is that he will take out the existing sell orders between $1.63 and $1.68, including some orders at $1.71 to ensure he gets the number of shares he wants. His alternative is to wait until more sellers come into the market at $1.63, which is unlikely when prices are rising.

What will this buyer do? In a market where there are many other buyers he is going to have to bid up or run the risk of missing out entirely. During the day he is likely to move his bid price up. When we compare today's depth of market information with yesterday's it is quite common to see the same orders move up the bidding scale over several days.

Sellers and potential sellers watch this action and use it to fine-tune their tactics.

Traders chasing this stock and looking to enter a new buy order will meet the offer at $1.63 knowing three things:

- The large buying orders at $1.62 provide a floor for prices, making his purchase safer.
- By meeting the offer he goes straight to the head of the line and gets a position in the stock.
- Prices have already risen by 4 cents, and the large orders, if they are to be filled, will push the bidding higher.

Using this information confirms the shift of the balance of probability in the trader's favor on this day. If every other analytical tool screams buy at $1.61 this depth of market information tells us it is unlikely we will get stock at this price. If our financial analysis allows us to chase the price to $1.65, then we shift the day's balance of probability in our favor by meeting the offer.

Traders looking to sell existing YDN stock have the opportunity to get a better exit. As prices move up many sellers back away, lifting their asking prices a few ticks above the current trade. With plenty of buyers chasing them they can afford to be coy. The order flow blocks further price rises at $1.71, but any sell order placed at $1.66, $1.69 or $1.70 is first in line. These points represent better selling opportunities — but only if they also lock in profits based on previous financial calculations.

Had these calculations indicated $1.71 as the best sell point then it is now too late to place the order. With over 173,000 on offer at this level even an enthusiastic market is going to have a little trouble swallowing the volume. A better exit is at $1.70 in front of the selling pressure. This is selling into strength and guarantees order execution.

GOING DOWN

Essentially, the same types of trading conclusions are drawn from Figure 15.11, but in reverse. The selling order overhang of 64,143 tells buyers they can get their desired number of shares any time, just by bidding a cent or two higher. There is no pressure on the buyers to bid up. Prices have dropped 5 cents since yesterday's close and the volume on offer is nearly the same — 64,143 compared to 70,000 sold yesterday.

By waiting there is a good chance the sellers will lower their price. With so many shares on offer the supply obviously outstrips the demand. Buyers don't need to jump ahead in the line because there is so much scrip on offer that nobody is in a hurry.

The seller looks pessimistically at Figure 15.11. Unless he is very close to the front of the order line at $0.27 there is a low probability of getting out. With at least 15 traders behind him stretching back to $0.29 it is certain one of them will act decisively to cut their losses by meeting the bid at $0.25. The entire sell order structure is likely to cascade towards $0.25.

With such heavy selling in place it is difficult to ask $0.26 and have it filled, even though this new order goes to the front of a new line. When prices are falling it is difficult to entice buyers to bid up by lowering the ask to the midpoint between the current bid and ask. Better not to quibble when the depth of market looks like this. Meet the bid and get out at, or just beyond, your stop-loss points.

The buyer sees Figure 15.11 in an entirely different light. For the trader placing a new order the danger is the buyer at $0.25 will see the market depth, pull his order out, and re-insert it somewhere between $0.23 and $0.17. When markets fall, buyers retreat in front of the selling pressure, realizing they do not have to pay as much as they originally estimated. An initial buy order, first in line, could be comfortably placed at $0.18, and monitored closely.

This bid increases only if more buyers flood in at higher levels, or if sellers refuse to lower their offer. This is a waiting game where the buyer holds the upper hand. Depth of market information allows the trader to see how best to implement his trading decision on the day.

CRYPTIC NOTATIONS

Institutions are not always comfortable with transparency. They like anonymity and in quote-driven markets they get this with market-maker co-operation. In order-driven markets they get it with an exemption from declaring the size of the order. In these markets the most exciting notation to appear on the Level 4 depth of market screen is *0 — meaning undisclosed.

There are a number of reasons for a buyer or seller to request his order be placed as *0, but the most common is because he does not wish to give away the size. Such orders are often very large — so large that they will have a significant impact on the operation of the market. As a buyer, if there is a *0 order below me I am comfortable because I know this will often act as a cushion against falling prices if it is confirmed by chart analysis.

As a seller, I am less comfortable with a *0 order below my intended exit point. Such an order suggests the market is going to have a hard time gobbling up all the shares on offer at lower levels before reaching my sell target. Such *0 orders do not invalidate my sell, but they do tell me patience had better be a profitable virtue.

Undisclosed orders do not have to be large. Traders use *0 for many reasons, including a desire for anonymity if they are using more than one broker. It is unwise to assume a *0 order is large without any supporting evidence, such as the proximity to a support or resistance level noted previously on a chart. This is discussed below.

Mining deep markets gives an advantage that bid and ask information alone cannot match. Access to this type of screen, either as a snapshot or in real-time updated live feed, more than pays for the costs of Internet access.

TOO FEW, TOO LATE

Although an entry at a specified price level may be very desirable on every level of analysis, it must be assessed against daily reality by looking at the number of sellers and buyers at that level. An ideal TARGET TRADE is shown in Figure 15.12, with entry at $21.50 on good support. Exit is planned at $26.00 for an 18 percent return.

Often when the price drops to the support level only a few shares change hands. We may have wanted 1,030, but only picked up 100 before the price reversed and climbed.

Now we have an uncomfortable dilemma, shown in the right-hand column of Figure 15.12 headed ACTUAL TRADE. One hundred shares is not enough to make the trade worthwhile. On one hand this is a satisfactory result because our analysis has proven correct with prices falling to the selected level. On the other hand we cannot profit from this because we hold too few shares to make the trade viable.

With only 100 shares, the financial status of the trade is destroyed. The break-even point, assisted by minimum brokerage for such a small trade, blows out a few cents from $22.02 to $22.06. We can

Figure 15.12

BROKERAGE		
Av brokerage rate %	**1.200**	
Total trade equity	100,000.00	
EQUITY DETAILS		
Equity name	TARGET TRADE	ACTUAL TRADE
Number of shares	**1,030**	**100**
Purchase price	**21.50**	**21.50**
Net cost	22,145.00	2,150.00
Av brokerage	265.74	29.95
Full cost	**22,410.74**	**2,179.95**
RISK PARAMETERS		
Equity risk @ 2%	2,000.00	2,000.00
Risk on this trade	**1,800.00**	**1,800.00**
Stop-loss exit price based on purchase price	19.75	3.50
Stop-loss exit price based on full cost	20.01	3.80
Break-even price	22.02	22.06
REWARD PARAMETERS		
Sell price (inc. brokerage)	**26.000**	**26.05**
Gross return	26,780.00	2,605.00
Av brokerage	321.36	29.95
Net return	26,458.64	2,575.05
Clear $$$$	**4,048.00**	**395**
%%% Return full cost/net return	**18.06**	**18.12**
%%% Impact on total trading equity	**4.05**	**0.4**

still get an 18 percent return and we look for sales at $26.05, just a few cents above the original planned exit.

The real problem is revealed by the dollar figures. An 18 percent return on the actual trade puts $395 in our pocket and adds just 0.4 percent to our trading capital. This is a long way from the original $4,048 target.

Our choices are to stay with the trade and unload the 100 shares perhaps months later at break-even. Or we chase the price, building the position to an economic size while at the same time shifting the goal posts. Every parcel bought at a higher price lifts the break-even level. If we still want the original 18 percent return our preferred exit price moves upwards and beyond the price targets initially based on the better balance of probability. When this happens the probability of success diminishes as we buy deeper and deeper into the mire.

At these times it is preferable to exit the position as rapidly as possible, take the loss, and reallocate the capital to better trading opportunities.

There are two ways to avoid this uncomfortable dilemma. The first, already discussed above, is to get in front of the order stream by placing orders ahead of size to ensure our order is filled as discussed above. Effectively this places our buy order just above current support and our sell just below current resistance.

The second way makes use of the average order size to ensure our orders are filled.

BULLY THE MARKET

A better use of depth of market information helps the trader to avoid this embarrassing situation where he is both right and ruined. We make even better use when we turn away from the trading screen and pick up the latest company report.

We look for the number of shareholders. A small company might have 2,398. A company on the upper edge of the mid-sized range has 10,984, compared with 700,499 shareholders for a well-established corporation. Add to this the number of shares controlled by the top 20 shareholders and we develop a three-dimensional market picture. The top 20 hold perhaps 82 percent of the small company, 40 percent of the mid-sized organization and 9 percent of the corporation. The top 20 shareholders are often funds and institutions with investment style holdings. Most of the time these shares are not for sale. We get to trade the rest and this determines appropriate order size against which we evaluate the screen information. The real size of the float is determined by those stockholders willing to trade.

The volume, or order size, information allows us to assess the probability of our order being filled. We plan our exposure to the stock based on the average order size within the context of shares available for trading. If our order is too large the market will not be able to digest it. Instead of working with the market, we run the danger of becoming the market, creating new support or resistance levels just by the very size of our orders.

We avoid this by taking the average size of orders at and near our preferred entry price. This average order size should match the capital we plan to commit to this trade. If we cannot get a position with the size we want, then although the trade may be worthwhile by all our other chart and financial criteria, it may be physically impossible to execute in the market.

If average order size over the past five or six weeks is 100,000, this sets our maximum order size. The proposed trade must be financially successful within these parameters. That is, if the trade cannot meet our financial criteria based on an order size of 100,000 or less, it must be rejected. This figure is inserted into the Number of shares cell on the trading calculation sheet and financial objectives adjusted accordingly.

In deciding the order size we use depth of market information to establish the number of buyers at the support level, or our entry level, and the number of shares they want. A single buyer who wants 60,000 destroys our chances of getting 1,000 at the same price if we are last in line where average turnover is 1,000 a day. The same applies when there are many small orders in front of us.

Larger than average orders can be filled, but they take time. Stocks test and re-test support levels. This process defines these levels. Although individual volumes at these points may be small, they are often sufficient to nibble away at a larger buy or sell order over time. I have completed several trades where my large sell order was taken out 100 to 200 shares at a time, day after day. This is difficult trading but if selling is consistent the trader may feel more comfortable in taking the risk of having his order filled over several days, or sometimes even weeks.

By matching our order size with the average order size we increase our chances of it being filled. When there is a problem in having an order filled the trader must factor this into his risk assessment when it comes to evaluating the potential for the trade.

VALIDATING CHART ANALYSIS

Level 2 depth of market information provides valuable tactical intelligence, but just as importantly, it provides a way to validate chart analysis. The core of our stop-loss strategy is that stop-loss levels ought to coincide with logical chart support levels. This is not a theoretical exercise. It should be validated using actual buy and sell order behavior.

Validation is a three-step process, starting with basic chart analysis.

The Australian gold miner Normandy Mining (NDY) is the basis of this example. With smaller stocks the features are more marked. With larger stocks high liquidity and order flow blur the certainty, but in all cases the correlations illustrated below do exist. These correlations give validity to our chart analysis in particular, and to market charting approaches in general.

The first step is chart-based. Experienced traders will quickly note the two salient features of the NDY daily bar chart in Figure 15.13. Apparently, tenuous support is at $1.45, but this is also a long-term support level in previous years. Fairly substantial resistance is indicated at $1.64/5.

This is by no means a sophisticated analysis, although it indicates a 13 percent return between the bands. As traders we might want to explore the behavior of NDY at greater depth using the tools discussed in previous sections. However, in setting potential profit targets and stop-loss points, we invariably return to support and resistance levels in one form or another.

The second step in validating this chart analysis is to look at the Level 2 depth of market. This comes with some fine print that we will consider later. This validation is only possible where the Exchange trading system leaves unexecuted or good-until-canceled orders in place across multiple trading sessions. It is not possible with Exchanges where all unexecuted orders are purged from the system at the end of each day or trading session. We do use the snapshot figures for tactical purposes, but this consistency over time means major orders tend to remain in place until executed. Like a

Figure 15.13 Basic support and resistance
Normandy Mining, Australia
Daily bar chart

dotted centreline on a road at night, they outline the shape of the curve.

Order flow is uneven, as shown in Level 4 detail in Figure 15.14. Some price levels have more individual orders, or order volume than others. These order bulges tend to coincide with the support levels identified on the NDY chart. The first major bulge in the depth of market buy figures is at $1.45.

Level 2 screens showing consolidated orders at multiple price levels deliver the same information. As the third step it is convenient to display this consolidated information as a bar chart, shown in Figure 15.15.

By using either display format the trader calculates the average order size from $1.61 down to $1.46 at 23,225. The orders in place

Figure 15.14 Verifying depth of market and chart analysis
Level 4 depth of market

NDY Last sale 1.62							
		Qty	BUY	SELL	Qty		
	40,000	10,000	1.61	1.62	5,000	3,800	
	87,018	40,000	1.60	1.63	2,064	70,000	10,000
		200,000	1.59		9,000	30,000	17,000
100,000	1,900	5,000	1.58	1.64	5,899	30,000	10,000
23,111	100,000	3,000	1.56		15,000	12,000	50,000
		4,000	1.54		34,000	15,000	4,500
		2,000	1.52	1.65	10,000	2,537	8,250
	4,000	2,000	1.51		5,000	5,000	2,000
30,000	2,000	3,500	1.48		2,000	19,000	10,000
6,000	10,000	14,000	1.46		25,000	13,500	5,000
2,000	10,000	3,000	1.45		7,300	4,000	10,329
50,600	3,500	14,000			45,000	5,000	3,500
2,500	10,000	5,000			3,300	10,000	4,500
25,600	30,000	3,500			700	4,000	6,000
5,000	50,000	30,000			7,000	50,000	3,800
		1,000			8,000	42,000	
				1.66	25,000	4,000	

Figure 15.15 Confirming chart analysis by bulges in the order volume

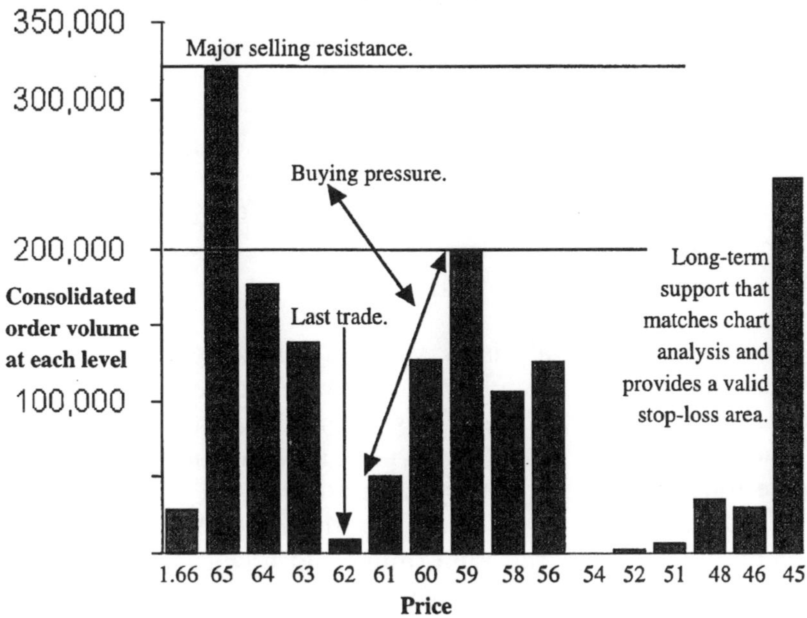

at $1.45 total 245,700. This massive block of buy orders, if left in place, provides firm support should NDY prices retreat.

This is the support level identified on the bar chart in Figure 15.13 and the large number of orders here are exactly where we expect them to be. This validates our chart understanding, and the placement of the support lines on the bar chart.

This is not coincidental in this hand-picked perfect example. It is a correlation repeated frequently across the market and it consistently provides the trader with important confirming evidence.

For the trader who had already taken a position in NDY and based his stop loss on the support level at $1.45, this depth of market information confirms his risk control strategy. If prices do fall to this level, the number of buyers gives the trader a better chance of making an exit at his preferred stop-loss level. This is as close to safety in the market as the trader gets.

UPSIDE INSTABILITY

Alas, the mother lode of information delivered by the depth of market screen thins out on the upper side. The same techniques can be used to establish and confirm resistance levels but they do not work as well. With NDY we anticipated substantial resistance around $1.64/5 and would expect this to be shown with an increased order flow. This is confirmed in Figure 15.14 with 29 sellers at $1.65. Smart traders have begun to cluster at $1.64 just ahead of the main resistance level.

Superficially, our analysis is verified. However, when people become sellers rather than buyers they take a different approach to value. Writing in *Against the Gods*, Bernstein discusses an example of the endowment effect of ownership. Students were given a coffee mug to keep. Later they were asked to set the lowest price they would be willing to accept for the mug. Another group of students were shown the same mugs and asked to nominate the highest they were prepared to pay. On average, mug owners wanted $5.25 while potential buyers would pay no more than $2.25.

The same endowment effect takes place in the market and makes using depth of market information for resistance-level calculations less certain. What we bought today for $1.45 we will not sell for $1.45. We buy in expectation of profit, so from the very first moment of ownership, we add a margin for this to the future resale price. This is reasonable, but we become unreasonable as the price increases, holding out for a higher price. This reaction is driven by what we think we can get.

For our purposes as traders this means the resistance levels indicated on the depth of market information are much more fluid than the support levels. Greed keeps moving the bar upwards. Fear pushes it downwards. Significant points of equilibrium are established in the market, and they often persist, but there is many a slip betwixt the ask and the sale.

FREEZE FRAME CAUTION

The market is full of annoying fine print and all depth of market information is no exception. Always remember it represents a snapshot of market emotions at a particular point in time. Markets change, and sometimes they change rapidly. Orders can be withdrawn, or re-entered at higher or lower prices. This is the dynamic of the market, jumping onto the bull and off the bear. Day traders use real-time depth of market information to initiate the trading process.

Position traders are less active in the market, making their initial trading decision after the market closes and after the end of day data has been collected. Position traders turn to depth of market information to confirm chart analysis, or to fine-tune an entry or exit. When we use this information it is at the end of the process.

From all this daily, hourly and by-the-minute froth and bubble in the market, certain points of ongoing stability emerge. Frequently they coincide with major points established by chart analysis. When depth of market information does so, it acts as additional confirmation. When it does not support chart analysis, the charts may need to be re-examined. In the trading world the market rules.

When depth of market is used as a confirming indicator it provides a valuable adjunct to trading decisions.

Ready access to full depth of market information is a distinct advantage. Just as learning to read a bar chart is a most valuable skill, learning to mine the depth of market information pays trading dividends. Depth of market gives us a glimpse of future intentions so we have the opportunity to match financial targets with market reality.

16

TRADING PLANS

In previous chapters we outlined the type of steps required to identify, select and manage trading opportunities. Every step takes the trader to a new level. Each level offers a variety of choices. A selection of these is shown in Figure 16.1. Just how you navigate through each level is an individual choice. No two traders will take the same route, or make the same choices even when looking at the same chart and indicators. The key difference between the novice and the professional is easily stated. The novice asks first about profits. The professional looks first at the risk.

Trading requires skill and just as the artist's skill and style distinguishes a Picasso from a Rembrandt your skill and trading style separates you from your competition. It is impossible to provide a single trading prescription that fits all. Our capacity for risk is different, our concepts of reward is too varied, and we all react differently under the goad of fear.

With these conditions in mind we look at a single application of a small selection of trading tools to a trade with the American company Goodyear Tire and Rubber. We apply the steps discussed in previous chapters. This plan has three stages:

- defining the opportunity
- getting to go, and to stop
- managing the trade, including the exit.

DEFINING THE OPPORTUNITY

To clarify the development of this trade we show the entire period in each of the charts. When discussing the entry conditions we consider the chart only up to a point defined by the vertical line

Figure 16.1 Levels and steps in developing a trading plan

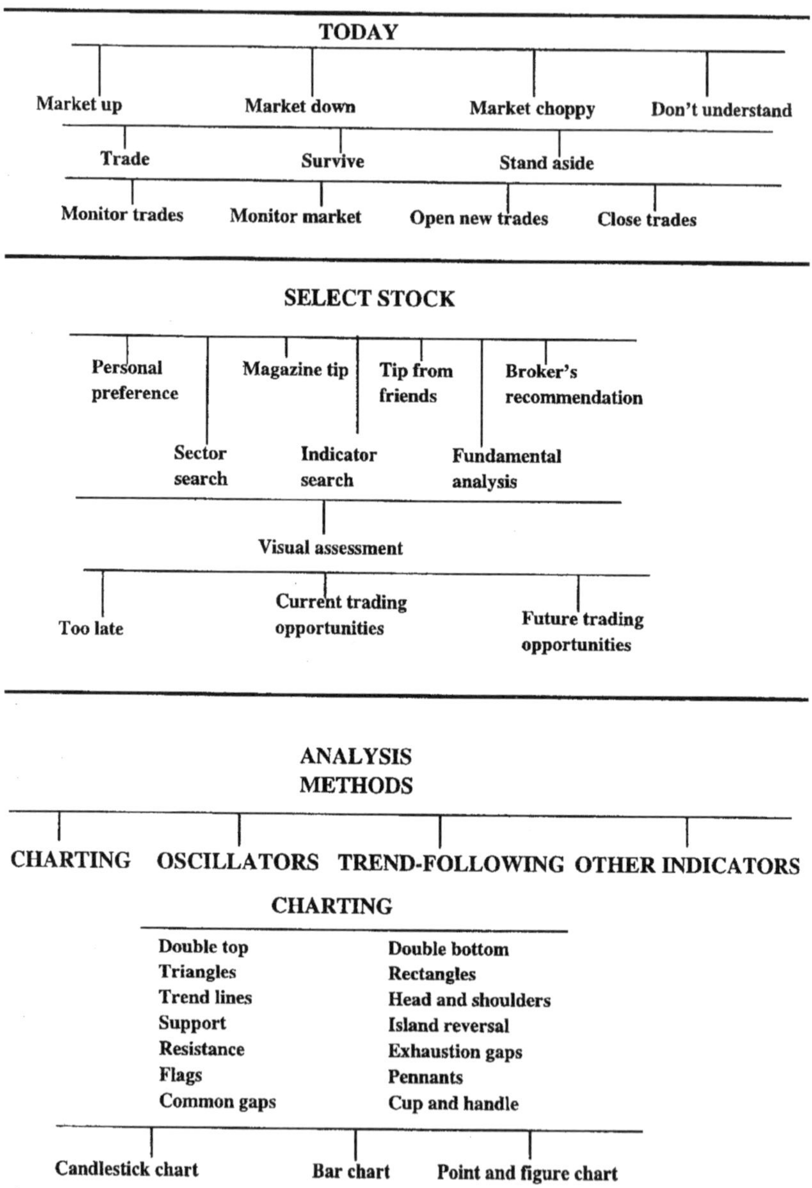

Figure 16.1 cont'd. Levels and steps in developing a trading plan

OSCILLATORS	TREND-FOLLOWING	OTHER INDICATORS
Relative Strength Index	Bollinger Bands	Count back line
Stochastic	ADX	Price% and volume
Rate of Change	MACD	Advance-Decline line
Williams %R	Moving average	Smart money
	2 moving averages	% retracement
	Guppy multiple moving average	New high-low index
	On Balance Volume	
	Trading bands	
	Average True Range	

EVALUATION

Trade · No trade · Uncertain · Proceed no further

STYLE OF TRADE

Aggressive · Speculative · Conservative · Defensive

TYPE OF TRADE

Trend - long side · Trend - short side · Rally · Momentum · Swing · Finger · Island in the sun

SET ENTRY PRICE

At market · Indicator value · Chart value

ENTRY/EXIT CONDITIONS

Establish profit targets	Establish stop-loss points
Financial targets	Financial stop-loss
Chart-based targets	Chart-based stop-loss
Indicator targets	Indicator-based stop-loss

EVALUATION

Improve profits · Analyse warrants · Risk OK · Profits OK · Proceed no further · Profits too small shown in all the following charts. Our entry analysis is based on what is shown to this point in time. Our exit analysis is based on all the information shown up to the last date recorded on the chart.

Goodyear is a stock in a downtrend. We follow these price movements down in Figure 16.2, looking for the best possible entry point to take advantage of any change in the downtrend. If we can catch a break-out we can ride the new trend for a long time. Although Goodyear has offered good trend trading opportunities in the past, it has been locked in a broad sideway's consolidation pattern. This offers trading opportunities between $46 and $58, which deliver a 26 percent return.

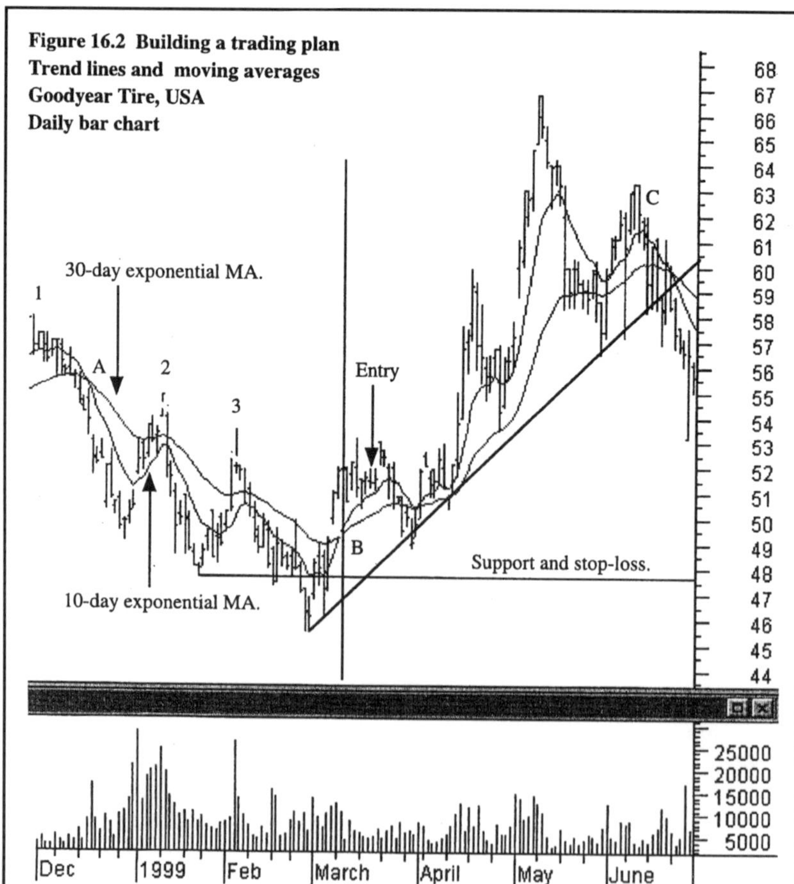

Figure 16.2 Building a trading plan
Trend lines and moving averages
Goodyear Tire, USA
Daily bar chart

Our initial strategy sets $58 as a potential exit target. Our first objective is to identify the break-out using the tools of charting and technical analysis. The gap-up opening has already drawn our attention.

GETTING TO GO

The downtrend is defined in two ways. The first is the straight-edge trend line. It is plotted to touch the maximum number of price extremes. It ignores the price spikes at points 2 and 3. A trend line placed along these points would touch only three points. The trend line plot as shown touches the maximum number of price extremes consistent with defining the trend. Plotting a trend line takes judgment, so where possible we back this judgment with other trend analysis tools as shown in Figure 16.2.

For this we turn first to a 10- and 30-day exponential moving average. The crossover of these two averages helped to define the beginning of the downtrend at point A. The crossover developing at point B signals another change in the direction of the trend. This confirms the break-out signal, alerting us to a potential trade.

We look for a further test of the strength of this change in direction. The Relative Strength Index (RSI) in Figure 16.3 shows a powerful divergence developing since December. When Goodyear made a new price low in December it was matched with a new RSI low. The Goodyear price lows in January and February were not matched with new RSI lows. This divergence pattern suggests the current break-out signals are most likely to lead to a trend change rather than just a short-term rally. We get set for an extended trade with initial targets set at the top of the consolidation band.

The MACD histogram shown in Figure 16.4 further confirms the trend change. MACD values continue to rise towards the zero reference line. Although traders may be cautious about using this type of MACD signal on a stand-alone basis we are more confident using it as a confirmation of previous analysis. The exact weighting allocated to each trading tool depends on many variables.

Figure 16.3 Building a trading plan
Relative Strength Index
Goodyear Tire, USA
Daily bar chart

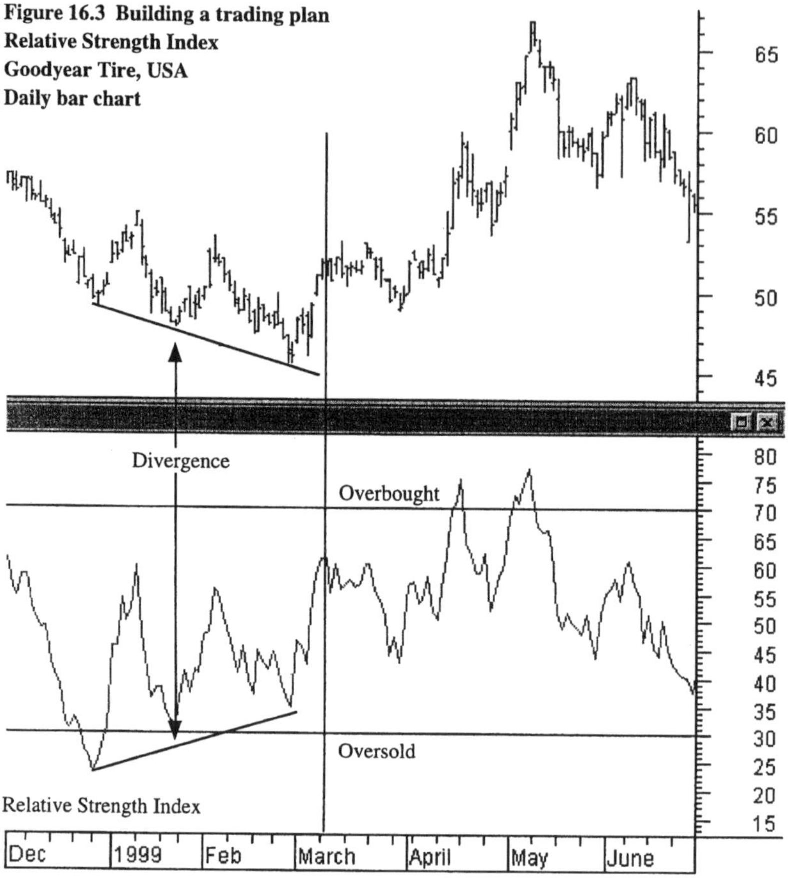

In some trades the MACD reading is critical so this indicator acts as the initiating signal for the trade. In this sample Goodyear trade, the primary initiating signal is the 10- and 30-day moving average crossover. The MACD signal is pushed further down the list. Which signals you decide to attach most importance to depends on how you define the trading opportunity and your preferred trading style.

Finally, we turn to the Guppy multiple moving average indicator shown in Figure 16.5. At the time of entry, defined by the vertical line, this delivers a signal for aggressive traders. The short-term

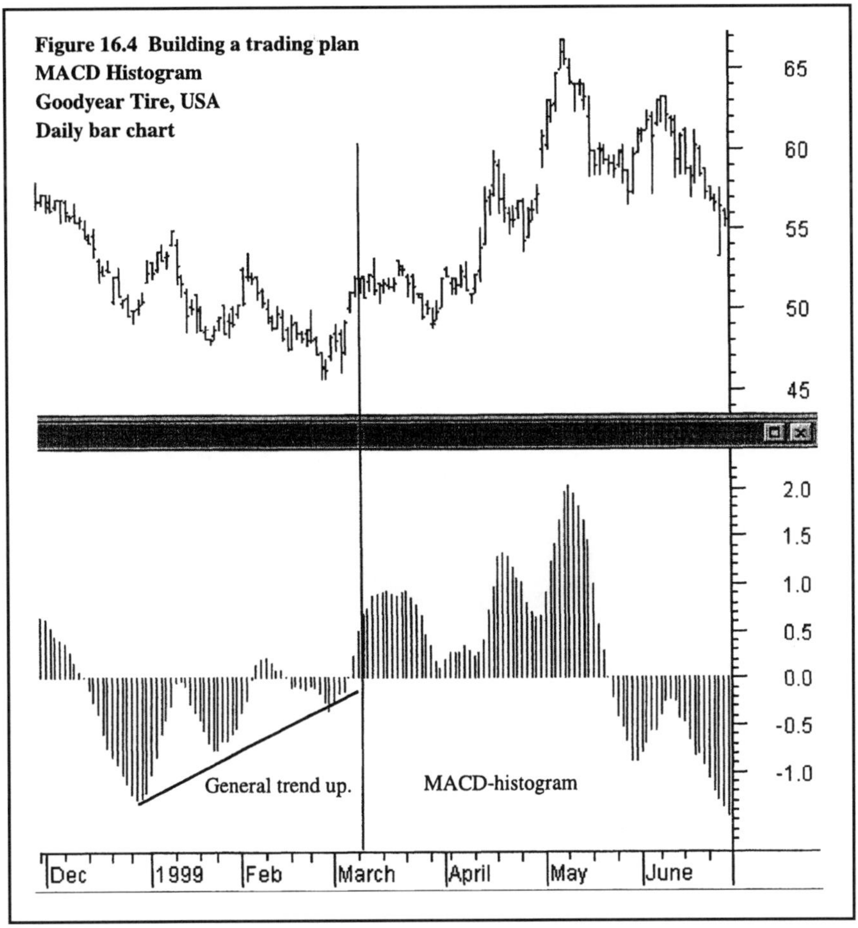

Figure 16.4 Building a trading plan
MACD Histogram
Goodyear Tire, USA
Daily bar chart

group of moving averages has tested, and re-tested the resolve of the long-term group on two previous occasions. This rally and retreat process is a characteristic on the multiple moving average downtrend display. Each test is more powerful than the previous ones so we are particularly alert for the third and fourth re-tests. We look for evidence that the long-term group of averages is weakening. This is provided either by a convergence of the long-term group, or a flattening out. This chart provides the second alternative so we take an aggressive position in anticipation of the trend break.

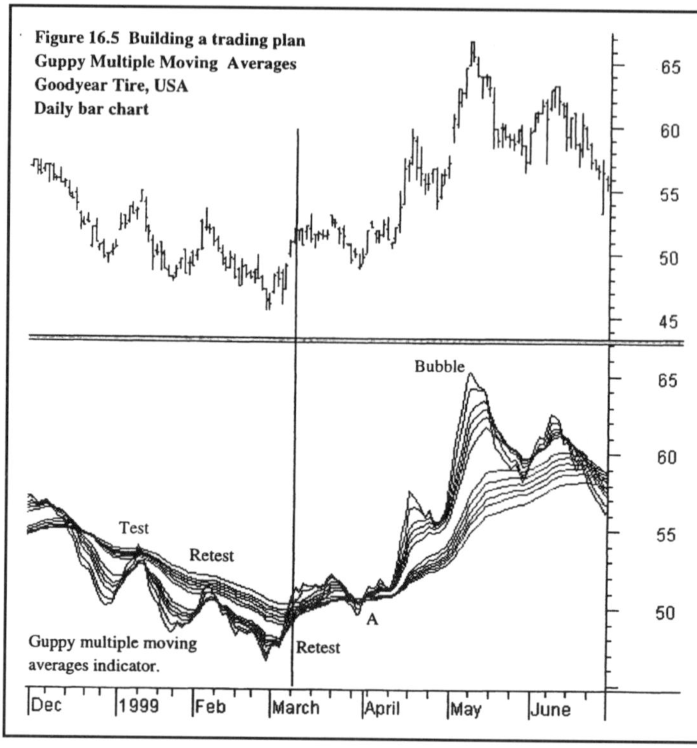

Figure 16.5 Building a trading plan
Guppy Multiple Moving Averages
Goodyear Tire, USA
Daily bar chart

Typically, this indicator shows a break past the long-term group of averages followed by a pullback to the long-term group. This provides an entry point for more conservative traders who would enter at point A. Although we are taking an aggressive position this does not mean we chase prices to the moon. We take an entry at $51 as prices pause after the first rally run.

MANAGING THE TRADE

The size of our position is determined by the money management method we use. In this trade we apply the 2 percent rule and the results are shown in Figure 16.6. The stop-loss point is an integral part of this calculation. As shown in Figure 16.2 the initial stop-loss is set at $47.50 and is based on the support level. We could apply other methods based on a count-back line technique, on a percentage stop loss, or a selected dollar figure. The exact calculation is your choice but you must select a stop-loss method.

Figure 16.6

BROKERAGE	
Av brokerage rate %	**1.20**
Total trade equity	**100,000**
EQUITY DETAILS	
Equity name	**GOODYEAR TIRE**
Number of shares	**487**
Purchase price	**50.00**
Net cost	24,350.00
Av brokerage	292.20
Full cost	**24,642.20**
RISK PARAMETERS	
Equity risk @ 2%	2,000.00
Risk on this trade	**2,000.00**
Stop-loss exit price based on full cost	46.49
Break-even price	51.20
REWARD PARAMETERS	
Sell price (inc. brokerage)	**62.00**
Gross return	30,194.00
Av brokerage	362.32
Net return	29,831.67
Clear $$$$	**5,189**
%%% Return full cost/net return	**21.06**
%%% Impact on total trading equity	**5.19**

Our preferred entry price is $51. Use a real-time Internet quote screen to manage your entry. With electronic trading where buyers are instantly matched with sellers — and if you are meeting the seller's offer — you should be able to confirm the trade as soon as it is executed.

In some markets you will have to ring your broker to get this depth of market information. When you get it, put the phone down. Analyze the information without pressure and ring him back to place the order. This is your buying decision, not his.

In other exchange systems do your best to have the trade confirmed as early as possible. If your broker is reluctant to provide service at this level, carefully consider how it impacts on your trading and adjust your approach accordingly.

The calculations in Figure 16.6 show the optimum trading size. This will need to be adjusted for lot or parcel size if your exchange does not allow unrestricted trading size.

While the trade is open we continue to monitor a handful of indicators. We plot a new straight-edge trend line to define the up trend. We also track the activity of the 10- and 30-day moving averages. These are shown in Figure 16.2 to the right of the vertical line. We look for closes below the trend line and movements towards a moving average crossover.

The RSI is used to track moves into the overbought area, although this generates warning, rather than exit, signals. Like all oscillator-style indicators the RSI tends to consistently signal overbought when a strong new up trend develops. It continues with this signal well into the new trend.

The main tools for monitoring the exit are the Guppy multiple moving averages. When these move too far away from the underlying trend established by the long-term group of averages they signal profit-taking opportunities based on the extreme rallies created by short-term traders. When these extremes exceed our initial profit targets they provide an opportunity to complete a better than expected trade.

Exits can also be managed with trailing stop-loss techniques including the count-back line, percentage stop loss, and selected dollar figure approaches. We do not apply these techniques in this example.

GETTING TO STOP

In the first planning stages we set either an exit target or exit conditions. Targets are usually based on old resistance levels. Sometimes they are built around what we consider to be a reasonable return for the risk in the trade. Plans that use exit conditions look for indicator readings, such as a moving average crossover.

We shoot initially for an exit target of $58 based on the upper level of the old consolidation band. When this level is hit all the trend indicators show the trend is still strong. We stay with the trade, basing our exit on trend indicators. These include the straight-edge trend line, the moving averages and the Guppy multiple moving averages indicator.

Deciding when to sell involves many of the same procedures as deciding when to buy. The decision is based on three factors. The first is aimed to protect trading capital, and the last to protect profits.

- The price level is equivalent to 2 percent risk of equity on the downside. When prices reach this level, you should be out immediately. If prices fall below this, get out anyway. The first loss is usually the cheapest.
- Profit objectives are achieved. If you are in the trade for a 10 percent return, then exit when it is achieved. If you must stay in the trade, do so only if other indicators are screaming 'Stay, Stay.'
- When other indicators call a trend reversal, or suggest a top, exit whether profit objectives have been achieved or not.

EXITS

Here we move to the right-hand edge of the chart, considering all the information gathered from April through June. We take our exit at $62 for a realized 21 percent return. This adds $5,189 to our trading capital.

Could we have done better? Of course, in theory. An exit at $67 is desirable, but rarely are these peak exits achieved by the same people who entered early in the trend break-out. We could bring home more dollars by increasing our position size, but only at the cost of increasing risk. We have to put more than 2 percent of trading capital at risk, exiting when prices fall to our initial stop-loss line at $47.50. Or we take an early exit when 2 percent of trading capital has been lost. Here is the potential for whipsaws because tight stops can take us out of good trends.

Trading reality is a long way from perfect. Our objective in this example is to show you how these trading plans are applied in the real world.

We exit at $62, shown as point C in Figure 16.2, for the following reasons. The straight-edge trend line is touched in May and June, and the two moving averages move close together. Additionally, the MACD histogram crosses below the zero reference line. These are the first indications of a weakening of the trend so we look for confirmation among our other indicators.

This pullback is shown as a bubble collapse on the multiple moving averages indicator display. The short-term group of traders have moved well ahead of the long-term investors' consensus of value. We are prepared to take advantage of the next rally and monitor this indicator closely. When the short-term groups begin to turn down we take an exit at $62.

We move in anticipation of the 10- and 30-day moving average crossover because of the earlier signal generated by the close below the straight-edge trend line. We are primed to take the best price possible on the rally.

In the same way as making a buy decision, we use a real-time Internet quote screen to fine-tune the exit. Internet traders who sell and meet the buyers' bid have their trades confirmed immediately.

If you have to ring your broker for the same information, when you get it, absolutely, definitely, put the phone down — fear clouds the judgment faster than greed. Ring the broker back when you have looked at the data and made your decision. A selling decision is often more difficult than buying. This is very much your decision, not his, so rely on your judgment. Phone through the sell order. Have the exit trade confirmed as a matter of urgency. If you are riding a loss you need to know the damage immediately so you can take appropriate action.

No matter which exchange you trade, the objective is to make an entry or exit, as close as possible to your preferred price.

TRADING REALITY

This example of a trade plan in action is only one of many possibilities. Aggressive traders will enter early in anticipation of the break-out. By using tight stop-loss control they manage the trade in a swing trading style, constantly probing for the bottom and riding rallies while waiting for trends. Conservative traders wait for the price pullback after the initial trend line break. They tend to enter a little later, and exit a little later. In return for an increased trend they accept a reduced profit.

The Goodyear chart offers rally trades, momentum trades and day trading opportunities. We have chosen to examine only a trend trade. Although we assessed the trade with five different indicators, some traders will select just one or two, perhaps the straight-edge trend line and the Guppy multiple moving average.

The market swamps us with choice. Clear trade planning is designed to avoid being overwhelmed. With clear objectives and appropriate use of trading tools we are in a better position to manage risk.

There is no universal trading system. The systematic approach described above is universal only in that it shows how method, indicators and techniques need to be related in a coherent and consistent approach to the market. This chapter has only summarized the process and shown you an example of how a trading plan is applied in the market. Your challenge is to apply the process and produce your own example.

Part IV

FAILURE WAITS UPON SUCCESS

17

OVER-TRADING

You might think after all this sound analysis, after all the chart examination, and after running the numbers, that trading success is guaranteed. The market failure rate suggests otherwise. This guarantee is not worth the paper it is written on because traders routinely commit financial suicide, often through over-trading, in response to instincts they don't fully understand.

Look in a mirror. It shows the traders' greatest trading enemy — ourselves — but most of us look to the computer screen for the culprit. In this section we want to look at some of the more creative excuses for failure: over-trading, inability to take losses, knowing when the market is wrong and gambling. I recognize many of them because I write from my own experience. Learning to look in the mirror is an important step towards trading success.

In this chapter we examine the relationship between how hard we work and how well we are rewarded. Our instinct to look busy — to over-trade — often costs us a great deal. After losing a million dollars Jim Paul decided the most effective trading approach 'if implemented properly, is actually quite boring waiting for your buy and sell criteria to materialize.' As private traders it is better to reach the same conclusion as Jim Paul without losing a million dollars. To save money we must learn to recognize when we are over-trading, usually because our wallet allows us, rather than trading with our brains.

Assessing our performance to decide if we are over-trading is made difficult by our accepted understanding of success. For most successful people there is a strong connection between how hard they work and the extent of their reward. Long hours, high levels of stress and frenetic office environments are tolerated because they deliver high pay, relaxing holidays and an upmarket lifestyle. Those who have this also have success. Those who do not have this obviously do not have success.

Success is a relative term. Those who are truly successful apparently no longer have to work. It seems as if there are hurdles placed at an important point in the work/reward equation. Once over the hurdle, the rewards come without apparent effort. These retirees from the shackles of work are admired and we wish to emulate them — either through hard work or luck.

Although these are generalizations, they play an important part in the way we see ourselves and our relationship with reward. In the centuries since Martin Luther hammered his 95 theses to the church door in Wittenberg, the protestant work ethic has gathered an ecumenical following. Trading alters this work/reward relationship in some very important ways because it has the potential to break the nexus between reward and effort. When this happens many novice traders feel uncomfortable and this impacts on their trading, turning success into honest failure.

Trading offers the opportunity of successful non-work and the markets continually lure hopeful novice traders with the hint of reward without too much effort. The Internet day trading frenzy in the last years of the century lured the inexperienced and the hopeful. For the full-time private trader, understanding and adjusting the relationship between work and reward to a personally comfortable level is an important challenge. Incorrectly handled adjustment leads to over-trading and potentially to a retreat from the market. The challenge is also issued to part-time traders and this tendency to trade with their wallet rather than their brain keeps many of them on the periphery of the market, trapped in a cycle of trading washout and recovery.

REWARD WITHOUT EFFORT

There are very few ways to come into riches and wealth without working that are applauded by the general community. Speculative trading is not one of them. Instant millionaires created by sweepstakes, lotteries, betting on the horses, or by successful casino gambling are accepted. People are envious, but not scornful. These windfall gains are the result of luck and we feel it could happen to anyone, including ourselves.

This is not wealth without work. It is wealth by luck. The return is not expected to be dependent on effort because this is a single event. If the win is substantial we retire and live a life similar to those really successful retirees. If the windfall is smaller, we return to work smug in the knowledge that life's little luxuries are no longer out of reach.

Win $30,000 in the Readers Digest sweepstakes or football pools and people congratulate you, but make $30,000 in the market and people are suspicious. The difference in reactions is important because it affects the way we approach trading.

To people outside the stock market the private trader appears to have an easy life, working a few hours a day and making substantial returns. The traders of fiction, often loosely based on flamboyant personalities such as Michael Milken or JP Morgan, make enormous returns for apparently little work. Professional traders employed by the institutions take home salaries and commissions of telephone number proportions and all they do is play with computers.

These public perceptions of traders are facile and inaccurate. They do not look beyond the surface gloss to see the amount of research, or analysis, or intellectual effort and emotional discipline required in the trading process. But these opinions cannot be ignored because the novice private trader brings these perceptions to trading, and later to his trading success.

These opinions are reinforced if the novice has some early successes. In return for a few hours of work in his spare time the market might pay him thousands of dollars. For workers whose wages look more like zip codes than telephone numbers this return represents substantial money. And it is paid for by so few hours of work — if you can call it work. That is, a bit of extra reading in the financial pages, listening carefully to the hot tip from a friend or broker, or perhaps just a lucky guess in a bull market or day trader's room provided by a friendly brokerage. Hardly work dictated by a boss, supervised by a clock and assessed against the number of voluntary and unpaid overtime hours.

At this early stage the novice trades in a way that is very close to gambling in many aspects. It is like an expensive lottery ticket, and sometimes the process is not much different. Real problems emerge when the novice decides to become more actively involved. Taking a real lottery or pools ticket for a few dollars each week is one thing. Taking new positions in the market is an act of a completely different order. Not only is it much more expensive, but it is also based on the assumption that consistent rewards can be gained in return for less work than our peers.

The prospect of large rewards for very little work is the initial appeal of the market for many traders.

REWARD WITH LITTLE EFFORT

Is this possible, and if it is, how is this possible? In answering these questions it is more helpful to start at the end and work backwards. How much time does the full-time trader spend in front of the screen? How many trades are completed in a year? These answers translate into hours worked.

By way of example let's consider an apparently modest ambition. We have $20,000 and we complete one trade every two weeks for 52 weeks. Each trade returns 5 percent or $1,000. By year end this represents $26,000 assuming only the original trading capital is used and profits are placed on deposit. This is a 130 percent return for the year. The trader starts with $20,000 and ends with $46,000.

Please understand this example looks easy, but reality has a habit of being more difficult. Readers should compare this with more realistic trading returns shown later in this chapter in Figure 17.2. Brokerage, slippage, transaction costs all eat into the 5 percent. Market liquidity has a significant impact on the trader's ability to execute the entry and exit at the desired price. To have 26 trades all moving in the desired direction represents very astute trading. Taking smaller returns, around 5 percent, may seem more modestly achievable than chasing larger 20 percent returns, but in practice it is still very difficult.

While still keeping an eye on reality, we will pursue this simple example to develop an approximate guide to the number of hours required each week. If an average of one trade a fortnight is sufficient to return a reasonable income, then how many hours does the trader need to sit in front of the screen?

The private trader does not have to trade every day. Unlike his institutional counterpart we wait until the best trading opportunities come along when the balance of probabilities is firmly lined up in our favor. In this example, we must make a decision once every two weeks. Our institutional cousins do not have this luxury.

Previous sections considered the processes involved in entering a position including identifying the opportunity using visual scans, or electronic scans of market data. Trading opportunities are evaluated using fundamental, technical or financial factors. The entry, the open position and the exit are all actively managed to meet financial objectives.

Although the time involved looks daunting, with experience the process is less so. If we have a number of open positions, these processes are all taking place simultaneously as we compare and reject multiple securities. For this example we want to separate these processes to estimate the time required for a single opportunity every two weeks.

Identifying the trading opportunity is the least time-consuming aspect of trading, particularly if our chosen market is relatively small. Identifying the single trading opportunity takes, we estimate, an hour a day on average.

Analyzing the trading opportunity is much more time-consuming. Perhaps five to 10 hours might be spent in analysis. This may include company research, reading balance sheets and assessing the fundamentals. Technical traders will spend much of this time applying and assessing various technical indicators and analyzing the price charts. If we take ten hours of analysis per position, this translates into one hour a day on average over a ten-day working fortnight.

The final trading step is managing the entry. Sometimes the entry is very quick, particularly if we meet the offer price. At other times the entry may take more time to be executed as we wait for prices to pull back to our preferred entry level. All order details are entered in a log for future reference. Once a position is opened the appropriate chart is printed and the summary trading plan attached.

Once the entry is made the trade is monitored daily. This may be as simple as checking the current trading activity waiting for the sell criteria to be met. Those using Internet access to real-time or snapshot prices do this in seconds. Others ring their broker and, if pleasantries are kept to a minimum, the task is completed in minutes. In slow markets traders check end-of-day data via the newspaper or data downloads.

Monitoring the open position takes a few minutes each day. Closing a position should be as easy, with the addition of a simple phone call to the broker to place the sell order. Trading records are updated and contract notes filed, both for portfolio management and for taxation purposes. Even with multiple open positions an hour a day should be enough. Again these are hypothetical figures, and actual hours may be more or less for individual traders.

Adding up the score card as shown in Figure 17.1 we record three hours a day — one hour for identification; one for analysis; one for management. For successful traders this is highly paid work. In return for a 15-hour week they are rewarded with a handsome income. This also makes trading a very appealing way to supplement income from our day job. With just a few open positions, an hour or so each evening with added weekend work makes trading possible. The old English trade union chant of 'Eight hours' work, eight hours' rest and eight hours' play' doesn't seem relevant. Just as importantly, the middle management executive refrain of 'Sixty hours a week with time for your family only when you retire' seems equally inappropriate.

Figure 17.1 Trading time

An example of daily tasks and time		
Identify trade opportunities		**1 hour**
* Database scan	20	
* Eyeball verification, bar chart	15	
* Indicator verification	25	
Analysis of opportunities		**1 hour**
* Check for bias	15	
* Assess stop-loss conditions	15	
* Assess profit targets	15	
* Rank by time/risk	15	
Trade management of open positions		**1 hour**
* Watch depth of market on entry	15	
* Place and execute buy order	5	
* Enter details in order log, print out chart with summary trading plan	5	
* With open positions, each day verify that original trading conditions are intact	15	
* Place and execute sell order	5	
* Enter details in trading records and file contract notes	15	

If a single trading position requires 15 hours, then logically two positions call for 30 hours and three for 45 hours. Fortunately, such linear logic does not apply. In reality trading opportunities tend to clump together. A single search may turn up several good opportunities, and then nothing for days. These multiple opportunities are considered together, and within reason, chart analysis is applied as quickly to one as it is to several.

Our example in Figure 17.2 is taken from our real-time personal trading records and shows the number of trades during a year. The average length of a trade is 28 days, but this fails to show how some weeks are very busy and others exceedingly dull. Extraordinary bull market returns from the last years of the century using around the same number of equity trades captured 94 percent and 102 percent annual returns. It has been fashionable to deride the equity market in favor of leveraged derivative and futures markets in the belief that good returns are not available with stocks. I do not agree with that view.

Before you rush to send e-mail please remember that relatively small size makes for nippy trading by private traders. Average position size is $20,000. Double this size for each position and the results suffer in thin speculative markets. Move to fund trading size and few of these trades would be contemplated, let alone executed.

For private traders such highly paid hourly work is a substantial part of the trading dream. Achieving it would not seem to create a problem. Nor would it if it were not for guilt. If greed and fear dominate the market, guilt is the shadow prowling beneath the surface of every private trader's success.

SO MUCH MONEY FOR SO LITTLE WORK

Having achieved this goal, some traders, perhaps many more of us than we would like to admit, feel uncomfortable. The roots of our discomfort lie in our long-held beliefs about work and reward. The protestant work ethic has certainly gathered an ecumenical following and we are not exempt.

For most private traders the path to trading has seen dalliance turn to commitment, part-time become full-time, and trading become serious. Every would-be trader reaches a turning point where a process used to supplement his income becomes a mainstay of his income. It comes at different stages in the trading process but once it is taken, our understanding of the relationship between work and reward is challenged. How we deal with this challenge will decide if we trade with our brain, or with our wallet. Our long-term success depends on this decision.

Figure 17.2 Real-time example of equity position trading over 12 months

Nominal trading equity is $100,000. Profits are swept into a cash management or at-call account. Position size is set around $20,000 for ease of comparison. Thirty trades were completed. Each trade was open for an average of 28 days. Losing trades took losses that were usually equal to 2 percent of the nominal trading equity. Winning trades were closed out when the initial trading conditions were met, even though price may have continued upwards.

Stock	Days open	Amount	$Profit	%Profit	W/L
LEG	42	$ 20,000	$ 2,775	26	WIN
ZPR	112	$ 20,000	$ 6,880	34	WIN
PRA	14	$ 20,000	-$ 780	-3.9	LOSS
CTR	21	$ 20,000	$ 230	1	WIN
LHG	21	$ 20,072	$ 3,330	16.5	WIN
NCM	14	$ 20,064	$ 334	1.6	WIN
DMR	42	$ 19,500	-$ 2,250	-11	LOSS
WRF	7	$ 20,150	$ 3,199	15	WIN
FIM	14	$ 20,040	-$ 2,505	-12.5	LOSS
TRY	21	$ 19,780	$ 1,840	9	WIN
VPE	49	$ 20,090	-$ 1,230	-6	LOSS
KGR	7	$ 20,700	$ 1,150	5.5	WIN
WSL	21	$ 19,916	$ 364	1.8	WIN
CXR	56	$ 20,400	$ 10,200	50	WIN
ADN	28	$ 20,075	$ 4,125	20.5	WIN
OCN	70	$ 20,800	$ 800	3.8	WIN
MEG	63	$ 20,250	$ 8,910	44	WIN
GGR	14	$ 20,160	-$ 1,440	-7	LOSS
LVG	56	$ 20,400	-$ 1,200	-6	LOSS
PRN	7	$ 20,150	$ 6,500	32	WIN
SCN	7	$ 20,060	$ 12,980	64	WIN
ZPR	7	$ 20,000	-$ 2,000	-10	LOSS
AHG	28	$ 20,540	$ 650	3	WIN
CRO	21	$ 20,020	$ 910	4.5	WIN
TAI	25	$ 20,150	$ 5,090	24.6	WIN
NBH	21	$ 19,964	$ 2,346	16.7	WIN
ASH	7	$ 20,900	$ 1,900	10	WIN
CFR	28	$ 20,025	-$ 2,225	-11	LOSS
IRO	7	$ 20,000	$ 6,250	31	WIN
LYG	21	$ 20,125	-$ 605	-3	LOSS
SUMMARY: CLOSED TRADES					
	Av days open	$ Traded	Year profit	% Return	22 Win/8 Loss
	28	**$ 604,331**	**$ 66,528**	**66.62**	**73% win**

The challenge is accepting that reward is possible without stress, sweat or long hours. If we cannot accept this the private trader is doomed to a life of make-work. Despite the computer revolution's promise of shorter working hours, more leisure and less paperwork most of us feel 40 hours a week is about right. This sets the parameters against which we often instinctively match the level of work required for a particular reward.

Now what happens if substantial reward, as suggested above, can be reached by working far less hours? This is not a trivial question. Trading turns our understanding of reward and effort upside down.

HOMEWORK

For full-time private traders the response is complicated further by a shift to a home-based office environment. Workers shifting to home-based businesses experience the same difficulty in adjusting to new conditions. Old habits die hard.

The habits are so persuasive that some people get in the car each morning, drive around the block and return to their home office in the same way they used to drive to work. More significantly, the home-based businessman, and private trader, must now accept the responsibility for creating, initiating and completing an appropriate workload.

The tele-office worker is exempt from this uncertainty because although he has the freedom to largely organize his own working hours, he is still driven by an external agenda decided by his employer. A set amount of work has to be completed, and in return he gets a set reward.

The self-employed businessman working from home finds the adjustment comparatively easy if clamoring clients are part of the business. Each project has a deadline, and the businessman recreates an environment of workplace stress through externally imposed agendas. Coincidentally, this equates stress, long hours and sweat with the level of reward.

External agendas are not automatic for the private trader. We have no clients demanding projects be completed in time. Time management is entirely our own, particularly if we are position trading and not tied to the screen all day. Ours is an entirely undisciplined environment where work activities appear to be almost optional. We have one master and it is ourselves.

Unusual questions have to be resolved. If I have no clients to visit, do I have to wear a tie to work? Why do I have to go to work today? What are the consequences of turning up late for work when I set my own hours? These bring up some worrying questions about standards, self-discipline, self-direction and guilt.

Your partner expects to see you glued to the screen and at least sweating over the market rather than finding you relaxed with a book in hand and a cup of coffee. It is no good explaining there is nothing you can do while waiting for the market to push prices up. If your partner works at a regular job it requires considerable understanding to appreciate the stress you experience during the trading day. It is a mistake to underestimate the impact of guilt on your behavior.

Not surprisingly, the entire situation can be extremely uncomfortable and we react in one of three ways. We fail as free agents and surrender to wage slavery, or we create our own work discipline. A third reaction is a break-up of the relationship with our partner.

MAKE BELIEVE WORK

Unfortunately it is sometimes difficult to distinguish between failure and creating our own work discipline. Working harder is a common discipline response because by doing so we justify the rewards. For full-time private traders this can lead to costly over-trading.

As suggested above, trading can involve as little as three hours a day and, without the distraction of a day job, we have the choice of deciding where those hours will fall: in a single clump, spread over the day, or deferred today in favor of a longer working day tomorrow. What do we do with the remaining five hours previously allocated to work? Potentially we have 25 hours a week of additional leisure time. With careful structuring the private trader can lead the life he has dreamed of, living and trading from anywhere in the world as his own boss.

Instead, typically we create more work related to what we are already doing. Some of it is useful study and development while some is over-trading disguised as necessary work. One way or another the amount of work seems to expand to fill almost exactly the number of hours we have available. Traders are not immune from this rule of modern management. Depending on how driven we want to feel, we can add more work to these hours, creating an artificial level of stress. This is when we start trading with our wallet.

The trader extends his activities by taking on new market segments or derivative markets such as options and futures or perhaps day trading, by taking many new positions financed by trading profits, by additional capital borrowed from other sources, or by margin borrowing. No matter which combination he chooses the effect is the same. He creates more activity to fill the empty hours and to justify the reward.

Top Australian trader Gary Smith notes, 'People with intensive work ethics have to stare at the screen all day to reassure themselves that they have worked hard.'

The trader may respond in this way because he cannot accept that the level of reward is commensurate with the amount of work he puts in. This terribly destructive response is driven by guilt based on our intuitive understanding of the work/reward relationship.

This problem applies to full-time and part-time traders. Both try to match the level of work with the increasing level of reward. Either the work increases, or the reward decreases. Over-trading, or trading with your wallet, usually decreases the reward in a subconsciously very satisfying way.

The reaction is destructive because we create the conditions of failure through overwork, through stressed and faulty decision-making. In the desire to be busy and to be seen as busy, we make haste and we make mistakes. We console ourselves that they are an inevitable part of the ups and downs of work and as seasoned traders we accept these mistakes.

A destructive feedback loop is constructed. Mistakes do mean we must work harder. We trade to win, and to win all the time. Losing is a sign of failure, so we drive ourselves harder when we make mistakes. We trade to fill in time without regard to financial objectives. With grim determination we unwittingly build a treadmill to replicate the conditions we used to work under in the corporate office.

Without realizing it, we do our best to make this new trading business into hard work because then, with sweat on our brow and a clear conscience, we accept the rewards — guilt free. We believe we are creating a working environment governed by self-discipline. Instead we set up the conditions of failure because we are trading with our wallet.

TRADING WITH YOUR WALLET

It is trading success that lets us quit our day job. It is this success that takes us back to our day job if we do not break the destructive cycle of over-trading made possible, paradoxically, by a few trading victories. This is how it develops:

Our behavior is driven by an uncomfortable feeling about easy money. We feel we have to trade because we have fallen into the trap that says busy hours are necessary to justify our reward. When the wallet is full, or replenished by a trade, we look desperately for new trading opportunities. To keep the hours busy we empty our wallet buying new positions as soon as the capital is available. If we fail completely, if the wallet is emptied and not refilled, then we retire from the field, exhausted but with trading honor intact. Nobody can say we didn't try to make a good effort of it. Just look at the hours we put in.

This is a danger faced almost solely by the private trader. Over-trading sneaks up disguised by the very success the trader seeks.

For the institutional professionals it may never come to this because they work in an office environment where the relationship between work and reward is clearly established and supported by peer group practices.

A TEST FOR OVER-TRADING

The essential defining feature of over-trading is not an absolute number of trades but the motivation behind each trade. Later we discuss how trading can slip into characteristic behavior patterns more closely associated with gambling, or more seriously, pathological gambling. Over-trading driven by a desire to experience the thrill of risk-taking rather than sound money management is one of the features of a gambling approach.

Over-trading takes a step in this direction when trading positions are opened primarily because the trader feels the need to do something other than wait patiently for the best opportunities to arise. This temptation is always present because somewhere in the market good money is being made every day. We suspect if we were more fully exposed, more fully committed, we too could take part in the great accumulation of wealth. This temptation is particularly strong in bull markets. Rather than miss out, novice traders rush into every reasonable opportunity they can afford. Trades are no longer based on good money management or risk control.

Different markets and different trading approaches dictate a range of trading activity. The day trader takes on more positions than an investor. A position trader completes less trades than an active commodities trader. In assessing the tendency for over-trading the primary test is money management. The test has four questions:

- Is each trade clearly based on sound financial analysis?
- Is each trade part of an overall money management objective based on matching position size with risk?

- Does each trade have clear financial objectives that determine the exit conditions?
- Does each trade only use capital allocated from previous trades?

Ask these questions of each new trade. If the answers are all affirmative the trade is well considered and part of a strategic market approach. If two or more questions are honestly answered 'No', the danger of over-trading is real. A 'No' answer suggests trading decisions are emotionally driven and this often draws on a need to justify the rewards.

The typical answers below to the test questions above suggest over-trading. This trader clearly relies more on the size of his wallet rather than his brain.

- Trade is quickly assessed on the basis of gross returns, or the current low with the highest high over the last year.
- Position size is determined by how much cash is currently available for trading.
- Exit is loosely based on previous highs or gut feelings. Some positions are closed early to free up cash for new more attractive positions.
- Money from other sources, such as the day job, is constantly added so new position sizes can be increased.

Over-trading is often a result of trying to fill in the available time or to make it appear through increased trading activity that the trader is really earning his rewards. A full wallet encourages over-trading because the additional cash makes it possible.

Over-trading is a relative concept without absolute measures. As a guide, the trades shown in Figure 17.2 are typical of those I take as an active position trader over a single year. These trades were taken in a notional portfolio developed on a weekly basis and traded in real-time. They give some idea of the frequency of trading and the spread of activity over time.

Trading with our brains means we are aware of our tendency to create work to fill the time available. It means we accept that significant rewards do flow from work that does not involve long hours, stress or sweat. It means the private trader appropriately values his intellectual and analytical contribution to the process of trading and accepts his rewards as commensurate with this. He understands no additional work is required to justify his income so his wallet stays in his pocket.

The work of a private trader is as hard and as honest as the next man's. You do not need blisters on your hands, nor stress leave to prove it. Most important of all, you do not need an empty wallet and a file filled with contract notes to measure your success.

18

NERVES OF STEEL — OR CHICKEN WIRE?

The destitute prospector who once mined a fortune in gold and, like many governments, threw it away, is a recurrent figure in literature. Destitution as a reaction to wealth is driven by emotional instability. Exposure to large sums of money is a heady experience magnifying emotional reactions. As the prospectors found in *The Treasure of the Sierra Madre,* wealth changes people and for some there is an almost irresistible urge to return to the time before wealth. This sounds unbelievable to those aspiring to wealth, but the consistent destruction of market fortunes suggests it happens more frequently than we imagine.

Our reactions to our search results and the implications of the supplementary numbers discussed in Part III ultimately determine our success or failure. Every journey starts with a single step and we start with the wrong foot when we let a little loss grow into a large one. This is a process we want to examine more closely in this chapter.

All good traders use a stop-loss calculation, but few traders consistently act on their stop-loss points, showing the best plans in the world are useless if we freeze at the point of decision. An effective stop-loss strategy matches the theoretical calculated stop-loss point with our psychological make-up.

Market myth proposes an excellent three-step trader's training course. First, the student is required to put $100 on a busy city side walk and wait until a passer-by picks it up. When the student is able to watch this happen without wincing and without tears he proceeds to the next step in the training course. The second stage is a repeat of the first, only using $1,000. The stage is successfully completed when complete nonchalance is achieved. The third step involves $10,000. The student must repeat this successfully, throwing money away without tears or fears, for several consecutive days.

Successful completion of the course entitles students to start trading.

I jest. The course is mythical, but the intent of the exercise is quite serious. All traders lose money, and they often lose it on a regular basis. The key difference is successful traders lose only small amounts of capital. They do this by using stop-loss methods and limiting losses to a small percentage or portion of their total trading capital.

This all sounds very sensible and straightforward. In practice it is much harder. Try the novice training course above, but using only $50. Unless you are particularly dedicated to developing trading attitudes you will find the process very difficult because we do not know in advance if our trading nerves are made of steel or of chicken wire. Most of us have an inherent inability to deliberately lose money, and this has a serious impact on our ability to trade and on our ability to set realistic stop-loss points. Many of us are quite comfortable with credit card debt and with frivolous wasteful expenditure consuming the weekly pay check. But this is not the same as taking a loss.

TAKING A LOSS

Market lore suggests you should 'Never trade with more than you can afford to lose.' This well-intentioned advice misses the point by assuming our total trading capital is at risk. Better advice is 'Never set risk levels at more than you can afford to lose.' Taking a loss is an integral part of trading and rationally we know money lost in trading is not really thrown away. Emotionally it just seems that way.

In trading securities, particularly on electronic exchanges, we get so little in return. After a $40,000 purchase we first receive a contract note and later a plain Holding Statement on a common sheet of paper, both plastered with a few figures. They are not exactly a trophy talking point. We cannot consume, display, use, or conveniently show them off as we would with a new car, swimming pool or house extension.

When we consider taking a loss — when the flimsy Holding Statement is suddenly worth $3,000 less than it was a day ago — it really does seem as if we are throwing money away. Lifelong attitudes to financial management subconsciously influence our decision, staying our hand when we should reach for the mouse button or telephone and exit the position. Being able to take this loss takes emotional courage and most cannot do it without a whimper. Emotionally we freeze when rationally we should act.

By a variety of mechanisms, all of us consciously avoid situations where we lose money. We do not like losing it so many of us could not complete the mythical three-step trader's training course. Unless we do complete it, albeit metaphorically rather than literally, the chances of trading success are greatly reduced. Trading success demands we move beyond these attitudes.

Is the private trader doomed unless he develops a devil-may-care attitude to losing money? The answer lies in the difference between courage and fearlessness. The trader needs courage — an understanding of fear and the ability to overcome it. The trader without fear cheats financial death — for a limited time. This is not a path we want to follow.

We understand only too well the fear of losing money and often this fear keeps us in losing trades rather than executing our stop loss. When we go too far, and too fast, fear overcomes our courage. The glimmer of an answer to the way we develop courage to efficiently execute stop-loss points is suggested by the ubiquitous slot machine found in casinos and clubs. They make a business of turning chicken wire nerves into steel.

THRESHOLDS

Casino players hate losing even though this is an inevitable consequence of chasing jackpot rewards. The key to understanding how they run the gauntlet of loss is not the size of the inducement, but the size of the wager and the way loss is limited to the wager itself.

For those with a high resistance to losing money, the 5-cent slot machine is heaven sent. Who will miss 5 cents? We all have different thresholds of tolerance and the casino operators thoughtfully provide opportunities for everyone to operate as close to their threshold as they feel comfortable. We have the choice to step up from the 5-cent machine to a 20-cent machine, or to $1- or $10-machines. We can change games and play with $50 chips at the roulette or baccarat tables, or join the high rollers at $1,000 a throw. By these graduated steps the casino takes advantage of differing threshold tolerances for loss.

The trader can learn from this management practice. The casino entices because the losses are small. Many gamblers accumulate large losses, little bit by little bit. The pain is reduced as every individual loss is affordable. In some important ways the process is the same as trading, except the trader actively monitors loss levels within an overall money management scheme designed to deal with uncertain rewards by containing risk. The casinos thrive because they match the tolerance for loss with the emotional maturity of their clients — and the number of slot machines accepting bets of a dollar or less says a lot about emotional maturity.

Many traders fail because they do not match the levels of loss, indicated by their stop-loss strategy, with their emotional ability to take them.

Each trader must first define how much he is prepared to lose should the trade turn against him. We have looked at some ways of mechanically calculating this, based on chart points and the 2 percent money management rule. However, the bottom line in practical terms depends on the individual trader. Some traders are comfortable with taking losses of several thousands of dollars while others feel extreme pain at several hundred.

Where is your pain level? All of us have a level of loss that we feel comfortable with. Once the loss grows beyond that threshold we increasingly find it difficult to pull the trigger on a trade. Our careful stop-loss planning is ignored. A loss of $100 is very easy to take. A loss of $1,000, or $10,000 less so. Every private trader should establish his tolerance for loss — his threshold — as early as possible. Every point is valid, be it constructed from chicken wire or steel. Knowing this figure in advance allows the trader to adjust his trading strategies so he does not expose himself to losses greater than he can bear.

This is an important additional consideration to include with the simple spreadsheet mechanics of the stop-loss calculations discussed in Chapters 13 and 14. In dollar terms the logical stop-loss points should be equal to, or less than, our loss tolerance level. If the stop-loss point, in dollar terms, represents more loss than we are comfortable with then we are less likely to pull the trigger when the time comes.

The stop loss may be perfectly logical, brilliantly analyzed, superbly placed, but unless it touches the right emotional chord it is useless because we will not execute it. And then the little loss grows into a substantial loss, further reducing our ability to realize it by selling.

The mythical three-step trader's training program proposed moving from $100 to $1,000 and then to $10,000. The private trader adopts the same approach, teaching himself to tolerate larger losses. If larger losses are emotionally tolerable, larger positions are taken consistent with wider money management objectives. As position size grows, so too does the dollar loss, even if the percentage loss remains the same.

For instance, a 2 percent loss on $4,000 of trading capital equals $80. Losing $80 is not the end of the world, and the trader can comfortably exit the trade and move into more profitable fields. If trading capital totals $100,000 then a 2 percent loss equals $2,000. This loss emotionally is of a different order, particularly when much of the $100,000 represents trading profits. Placing the sell order and taking this $2,000 loss is much more difficult to do, even though it still represents exactly the same percentage failure as the smaller account. Beginners find it difficult to fully convince themselves that it is the percentage figure that counts and not the dollar figure.

When they look at the trading calculation screen used in Chapter 13 they glimpse the dollar loss figure on a $100,000 account and flinch. Despite having $98,000 remaining, emotionally the loss of $2,000 is too difficult to contemplate. So the loss is permitted to grow, and with each dollar increase beyond $2,000 the chances of closing the position and realizing the loss are diminished. If they cannot act on a $2,000 loss, it is much more difficult to act when it grows to $3,000 or $5,000. Trading success demands we turn from this grim reality and develop strategies to overcome this emotional paralysis.

A TRADING COURSE

Changing deeply held emotional attitudes is a difficult task. The film *What About Bob?* popularized the concept of baby steps — taking many small steps towards a distant objective. The trader emulates this by determining his tolerance for 'throw away' money. If we know we will execute an exit when facing a $1,000 loss, but cannot really pick up the phone or click the sell button when the loss is $1,500, we need to make sure our trading tactics reflect this knowledge.

The trader needs to take positions where the dollar loss — in this case $1,000 — is at least equal to the logical stop-loss point. This is decided by manipulating the trade calculation screen to determine the position size to match the emotionally acceptable figure. The starting point is provided by the logical stop-loss point based on chart analysis.

Figure 18.1 shows two steps in adjusting the position size to reflect an ability to act on stop-loss points. We have three sample traders, Advanced, Beginner and an Emotional Loser. In all cases the logical stop-loss point, based on chart analysis, is at $41 and total trading capital available is $100,000 with the proposed entry at $43.

Trader Advanced has no problems with taking losses of $2,000 so the limiting factor is the 2 percent of equity figure. He matches the 2 percent loss level of $2,000 with position size. The calculations show an entry at $43 and position size limited to 700 shares or

Figure 18.1

Adjusting stop-loss to tolerable levels

Av brokerage rate %	2.000		
Total trade equity	100,000.00		
	TRADER ADVANCED	**TRADER BEGINNER**	**TRADER EMOTIONAL LOSER**
EQUITY DETAILS			
Equity name	STOP THE LOSS	STOP THE LOSS	STOP THE LOSS
Number of shares	**700**	**350**	**700**
Purchase price	**43.00**	**43.00**	**43.00**
Net cost	30,100.00	15,050.00	30,100.00
Av brokerage	602.00	301.00	602.00
Full cost	**30,702.00**	**15,351.00**	**30,702.00**
RISK PARAMETERS			
Equity risk @2%	2,000.00	2,000.00	2,000.00
Preferred risk on this trade	**2,000.00**	**1,000.00**	**1,000.00**
Stop-loss exit price based on full cost	41.00	41.00	42.43
Emotional Loser real loss at $41.00 chart stop loss			2,000.00

$30,702. With this combination the calculated dollar loss figure coincides with the $41 stop-loss level derived from the chart.

Trader Beginner is less experienced. From previous trades he knows once the loss grows beyond $1,000 he has great emotional difficulty in closing the position. Like Trader Advanced his available trading capital puts the maximum loss at $2,000 using the 2 percent rule, but he wants to limit any potential loss to $1,000. To do this he reduces his position size to 350 shares or $15,351. This combination still calls for an exit at $41 — the chart-derived logical stop-loss point. With only $1,000 at risk if the trade does turn against him, Trader Beginner is now more confident he will execute his stop loss.

In setting the stop-loss point both sample traders matched their emotional tolerance for a loss in dollar terms with the logical stop-loss point based on chart analysis. Trader Emotional Loser only looks at the chart-derived stop loss so the problem rapidly becomes serious.

Trader Emotional Loser fools himself by taking a large position size of 700 coupled with a small dollar stop loss. If he does act on the exit signal generated by the dollar loss — when price falls to $42.43 — he is whipsawed in and out of the position time after time just by the normal range of daily price action. Before long he concludes this is a losing strategy so he selects the chart stop-loss point as the exit trigger.

The consequences are fatal. When prices do fall, they pause, or consolidate around $41. Trader Emotional Loser now faces a $2,000 loss. Emotionally he is paralyzed and ends up trapped in a losing position.

Most of us have visited this scenario at some time in our trading career. It generally happens this way. When prices fall to $42.43, just a few cents below our entry price, we lose our emotional maximum of $1,000. With $1.43 left to reach the chart-derived stop-loss point we hold on, convincing ourselves that prices will pause at this level. We make a fake promise to ourselves to exit if prices fall below the chart-derived stop-loss point. Now an exit at $41 costs $2,000. When prices do fall to here, we hold tight unable to face the extra loss. We quibble, making another fraudulent personal promise to exit when prices rally back to $42.43.

This scenario does not disappear by itself and unless we take action we return to it again and again until we no longer have the money for the entry fee. We avoid this scenario by manipulating position size with reference to the logical stop-loss point so the dollar value at risk is within our emotional threshold.

When Trading Beginner is able to consistently take a $1,000 loss calmly, quickly, unemotionally; if he can click the mouse to send the sell order or pick up the phone, sell the position without his voice quavering, and without feeling rotten about himself when he puts the phone down; if he can watch the order executed on the screen in real-time without a sniffle or morsel of regret, then he is ready to move on. Now he is emotionally ready to accept larger losses if required.

Just like the mythical three-step trader's training program, Trader Beginner increases the dollar amount he is prepared to lose. This is done in small increments, perhaps $500 in this case. The jump from $1,000 to $2,000 may be too much. It is very much a trial and error process finely tuned to suit every trader.

The key is the dollar size of the loss. In searching for real trading success we match the theoretical money management and risk management objectives with our practical ability to initiate the loss. It is the latter that determines the position size.

Perhaps our trading capital gives $5,000 as an outer limit under the 2 percent risk rule. If the trader finds he cannot tolerate more than a $4,000 loss on any position, he should limit his position size to a level where $4,000 is the dollar value of the potential stop loss.

We do not change the stop-loss level, moving it up so it hangs in mid-air, unrelated to any logical stop-loss point. It is always based on chart analysis of logical stop-loss points. This includes making use of support areas, or setting a trailing stop-loss in an open position. Instead, on entry, we manipulate our position size so the dollar loss is within the practical rather than theoretical limits. Emotions are powerful influences on behavior, and trading exposes people to the full range of the most powerful of them all — greed and fear. Understanding these emotions and the role they play in sabotaging, or supporting, our trading gives us an important trading edge.

TRADING WITH MATURITY

Trading is not just business by another name. Despite technical mastery of trading mechanics, many novice traders still fail. Private trading requires emotional maturity. This is reflected in many ways. Some of the young institutional traders and brokers splash their windfall earnings in glitzy shows of wealth and earn the opprobrium of the general public. These people trade OPM, usually pronounced 'opium', an abbreviation for 'other people's money'. OPM is just as addictive and mind-bending as its sound-alike namesake. Do not confuse this bull market behavior with the attitudes and skills required for private trading.

Private traders tend to be more restrained, reflecting the same emotional maturity to the display of wealth as they apply to the attainment of it. Next time you attend a trading seminar try to estimate the trading net worth of individual participants. It is difficult because there are few physical clues in dress or decoration. The only clues come from the quality of the questions asked.

If we find it difficult to act decisively on stop-loss points — and most of us have this problem initially — then we must develop this ability in small steps. In the beginning this appears to limit profits, but as we develop as traders we understand this emotional maturity acts as a brake on losses and allows profits to flow and grow naturally.

19

COMMAND AND CONTROL

Size is a bully in the market. When an institution chooses to sell its holdings, the shares it unloads on the market create a solid resistance level. Buyers find no reason to bid higher when thousands of shares are on offer at $40.00. Because institutional traders are often patient there are also few bargains below $40.00 as bids of $39.00 leave the institution unperturbed. Of course, in general market collapse the institutions are just as eager to unload as everybody else.

The unwise private trader has ample opportunities to bully the market down at the speculative end. We touched on the mechanics of this in Chapter 15. On the one hand low liquidity hinders our entry and exit strategy. We must adjust our position size so it equals, on average, the volume over previous weeks. The relationship between volume and position size is critical in low liquidity stocks and easily observed on depth of market screens, as well as on the daily chart. When our buy order is first in line at $12.77, and with no trades today, the horizontal line on the bar chart seems to stretch infinitely into the future.

We also know, should we raise our bid to $12.79, or meet the offer at $12.80 that our action alone will be solely responsible for a new line on the chart, perhaps setting the high or low for the day. At first this idea is intriguing, but left unchecked it grows into a dangerous misconception that we can bully the market into doing what we want. Like a surreal Salvador Dali painting, in a particular light and at a certain angle, this picture turns ugly as a hidden bully emerges from the background.

How often have you had the dubious distinction of being the only buyer at the absolute high? Have you succumbed to the dangerous idea that your buying can create break-out conditions, and, that by implication, others will follow? The fallacy here of course is that a break-out, or a new high, are only valid when set by the general market and not when set in anticipation by eager but misinformed individual traders. Wishing will not make it so, not even when backed with your capital.

As private traders we would never dream of such action with a large blue chip stock like General Electric, Glaxo Wellcome, Overseas-Chinese Banking Group or National Australia Bank. Our tiny order is swamped in high liquidity and heavy volume, so our market impact is reduced. With smaller stocks our orders have significance. The step from observing the impact of our orders to deciding if our orders have impact is small, and dangerous.

BULLIES LOVE CONTROL

Quite obviously we need to avoid and discard this idea that we can have an impact on market behavior out of proportion to our size. We would discard this in favor of more relevant trading issues if not for the fact that many private traders, at one time or another, fall victim to this idea. Nobody openly admits to believing they can control the market, but often their action speaks louder than their denials. This happens in three ways.

The first is when we step from the audience onto the stage as an actor. As soon as we place an order we are on stage. The trading shows at the small end of town provide the opportunity to play out the fantasy of the market bully. It is not recommended, and if undertaken deliberately and systematically to 'ramp' or push up a stock price, such action is illegal.

Ramping a stock involves creating the illusion of price activity, usually by controlled buying and selling between several related parties. Volume increases and prices churn within a tight band. Other traders are attracted to the action, bidding up price based on the volume activity. The original traders ride the price action, selling into the growing strength. There are many variations on this theme — all illegal — and all based on creating unusual trading volume in a sleepy stock.

Such activity is substantively different from our observation as private traders that our buy or sell order does have an observable impact on the market when trading small speculative stocks. This is not control and when we try to bully the market we usually end up worse off. When we try to buy too much we push the price up. When we try to sell too much, the price falls because we choke the market with our sell order. When our position size is greater than the average size of trades we run the risk of not being able to execute our trade at the best price.

The second way our actions speak louder than our denial of the bully charge comes when we slide, trade by trade, into gambling mode. The pathological gambler believes in his omnipotence and the gambling trader works with the same delusions. These issues are more fully explored in the following chapter.

It is the third approach we want to consider in this chapter. Fertile ground for this belief about ability to control the market is provided when we build the false link between success in the market and successful prediction. This belief grows into a particularly nasty weed when combined with the observed impact of our orders on stocks with low liquidity.

Insidiously and erroneously the idea grows that the trader is somehow able to control or improve the outcome of his position by superior predictive analysis. The command and control fallacy entices when profits follow prediction.

If this sounds unreasonable then consider any of your open positions currently showing a loss. Ask yourself why you haven't exited the trade — and answer truthfully. Despite good chart analysis and stock selection, too often we kid ourselves with excuses: 'The sell off was overdone,' or 'This company is fundamentally sound with good management,' or even the most optimistic and emotionally fraudulent of all: 'Fools. Don't they realize the global potential for this product!'

This last excuse is sometimes presented by fund managers as a virtue because 'there is always a handful, only a scant handful of investments around the globe that have been mispriced by the markets', and by implication their funds management team has the skill to uncover these investments. When this approach is applied to private trading the effect is insidiously disastrous.

Satisfied with any of these excuses, just like a bully, we fight the market, pitting our ego against it trying to prove ... what? ... that we know better than the market. Stripped of the self-justifying rhetoric our actions sound feeble, so why do so many traders persist with this? Exploring the roots of our confusion hands us a trading edge. Paradoxically they are often entangled with the roots of business success.

Many private traders turn to the market after a successful career in business, or the professions. Initially, trading income is a supplement to their day job and because they are still working it is easy to confuse the command and control skills that breed success in one sphere with the skills needed for success in the other. Some strategies that bring success in business bring disaster in the market.

Consider as an example a successful condominium entrepreneur who, in the start-up days, and in the construction slowdown held on grimly only to emerge victorious and profitable. Success came from tenacity and the ability to control the external factors in his segment of the market and to outlast his competitors.

Certainly our entrepreneur analyzed the housing market and predicted a shortage of apartments. This command of analysis gave him the power to control events by building apartments to meet the identified demand. To him it seems superior analysis meant early action that gave control and this equates with success. This is the core message of many modern management books. The message is not heard in the financial market, but the idea is hard to shake because it gives our entrepreneur the wealth required to trade.

Past business success develops the unspoken conviction that if he understands key information he can control his local market and make a profit. From here it is a short insidious step to the idea of stock market control. Even a small string of trading successes are equated with successful market predictions. Bit by bit, trade by trade, he comes to believe in his ability to master the market by throwing money at it. The baby bully is born.

BABY BULLIES

Business success sometimes breeds arrogance. In contrast, trading success always breeds humility. We do not need to be a successful businessman to become a baby bully. Any of us can shove the market around when volumes are low enough. All novice traders pass through a developmental stage. They flirt with the idea that their understanding of the market means when they take a position the market will move in their favor. Although this growth phase is often most marked in traders with a business background, none of us is immune.

Inevitably one of our favorite positions — usually the one perfectly selected by our database scan, the one superbly analyzed and entered at just the right price — turns against us and when it does, we are stunned. So we hold on, waiting for the market to reverse and match our previous market call. We rationalize our inaction in the jargon of our business success. 'I was right in the '97 currency slowdown so this will come good,' or 'Perseverance paid off when the Shanghai negotiations collapsed, so I will stay put.' The longer we have traded the more likely we are to use the jargon of trading, telling ourselves and others: 'The sell-off was overdone.'

Even more perversely, some novice traders feel if they can carry a large loss it says something positive about their wealth. The 1987 Crash showed how flimsy high net worth is as protection against the power of the market.

Stripped of fancy bravado, all these excuses are really attempts to exert personal control over the market via an open position. This quest for omnipotence can balloon into the gambler's friend as shown in the next chapter. Most of us do not go this far, but our belief in our ability to control events is a serious impediment to better trading. Professional traders are not immune as hubris lurks on every trading screen. For an extreme example of this phenomenon take a look at *Going for Broke* or *Rogue Trader,* both accounts of Barings Bank trader, Nick Leeson. Similar stories exist about the Japanese copper trader, Yasuo Hamanaka, but they are not as well documented. All show how traders can go bad in a very big way, but every day there are traders quietly doing the same thing on a smaller scale — financially backing their predictions against the market reality.

RIGHT IS SOMETIMES WRONG

We overcome this tendency when we accept that trading the market is not about being right. It is about being profitable. In an objective sense we have shown how a trade can match all our criteria, but still show such an unprofitable low percentage or dollar return. In these circumstances we are right, but also wrong. In an emotional sense, when we manage a trade dominated by the need to be right we can be very wrong. This need to be right is a powerful barrier to profitability.

The need for control — the need to be right — produces some creative excuses for trading failure. Check your repertoire for matches.

'I bought too early, but I can see the bottom forming', or 'I am surprised the market doesn't realize the potential of this stock. I will buy more now it has gone lower', or for technical analysts, perhaps 'My Elliott wave count is out by one.'

We generate these excuses when we falsify the links between success, prediction and control. No matter how foolish these excuses seem in retrospect and in the cold light of substantial loss, the 'wanna-be' trader has many reasons, often counted in dollars, to convince himself they are valid. To do otherwise is a larger threat to his self-esteem as a trader, and perhaps as a successful businessman and professional. Essentially, he struggles to control the market because control of the business environment has brought him success in the past.

CONTROL THE CONTROLLABLE

We cannot control the market, despite the illusion of our order impact in low-volume equities. We must accept the inevitability of powerlessness to develop the humility required for success. The similarity to some Asian philosophical concepts is striking. Richard McCall in *The Way of the Warrior Trader*, and others, follow this path to its extremities. It is too easy to be sidetracked by this philosophy at depth, but traders do benefit from an understanding of the relationship between self and unreasoning infinity. Those uncomfortable with the way of the Samurai may find more comfort in the existentialism of Camus, or at *The Edge of Chaos* with Bernice Cohen, or perhaps with Ian Stewart debating *Does God Play Dice?*

We want to believe in an ordered universe and all that this implies. This suggests order does exist in complex and chaotic situations. It implies a key can be found to unlock the secrets of a chaotic market and the key is forged from superior analysis backed by cash. Success builds on predictive analysis that is right and is coupled with control over external events. This self-reinforcing system does build business success. It is not as useful in trading success.

The novice trader steps back from the tangled relationship between success and control by redefining what we mean by control in terms of trading. Business success often comes from controlling events. Trading success usually comes from reacting to those events. The control required is personal rather than external.

Traders understand the only events we have control over are the timing of our entry and our exit. This does not destroy the need for analysis but it does change its relationship with control. An understanding of demand and supply factors, of management strengths and weaknesses, of statistical measures of performance, or of technical indicators used with charts is a vital part of the trading process. Good analysis helps to make the entry and exits much better.

But trading discipline — the timing of entry and exit — turns these skills into profits.

So what is our key? The trader truly understands his analysis does not shape the market. The length, the complexity, the time spent on the search bears little direct relationship to the outcome of the trade. Within reason, more research is better than less, better analysis and analysis tools are more effective than cheap software and gut trading decisions, but more does not automatically improve the chances of success.

Successful traders recognize these activities help us to define the market and a trading opportunity, but not to influence it. The trading wheel turns a half revolution so we stand directly opposite the business relationship between analysis and control.

In our simple housing example, the entrepreneur, as a result of his analysis, takes control of events or activities by building apartments. In contrast, the trader increases exposure to the housing market segment in reaction to price activity. More subtly, the trader may look for leveraged exposure via related economic activity through construction material manufacturers, suppliers of household goods and furnishings, or mortgage securitization derivatives. The trader profits by controling the time and place of his entry and exit, not the underlying building activity.

Irrespective of whether the markets are the result of a random walk, of a pattern, of cycles, or a product of chaos, we make our profit by controling the only element we can realistically control — ourselves. We decide the time, place and size of our exposure to a dynamical system that is beyond our control in every other sense. We apply an analytical framework to improve our understanding of the market so we make consistent decisions about how we are going to trade the market as it is, rather than the way we would like it to be.

Sometimes the market looks like a rich man's playground where size is king. Bullies aim for size believing it confers control. Such belief is fatal because unlike the schoolyard, the penalty for bullies is not detention. The market, indifferent to your existence and survival, quietly accepts financial ruin as a just punishment.

Bullies are unable to say, 'I believe the market is wrong, but I will trade the chart signals rather than my opinions.' The consistent profits come from controling the time of our entry and exit. The most successful traders are those who understand that the rules which allowed them to accumulate business wealth are not always the rules which favor trading profits. The key behavior that saves us from the fallacy of market control is the way we consistently profit from trading ability rather than prophecy. Only then have we swapped fictitious control of the market for better control of our trading.

20

GAMBLER OR TRADER?

Paul I Munves, *PhD.**
Contributing Author

For many readers, trading is the most interesting and exciting activity they know. The excitement does not come from a frisson of fear or from the horror, vicarious or otherwise, of loss and potential loss. It comes from the daily challenge to trade the market effectively by managing risk. The task of aggressively managing risk places trading activities in the room next to the one labeled gambling, but the connecting door should be forever locked.

Sadly for some traders the door is left ajar, and the trader's relationship with risk slips out of control, sliding into the next room. This chapter briefly explores how you can recognize when real trading stops and when gambling in the financial markets begins. Very little research has been done in this area. Nonetheless, we are suggesting that when trading behavior resembles gambling behavior, the trading activity may reasonably be understood in the same way gambling is understood.

Later we look at some simple self-help measures to regain more appropriate control, but first we search for guiding clues helpful in recognizing pathological gambling because these may be useful indicators of when trading starts to slip into gambling mode.

PROFESSIONAL GAMBLING

How do we distinguish trading from gambling? There are important differences between the phenomena of gambling and of trading. Gambling selects defined events with known rewards and the gambler has no control over relatively unknown risks. It is an activity with a defined beginning and end, such as a horse race, a throw of dice, or a hand of cards. The gambling event itself creates and circumscribes risk as it does not exist before or after the event. Gambling provides multiple defined and transitory events from which the gambler makes a selection.

In contrast, trading is very different. Trading is the practical limitation of risk in pursuit of unknown reward. Traders participate in an ongoing, continuous event where the beginning and end are entirely defined by the participant. The trader manages a user-defined segment of risk that is already in existence prior to his participation and which will certainly continue after the trader withdraws from his position. The market thus provides continuous risk. The trader selects the management strategies to control risk partly by achieving control over himself. This is demonstrated in his ability to make controled, astute decisions about the point of entering and the point of exiting a trade. Unlike gambling, which relies on predictions and betting, trading depends on managing and controling risk. There are, therefore, extremely important motivational differences between the gambler and the trader that we shall discuss at greater length below.

You might not agree with these distinctions built around behavioral phenomena, but if you are serious about trading then please develop your own consistent set of understandings so you can avoid the trap of gambling in the financial markets while pretending you are trading. The definitions above are at the core of the way we understand and discuss gambling below. The impact of this distinction on traders varies. For some the impact is fatal, for others an uncomfortably close shave, and for the serious traders, it provides a useful way to understand and avoid financial oblivion while still enjoying their chosen pursuit.

We trade the financial markets to make money and this is the ultimate criterion in deciding if our activities are warranted and successful. Reading this book may be pleasurable, but you invest the time and effort in the hope that it will in some way help you make money and preserve wealth. Whether you are investing in the markets with relatively longer term time horizons or more actively trading in the markets with shorter term time horizons, the primary goal should be the same — to make money. This is self-evident for the full-time professional trader, but even a part-time trader is quite 'professional' when his activities are guided by this simple and overarching principle.

The danger for both short-term traders and long-term investors is when their attitude towards risk deteriorates due to an emotional unwillingness or even psychological incapacity to manage it. The professional trader accepts risk as an inescapable fact of life in the markets, but he devotes himself to the task of controling risk by becoming adroit at calculating and managing it assiduously. Calculated risks are taken as part of the business of trading in much the same way that a retailer takes calculated risks in purchasing inventory for his store.

In this way trading is akin to professional gambling as the professional gambler makes his living using gambling as his primary source of income. As with trading, there are far more 'wanna-be' professional gamblers than successful ones. Those who are successful are devoted to calculating risk and controling it in ways specifically applicable to the way gambling risk is packaged. These are individuals capable of extraordinary self-control and very capable of waiting for the 'best bet'. Similarly, successful traders will invariably become adept at developing and utilizing a set of tools for calculating and managing risk. While successful traders may vary widely in their reliance on diversification, asset allocation by percentage of total assets, percentage of cash equivalents in their portfolio, fundamental analysis, technical analysis, stop-loss techniques, system development, and orthodox, automated system trading, they will nonetheless be unwavering in their devotion to managing and controling risk.

Both professional gamblers and traders rely on profits alone to evaluate whether their methodology is indeed worthwhile. They do not include an element of excitement or thrills in the reward calculation. Trading, then, is best understood to be a disciplined activity aimed at taking calculated, managed risks for profit in the financial markets. As Confucius wrote, 'In all things, success depends upon previous preparation, and without such preparation there is sure to be failure.'

Professional risk management is a common feature of professional trading and of professional gambling. It would be foolish to deny this commonality. It is equally foolish to next decide that both activities amount to the same thing. The novice trader often fails in trading because he brings to his trading activity an inappropriate attitude towards risk more similar to that seen in the usual understanding of gambling as simply a pass-time activity. It is this failure to manage risk that we most commonly associate in a pejorative way with gambling. It is this slipshod approach that we want to isolate, explore and banish from our trading activities.

THE FIVE 'E's' OF GAMBLING

When we use the terms gambling and gambler in a pejorative sense we are not referring to the professional gamblers discussed above. Instead we mean the garden variety gamblers, those who choke the casinos, rooted in front of a slot machine, draped over the roulette table, and clinging to the last hand of poker. This understanding of gambling is our primary concern.

Pathological gambling in the financial markets is a strong term applied to the end product of several developmental stages. The variety of behaviors is a continuum as shown in Table 20.1. As in alcoholism, denial is often an important characteristic reaction. With denial, selected perceptions are rejected in the service of avoiding psychological pain. Inherent in maintaining the denial is the use of fantasy, so the pathological gambler believes, in the face of evidence to the contrary, that he can gamble in a normal and controled manner. Furthermore, he will ignore past losses, no matter how heavy or continuous, and believe he can win at gambling.

Pathological gamblers routinely deny their loss of control, but this is not the first, nor the only development suggesting that a pathological process is under way. We want to explore these psychological developments and attendant behaviors for their heuristic value, so we can avoid unlocking the door from the trading floor to the adjoining room where gambling takes precedence. Gambling in the financial markets will most assuredly result in self-destruction. Efforts at self-help will most likely fail if not buttressed by participation in Gamblers Anonymous and preferably with simultaneous treatment with a mental health professional specifically familiar with this kind of problem.

People gamble for a variety of reasons, often classified as the five 'E's' of gambling:

- entertainment
- excitement
- escape
- easy money
- ego.

All of us enjoy the contribution these five 'E's' make to our trading day, but they are not the primary motivation for trading. Traders who are primarily motivated by any or all of the five 'E's' are actually gambling. Traders who are pathological gamblers have permitted these needs to gain ascendancy over earned profits and contaminate their risk management capacities. This difference in the weighting of one's motivations is the key factor in deciding if we have slipped from trading into gambling. When profits alone are not enough, we have begun to gamble.

In the casino a $2 slot machine delivers the five 'E's' at the push of a button. In the market, delivery is just as certain, but comes at a much higher price. There are six types of gamblers as described in Table 20.1. These can be used as a proxy to recognize gambling behavior in traders. Perhaps the most important variable between types is the degree of control the trader has over his trading activity. The more he is involved with risk-taking to fulfil emotional needs, the more likely it is that he is gambling rather than trading.

Trading slips into gambling mode when it is predominantly engaged in for any or all of the five 'E's' listed above rather than a systematically organized activity endeavoring to calculate and manage risk in the pursuit of profit in the financial markets. It is the devotion to managing risk that distinguishes trading as a professional activity. The less control an individual is able to exercise over his trading activity, the more likely it is that gambling better describes the activity than does the term trading.

Table 20.1 Types of traders and gamblers

Type of trader	Type of gambler	Description	Degree of control	Length of stay at this level
Well-functioning trader	Professional gambler	Trading/Gambling is his primary source of income; makes his living trading/gambling. Note: There are more 'wanna-be' professional traders and gamblers than successful ones.	Very controlled; patiently waits for the best trade/bet.	Indefinite.
	Antisocial personality	Has a criminal mindset. Was committing crimes before gambling problem developed.	Committing crimes driven by criminal thought process.	Indefinite; gambling continues even in prison.
	Casual social gambler	Gambling is one of many forms of entertainment; gambles infrequently.	If he could not participate in gambling, he would rarely miss it.	Rarely escalates to a higher level; if he does move, it's in response to a trauma or fueled by a Big Win.
	Serious social gambler	Gambles as a major source of entertainment; plays regularly at one or more types of gambling and does so with great absorption and intensity; comparable to a tennis or golf 'nut'; gambling is still just a pass-time activity.	Can stop gambling but would definitely miss it.	May be able to keep serious gambling under control. Is especially vulnerable to external factors that could cause him to escalate his gambling and become a pathological gambler.
Deteriorating trader	Relief-and-escape gambler	Trades/Gambles to escape troubles in personal or business life. Spends more time trading/gambling than he did prior to his need to escape from personal problems. Differs from pathological trader/gambler in that he has some degree of control over his trading/gambling. If another solution could be found to relieve tension over his problems, he would probably trade/gamble less.	Can probably stop trading/gambling, but with more difficulty than the well-functioning trader or the professional and social gamblers who exhibit more control.	Is very vulnerable to slipping into becoming a pathological trader/gambler. Debts incurred by diverting bill money to trading/gambling may result in entering the 'chasing' phase of the pathological trading/gambling cycle.
Compulsive pathological trader	Compulsive pathological gambler	Driven by an uncontrollable urge to trade/gamble: trading/gambling seriously compromises, disrupts or damages personal, family, or career pursuits. May incur excessive debts, loss of family, loss of job, and may even commit crimes to continue trading/gambling.	Difficult to stop trading/gambling without professional intervention no matter how hard he tries. Loss of control evident and indicative of a disorder of impulse control. These individuals are very likely to satisfy 5 of the 10 criteria for pathological trading or gambling seen in the accompanying Table 20.3.	Goes through Winning, Losing, and Desperation Phases that may last for 15 years or longer. Left untreated, the disorder can ultimately destroy everything important to the compulsive pathological trader/gambler.

Adapted from the Texas Council on Problem & Compulsive Gambling, Inc.

Likewise, the greater the inability to control the activity in terms of time devoted to it, amount of risk taken on, emotional involvement, and impact on lifestyle stability, the more likely it is that gambling may become a bona fide disorder of impulse control formally designated as pathological gambling. Pathological gambling quite frequently exhibits three distinct phases. Table 20.2 provides a formal summary of each phase and has been included to illustrate how a problem with gambling can evolve over time in an individual's life. Readers who recognize themselves should make every attempt to withdraw from the market and seek professional help. For those who see this process as reflecting what is going on with their 'trading', this could be the most important item addressed in this book for their very survival could well be at stake.

While normal gambling is a risk-taking activity aimed at satisfying normal desires for entertainment, excitement, escape into fantasy, good fortune, and winning some people get hooked on risk-taking as an end in itself. Fyodr Dostoyevsky, himself a pathological gambler, knew this. In 1866 in *The Gambler* he wrote:

> *"I am sure vanity was half responsible for this; I wanted to astonish the spectators by taking senseless chances and — a strange sensation — I clearly remember that even without any promptings of vanity I really was suddenly overcome by a terrible craving for risk ..."*

The fascination with risk-taking as an end in itself can be understood in various ways. Although the emotional 'logic' may strain your credulity, gambling offers the possibility that anything may in fact happen, that one risk is essentially no greater than any other, and that someone may, therefore, not be accountable for the choices they have made. For some, the allure of risk, of the improbable, of the chance occurrence is that it affords them the delusion that they will escape accountability and guilt. There is yet another way gambling offers a psychological escape. The taking of huge risks may also be sought for the intensity of the experience it affords, for the adrenaline rush, and for the distraction from unwanted feelings such as stress, helplessness, guilt, anxiety or depression.

Table 20.2 Phases in a gambler's career

Characteristic	Winning phase	Losing phase	Desperation phase
Reason for gambling	Gambling for entertainment, ego, excitement and easy money.	Gambling to recoup losses; has some wins but has more losses; chases losses to tyr to win back what he has lost.	Gambling because he cannot keep from it.
Gambling attitude	Plans careful and cautious bets.	Wagers are impulsive and rash; bets on things with high odds to maximize payoffs.	Unreasonable; panicky; bets hunches, super-situations, long shots.
Mood	Eager, unreasonable optimism.	Frequently angry and depressed over losses; even winning does not make him happy.	Feels powerless; blames others; feels remorse and panic; becomes a zombie.
Driving force to gamble	Euphoria of winning; consuming desire to perpetuate that high; fantasizes about winning.	Overwhelming need to quell depression over losing; desperately trying to recapture the glow of the Winning Phase.	May cheat, steal, lie and manipulate to stay in action. Tries to juggle dwindling resources between bills and gambling money.
Time spent gambling	Gambling is a part-time, leisure activity.	Most of life devoted to chasing his losses.	Dominant thing in life.
Work activity	Works in usual pattern, although begins to spend working time thinking about gambling.	Begins to miss work to go to the track, casino or watch sports; conversely, may have two jobs to get more money.	Probably has been fired from his job; reputation ruined.
Family life	Begins to split his time between gambling activities and family.	Preoccupied with gambling; wife and children stay out of way; home life is unhappy.	Life is out of control; alienated from family and friends.
Source of gambling money	Winnings and money allotted to entertainment or leisure activities.	Becomes a con man; starts to convert assets into cash; heavy borrowing; has outstanding debts and several loans.	Gets money wherever he can; often resorts to criminal activity.
Personal habits	Life continues in normal pattern. Family enjoys presents and extra income from the gambling proceeds.	Frequent absences from home; virtually ginores children and wife; lying becomes full-time activitiy; personality changes; is irritable, restless, withdrawn; unable to pay debts.	Everything he does seems out of character; irrational and desperate thinking; little consideration for family or health.
Length of phase	Varies: usually no longer than 3 years.	Varies: up to 15 years or longer.	Usually shorter period.
How phase ends	May experience a 'Big Win' or what some gamblers think of as beginner's luck. This Big Win results in thinking he can win money often. However, he hits what he thinks is an unlucky streak and starts to lose instead of win,	Gambler runs out of sources of ways to get bailed out of his financial problems; his sources of getting money with which to gamble become more limited.	Either seeks help from Gamblers Anonymous or counselling or things continue to get even worse (family leaves, he loses his job, commits crimes, goes to jail, tries to commit suicide).

Adapted from the Texas Council on Problem & Compulsive Gambling, Inc.

Some satisfy these cravings by jumping out of perfectly sound aircraft at high altitude, bungee jumping, or driving expensive fast cars at three times the speed limit. Some of us find it more convenient to ring our broker.

By examining the extremes we are able to identify and manage the tendency in ourselves. An authoritative list of criteria for pathological gambling can be found in the Diagnostic and Statistical Manual, DSM-IV, of the American Psychiatric Association. We have included an adaptation of these criteria in Table 20.3 once again to familiarize the reader with criteria used by psychiatrists in assessing pathological gambling.

Why we gamble is an issue beyond the scope of this chapter. Broadly, we note there is now a trend towards taking a multidisciplinary approach to the understanding of pathological gambling. Quite probably, sociological, psychological and biological processes are involved in an interactive and complex fashion. A person's developmental experiences, personality structure and dynamics, as well as constitutional vulnerabilities may all be involved in the manifestation of this disorder of impulse control. Compulsive pathological gambling has also been likened to other addictive disorders as a dysfunctional attempt to resolve underlying emotional disturbances.

Our concern here is early recognition of similar characteristics in traders and to indicate possible preventive action. Pathological gamblers will typically exhibit some, but not necessarily all, of the following narcissistic characteristics. We have added an example of a typical statement a trader might make when exhibiting the particular characteristic:

Grandiosity — 'I take very large positions because I'm a better trader than most.'

Omnipotent strivings — 'I have been right before so this will come around.'

Magical thinking — 'I know this trade will work because it has to.'

Table 20.3 Diagnostic criteria for pathological trading and/or gambling

A	Persistent and recurrent maladaptive trading or gambling behavior as indicated by five (or more) of the following:
1.	is preoccupied with trading or gambling (e.g. preoccupied with reliving past trading or gambling experiences, handicapping or planning the next venture, or thinking of ways to get money with which to trade or gamble)
2.	needs to trade or gamble with increasing amounts of money in order to achieve the desired excitement
3.	has repeated unsuccessful efforts to control, cut back, or stop trading or gambling
4.	is restless or irritable when attempting to cut down or stop trading or gambling
5.	trades or gambles as a way of escaping from problems or of relieving a dysphoric mood (e.g. feelings of helplessness, guilt, anxiety or depression)
6.	after losing money trading or gambling, often returns another day to get even ('chasing' one's losses)
7.	lies to family members, therapist, or others to conceal the extent of involvement with trading or gambling
8.	has committed illegal acts such as forgery, fraud, theft, or embezzlement to finance trading or gambling
9.	has jeopardized or lost a significant relationship, job, or educational or career opportunity because of trading or gambling
10.	relies on others to provide money to relieve a desperate financial situation caused by trading or gambling.
B	The trading or gambling behavior is not better accounted for by a Manic Episode.

These criteria, with minor revision simply to include reference to trading activity, are adopted directly from the Diagnostic and Statistical Manual, DSM-IV, Code 312.31 of the American Psychiatric Association.

Exploitative tendencies — 'If you really care you can help me by giving me your money to trade so I can make back the loss.'

Poor reaction to criticism — 'Who are you to judge?'

Excessive sense of entitlement — 'Of course I want the benefit of the doubt on that order.'

Recurrent fantasies of unlimited success — 'I'm going to trade myself right into a new car and a new house.'

Chronic feelings of envy — 'My turn for a lucky streak is certainly due now.'

Notable deficits in capacity for empathy — 'How can you ask me about the margin debit when you know I'm working off that last loss?'

Profound craving for attention and admiration — 'It's no problem for me to let the loss run because I've got the courage and enough capital to wait for the market to turn.'

Feelings of uniqueness — 'The market doesn't understand the true value of this stock but I do.'

'Black or white' thinking and 'All or nothing' tendencies in the way they view themselves and others — 'Why take a small position when I know this stock has already completed its bottom?'

The common link here is a false feeling of omnipotence. Instead of managing risk, the trader begins to think he can somehow control the market. He adopts an illusion of power and control often intended to defend himself against intolerable feelings of helplessness, depression or guilt. The tendency is to experience oneself as omnipotent or all-powerful at precisely those moments when one is actually most helpless and out of control. This is profoundly self-deceptive and maladaptive.

Simply put, such a sense of omnipotence is more likely born out of desperation. Richard J Rosenthal suggests that 'pathological gambling is basically an addiction to a false state of mind.' Those readers who wish to explore this further will find Rosenthal's 'The Pathological Gambler's System for Self-Deception' in the *Journal of Gambling Behavior* and his, 'The Psychodynamics of Pathological Gambling: A Review of the Literature' in *The Handbook of*

Pathological Gambling edited by Galski a useful introduction to this engrossing field. Additional references are in the annex at the end of this chapter.

Irrespective of whether the markets are the result of a random walk, of a pattern, of cycles, or a product of chaos, the trader makes his profit by controling the only element he can realistically control — himself. He applies an analytical framework to improve his understanding of the market so he can make consistent decisions about how he is going to trade the market as it is rather than the way he would like it to be.

MIRROR, MIRROR ON THE WALL

Under the extraordinary light of pathological gambling our everyday trading foibles lose intensity, but if your trading becomes prominently motivated by more than one or two of the five 'E's', it is time to recognize that what you may wish to think of as trading is, in fact, gambling behavior. While you may still possess control over this form of gambling that is masquerading as trading, continued self-deception will blow you out of the markets. The similarity of these behaviors suggests ways to explore why the discipline of trading has given way to seeking entertainment, thrills, distraction, wishful thinking and a variety of narcissistic needs. The list of 20 questions in Table 20.4 are a guide that can be used by traders to assess whether their trading has gotten out of control.

This list is adapted from the Gamblers Anonymous Twenty Questions which are usually accepted as the best layman's tool for purposes of self-assessment. A 'yes' answer to seven or more of these questions suggests that your trading is slipping towards gambling behavior. Every trader can benefit from answering this list of questions as honestly as possible. We all have occasional lapses in self-discipline. Answering these questions will help traders to identify trading inclinations that interfere with maintaining optimal trading self-control.

The gambler's memory distorts the world in a way that written records cannot. Just as sound identification of trading opportunities points us in the direction where the balance of probabilities is

Table 20.4 The traders' twenty questions

1 Has trading routinely caused you to neglect necessities such as time with family, record-keeping, leisure time activities, household maintenance, and so forth?
2 Has trading ever made your home life unhappy?
3 Has trading ever adversely affected your reputation?
4 Have you ever felt remorse after trading?
5 Have you ever traded to get quick and easy money with which to pay debts or otherwise solve financial difficulties?
6 Do you resist efforts to carefully develop or follow a trading plan?
7 After a losing trade do you feel you must trade again as soon as possible and win back your losses?
8 After a winning trade do you have a strong urge to win even more regardless of your original trading plan?
9 Do you ever trade with positions that are large enough to seriously damage your entire account?
10 Do you ever borrow outside of your trading account to finance your trading or have you had difficulties due to margin calls?
11 Have you traded just to prove you were right or to impress someone?
12 Have you ever traded with money that you have previously allocated for payment of still obligatory non-trading expenditures?
13 Has trading ever made you careless with regard to your own welfare or that of your family?
14 Have you ever traded mainly for excitement rather than according to a trading plan?
15 Have you ever traded to escape worry or trouble or even boredom?
16 Have you ever committed, or considered committing, an illegal act to finance trading?
17 Did trading ever cause you to have difficulty in sleeping?
18 Do arguments, disappointments or frustrations create within you an urge to trade?
19 Did you ever have an urge to celebrate any good fortune in your life by trading?
20 Have you ever considered self-destruction as a result of your trading?

These questions are an adaptation of the Gamblers Anonymous Twenty Questions. Seven or more affirmative answers to these questions would be considered to be an indication that trading activity is deteriorating and/or becoming pathological as described in Table 20.1 and Table 20.3.

weighted in our favor, so too does the careful identification of the tendencies that are interfering with the discipline of sound trading practices.

Pin the following list beside your trading mirror. The first two listed activities are valuable for any trader, and we would recommend they be retained as a matter of course. These notes can be written in the margin of a chart, then printed and pinned to the wall when each new trade is opened.

The activities further down the list are designed for those who fear they have a more serious problem where the slide from trading to gambling has begun in earnest. This is a slippery slope, but recovery is possible.

- Keep a diary of feelings before, during and after putting on a trade. Reflect on why you think you had those feelings and whether they are a sound basis to make judgments about either market action or oneself.
- Write down all the reasons why a disciplined, controled and systematic approach to trading is distasteful. Note all of the aversive thoughts and feelings that occur to you about the labor of calculating and managing risk.
  This includes the inclination to have another cup of coffee, to walk the dog or hope the telephone rings. These diversionary tactics are designed to defer the more unpleasant tasks. Reflect carefully on how you think you came to have these feelings and whether in your considered judgment these feelings are an asset or a liability to your ability to trade. Tusche Chande's $ecure software is the first attempt to build a useable database of personal trading responses. A demo copy can be downloaded from the link on the Guppy Traders site at *www.guppytraders.com*.
- Write down everything that you consider as a current source of stress and anxiety. Ask yourself if you can acknowledge feelings of helplessness as a normal part of the human condition. Seek appropriate understanding of and solutions to your frustrations rather than seeking escape, distraction and pseudo power through a 'Big Win'.

Sometimes our sense of helplessness is engendered by the market itself. The market is infinite, uncontrolable, uncaring and unforgiving. At times traders try to impose their will on the market as discussed in Chapter 19. Successful traders accept this inherent uncontrolability and trade on the edge of the implied chaos. Those likely to be unsuccessful traders swap this existentialist existence for the fleeting power conferred by the trade of a lifetime. Be honest with yourself. If you feel uncomfortable with uncertainty, then trading is not a fruitful activity.

- Write down all of the significant affronts to your self-esteem that have occurred in the past or currently. Write down how vulnerable you feel to these unwanted occurrences and what strategies you typically employ to cope with them. Write down how you maintain your feelings of self-worth and your emotional equilibrium. Reflect carefully on whether these tactics seem optimally appropriate and effective. Trading activity should not be employed as a strategy to cope with diminished self-esteem.
- Repeat steps 1–4 noting how you think those who know you the best would have responded about each of the issues related to your functioning. Consider carefully how many of their imagined responses reflect your own best judgment about your own functioning.
- Discuss steps 1–5 with at least one of your most trusted and reliable confidants. If fear or shame would deter you from discussing these items with anyone you know, consider seeking a consultation with a mental health professional.

LIFE IS A GAMBLE, BUT TRADING IS NOT

We have attempted to provide some guidance above to help you recognize when you stop trading and start to use the financial markets for gambling. For those well down the path we included some guides to recognizing pathological gambling so you can decide if professional help is warranted.

Both trading and professional gambling rely on the effective management of risk. Emotions play a useful role in each activity, but they do not provide the dominant motivation or reward. In essence, trading becomes pathological gambling when there is a shift in the predominant motivational orientation accompanied by needs to alleviate psychological pain in an inappropriate, unrealistic and compulsive manner. We all have our momentary lapses, our bouts with temptation, our narcissistic indulgences, and as we are all subject to the slings and arrows of outrageous fortune, we may not always be at our best. But these transitory occurrences are evidence that we are all more simply human than otherwise. If we can acknowledge our failings, if we can reflect honestly about how we all sometimes mishandle our feelings and deepest desires, we can learn from our indiscretions and imprudence, becoming even more adept at our task as traders, which is the effective management of risk.

Superficially, in many ways the trading floor is next to the gambling floor. At times the smooth glow of numbers on the trading screen is almost indistinguishable from the soft rattle of electronic slot machines. Good trading demands we look beyond the superficial. The two floors are in rooms decorated with different patterns of risk and the connecting door should always remain locked.

*ABOUT THE AUTHOR

Paul I. Munves, PhD. earned the Certificate in Psychoanalysis at the William Alanson White Institute in New York and returned to his home town of Dallas, Texas in 1982. He established the Dallas Society for Psychoanalytic Psychology and served as its President for two terms. The Dallas Society for Psychoanalytic Psychology awarded him the Distinguished Psychologist Award in 1984. He continues to serve as Associate Professor in the Division of Psychology at the University of Texas Southwestern Medical Center and maintains a private practice devoted to working with adults. He very actively follows the markets and his observations are based upon his experience with market participants.

ANNEXE

References

Lesieur, Henry R. and Rosenthal, Robert J. (1991), 'Pathological Gambling: A Review of the Literature' (prepared for the American Psychiatric Association Task Force on DSM-IV Committee on Disorders of Impulse Control Not Elsewhere Classified). *Journal of Gambling Studies*, 7 (1), 5–42.

Rosenthal, Robert J. (1986), 'The Pathological Gambler's System for Self-Deception'. *Journal of Gambling Behavior*, 2, 108–20.

Rosenthal, Robert J. (1987), 'The Psychodynamics of Pathological Gambling: A Review of the Literature'. In T. Galski (Ed.), *The Handbook of Pathological Gambling* (pp. 41–70). Springfield, Illinios; Charles C. Thomas.

For Further Reading

Journal of Gambling Studies. Edited by Henry R. Lesieur, PhD. Human Sciences Press, Inc. Subscription Department, 223 Spring Street, New York, New York, 10013–1578.

The Psychology of Gambling, Edmund Bergler (1958), New York, International Universities Press.

Behind the Eight Ball, Linda Berman and Mary Ellen Siegel (1992), New York, Simon & Schuster.

When Luck Runs Out, Robert L. Custer and Harry Milt (1985), New York, Facts on File Publications.

The Chase: Career of the Compulsive Gambler, Henry R. Lesieur, PhD (1984), Cambridge, Mass., Schenkman Books.

Compulsive Gambling: Theory, Research, and Practice. Edited by Howard J. Shaffer, Sharon A. Stein, Blase Gambino and Thomas N. Cummings (1989), Lexington, Mass., Lexington Books.

Where To Turn For Help

In The United States
The National Council on Problem Gambling, Inc.
445 West 59th Street
New York, New York 10019
USA
(212) 765-3833
(800) 522-4700

Institute for the Study of Gambling and Commercial Gaming
University Of Nevada, Reno
Reno, Nevada 89557-0016
USA
(702) 784-1477

Gamblers Anonymous
PO Box 17173
Los Angeles, California 90017
USA
(213) 386-8789

Gam-Anon
PO Box 157
Whitestone, New York 11357
USA
(718) 352-1671

Institute Of Certified Financial Planners
Two Denver Highlands
10065 East Harvard Avenue
Suite 320
Denver, Colorado 80231
USA

International Association of Financial Planners
Two Concourse Parkway
Suite 800
Atlanta, Georgia 30328
USA

Internationally
Canadian Foundation on Compulsive Gambling (Ontario)
505 Consumers Rd, Suite 605
Willowdale, Ontario M2J 4V8
Canada
(416) 499-9800 (business hours)
(416) 222-7477 (after hours)

Gamblers Anonymous/Gam-Anon
17–23 Blantyre Street
London SW 10 ODT
England

The Society for the Study of Gambling
C/o Dr David Miers
Cardiff Law School
PO 427
Cardiff CFI 1XD
Wales,
UK
0222-87400

Jellinek Consultancy
Ostende 9
1017 WT Amsterdam
The Netherlands
020-6220261

Australian National Council on Compulsive Gambling
PO Box 114
St Pauls
NSW 2031
Australia

21

INSIGHT AND IRONY

This prospecting expedition was about finding nuggets of trading opportunity. We expected to find nothing else — or so it seemed. Chaucer's company of pilgrims in the *Canterbury Tales* expected to wend their way to Canterbury ostensibly 'The holy blisful martir for to seke' and nothing else. With sustained insight and irony Chaucer exposes a multitude of expectations, some of which are only loosely associated with such pious ambitions.

The market allows both insight and irony and our prospecting expedition is no exception. Working in our home office we may think we are prospecting alone, but we are part of a new gold rush. Linked by the power of information, equipped with electronic tools, and connected to a market beyond the power of any individual, organization, or government to control, we travel with a company of prospectors working the same ground.

Chaucer talks of 'a compaignye of sondry folk, by aventure yfalle in felaweship, and pilgrimes were they alle.' Pause for a moment, forget the institutional traders, and survey the company of fellowship at our level, clustered not in a tavern at Southwerk, but dispersed in market cyberspace.

Some 'wanna-be' traders are really prospecting for thrills. Their jungle adventure is not about survival. They look for a near-death experience as an antidote to an otherwise dreary working life. When charting software empowers these people they reach stupid decisions much faster.

A few are excited by the sheer risk of it all. These gamblers pose no serious competition. The stakes are too high for them to survive more than a few trades. Their prospecting technique involves scattering money at random with the demented excitement of the truly financially insane. Their behavior is mildly infectious so we are well advised to observe them from a distance.

Other prospectors are tradesmen. We tell them by their expensive software tools and the suite of technical indicators spread across half a dozen charting and analysis packages. Some of them are so enchanted by screen patterns that they fail to see the nuggets in plain view. Their technical virtuosity must match the reality of the market, but does not always do so. These prospectors improve their chances of success by their mastery of tools rather than processes.

The huddle of day trader screen jockeys jammed next to a monitor confuse action with profitability. For many, getting closer to the action — a real-time feed — is a substitute for an inability to trade well. Some are temperamentally suited to day trading. Others, like moths to a flame, are drawn towards it because they cannot trade successfully on longer time scales.

Skulking in a corner, looking for victims are the command and control kings. They would wrench a nugget of opportunity from the market's reluctant grasp — if only they could make it so. We tell them initially by the wad of cash and sheer brute force they bring to the delicate task of discovery and exploitation. Like the others above, they are led by ambition.

At the back of every prospector's mind is always an ambition to 'strike it rich' or 'hit the jackpot'. This ambition has carried us beyond the daily grind of work for wages and at the start of this expedition it now demands a revision of established relationships. Harnessed properly this ambition drives us forward. Unharnessed it leads to unpredicted destinations.

We all want the opportunity to prove that money can make us happy. If we were honest with ourselves, and we rarely are in public, then we acknowledge this as the primary motivation in this market-driven treasure hunt. These ambitions are no different from those that fueled the American and Australian gold rushes of the mid-nineteenth century; that enticed Spanish peasants to destroy a civilization in their search for the man of gold — El Dorado; that encouraged men to push wheelbarrows across deserts to distant goldfields or to hack through the jungles of Borneo looking for another Bre-X. How we use this ambition, not our prospecting tools, decides our success or failure.

Scattered among the soon-to-be disheartened and defeated prospectors are a few successful traders, not necessarily distinguished by wealth. Their ambition harnessed as a driving force, they combine technical mastery of their tools with an artistry that at first glance appears intuitive. Closer inspection reveals they carry, in addition to the basic pick and shovel charts and metal detecting technical indicators, spreadsheets for risk calculation and financial analysis.

They are risk managers comfortable with the enormity of the market and their personal insignificance in it. It is this acceptance more than any other factor that facilitates the identification and successful exploitation of trading opportunities when equipped with even the most basic of tools. They have asked the question 'I am a trader because ...' and found that the answer does not begin with $$$. This is the group we wish to emulate.

These are our fellow travelers on this prospecting expedition. It is not just a pilgrimage on a trail of wealth any more than Chaucer's company sought only spiritual enlightenment. As private traders we participate in the most fascinating modern expedition of all, but watch out for the irony.

Search hard and trade well.

GLOSSARY

2 percent rule Money management rule that says you limit risk to no more than 2 percent of your total equity on a single trade.

Ask The price sellers are asking for a stock.

At market order Buy, or sell, at the current market price.

Average down A strategy where the trader holds stock bought at a high price and buys more when it falls lower. This reduces the average price paid and theoretically makes it possible to trade out of the loss on the first lot of stock.

Bar charts A chart that uses a vertical line to show the low and the high of the day. The open is shown as a bar on the left of the line, and the close as a bar on the right.

Bears People who believe prices will fall.

Beta A ratio measuring an individual stock's return against the historical return of the market. If a stock increased in value by 12 percent and the market by 10 percent, the stock's beta is 1.2.

Bid The price buyers are willing to pay for a stock.

Black box Computerized trading system where the parameters are set by the software developer and cannot be changed by the trader.

Blue chip Quality stocks with consistent earnings, large capital base and good dividends.

Blue sky Applies when there is an unknown upper limit on prices. From a fundamental perspective this may be because the true value of a mine, or a technological process is unknown. From a technical analysis perspective, it is when price moves beyond its historical highs.

Bollinger bands Popularized by John Bollinger, these are essentially trading bands marking the upper and lower standard deviation from a moving average price element, such as the close. Other trading bands use a percentage movement.

Bonds These are fixed interest financial products commonly offered by government and semi-government bodies. The capital value fluctuates depending on interest rates. Bond traders try to maximize returns by trading the capital value.

Break-outs A price movement above or below a trend line or chart pattern. This often signals a trading opportunity.

Broker The link between the trader and the market. A commission fee is paid in return for executing an order. The broker ensures all other documentation is properly forwarded and trades settled. Brokerages also provide research, advice, underwrite new IPOs, and so on.

Bulls People who believe prices will rise.

Buy and hold An investing strategy based on the historical tendency of the market to rise over time.

Candlestick A Japanese charting method. The price movement between the open and the close is shown as a vertical box. Lines extend from this to the high and low for the day. This makes the bars look like they have candle wicks. Down days are filled in, and up days are left blank with most computer versions of this charting method.

Capital gains Additions to trading capital due to a rise in the stock price.

Cash Management Account (CMA) An 'at call' interest-bearing account operated by a bank or a brokerage firm.

Consolidation pattern A sideways pattern where prices cluster around a single price level. It suggests most market participants agree on the value of the stock.

Correction A retracement or pullback of prices after a dramatic or prolonged price rise or fall.

Day traders Traders who try to buy and sell on the same day.

Depth of market How many current buyers, or sellers, there are at each price level beyond the current bid and ask.

Dow, the A widely quoted US market index based on a basket of stocks trading on the New York Stock Exchange. It is the most visible evidence of the Dow theory of market behavior based on technical analysis of price patterns.

Electronic Communication Network (ECN) Used to show quoted market prices. Some are operated by third-party groups like Reuters, while others are operated by an exchange, like NASDAQ.

Exponential Moving Average (EMA) A mathematical statistical method of calculating an average where greater weight is given to more recent price action.

Entry The price at which you buy a stock.

Equity The total dollar value of your trading account. Also a stock, as in equity trading.

Equity market A market where company shares or stock is traded.

Exit The price at which you sell a stock.

False break-outs A price movement above or below a trend line or chart pattern that does not continue in its initial direction.

Filled When your buy or sell order has been completed.

Floor trader Someone who trades on the floor of the exchange for personal profit or for an institution. Trading floors exist only in open outcry Exchanges.

Front run Using depth of market information to get in front of buying or selling pressure. It is unethical and in some cases, illegal, practice when a broker places his own order in front of a customer's order that he thinks will move the market.

Institutions Large companies, such as banks, mutual funds, superannuation funds and insurance companies that are active traders or investors in the market.

Intermediate term From a position trading perspective it means more than a few days, and less than a few months.

Intraday Price movements during a single day.

Liquidity Liquid markets have plenty of buyers and sellers at each price level, making it easy to buy or sell. Illiquid markets have few buyers or sellers.

Live feed Price data updated instantaneously via an open modem link.

Long A position that profits from rising prices. That is, people who buy low and sell high.

Long term From a position trading perspective it means more than a few months.

Lots The minimum number of shares that must be purchased. Shares over and above this amount are called Odd Lots. As Exchanges become fully electronic the idea of lots disappears so traders can buy any number of shares.

Moving Average Convergence Divergence (MACD) An indicator that plots the way two exponential moving averages move above and below a zero line. The crossover, and divergences, can be used to generate buy and sell signals.

Margin trading Using commercially borrowed money for trading. The amount loaned is usually tied to a percentage value of the stock purchased. It is recalculated daily on a marked-to-market basis. If the value of the stock falls too much, the trader will be asked to deposit additional money to meet the margin so the loan as a percentage of the stock value remains within acceptable limits.

Marked to market The value of open positions when calculated using the closing prices. This includes unrealized losses or gains.

Market fund A fund that uses investors' money to invest in other listed companies, or to trade the indices on the futures market.

Market wizard A consistently excellent trader. A term applied to any of the traders interviewed by Jack Schwager for either of his two *Market Wizards* books.

Mutual fund A fund that pools investors' money and invests in other listed companies. Also called a market fund, or a fund of funds.

Noise Insignificant price movements that do not signal a trend change or break-out. Separating noise from significant price movements is one of the objectives of technical analysis.

Non-equity market Markets dealing in other financial products, such as currencies, futures, commodities, bonds and other financial derivative products.

Offer The price sellers are asking for a stock.

Options An option is the right, but not the obligation, to buy or sell a security at a certain price within a given time.

Oscillators These help identify turning points by tracking the speed and momentum of price changes. They are leading, or coincident indicators. Typically, an oscillator chart oscillates around a horizontal centre line.

Other side of trade The person you have bought shares from, or the person you have sold shares to.

Overbought/Oversold A technical indicator that defines when prices have risen, or declined, too far. This suggests prices might correct towards a median level.

Paper trade To duplicate the trading process without using money. It can be used t verify a trading approach before using real money, or it can b used to keep in touch with the market while your trading capi l is fully committed to other positions.

Parcel The minimum number of shares that must be purchased. As Exchanges become fully electronic the idea of parcels disappears so traders can buy any number of shares.

Pivot points The absolute low, or high, of the current trend. Prices reverse direction in a new trend from this point. Exactly where you place a pivc point will depend on if you track short-, intermediate- or l ng-term trends.

Point and figure A arting method that records only changes in price direction.

Position Holding, or intending to hold, equity in the market. Open positions have been bought, but not sold. Closed positions have been sold. A flat position is where a trader has no money in the market, but is looking for opportunities.

Position traders Tra rs who hold a position for a few days, or months, with the tention of selling for capital gain.

Quote on demand service that provides a 'snapshot' of the current bid and ask. It is not updated on your screen when a trade takes place. To get an update you must take another 'snapshot.'

Reversal When price changes direction. Can also mean a change in the direction of the trend.

Scalp the market To take small returns by trading large position size.

Scrip A term for are certificate, now used to mean any documentation, paper or electronic, that proves ownership of the shares.

Security Another term for shares issued by a company.

Short A position that profits from falling prices. That is, people who sell borrowed equity at a high price and buy it back at a lower price for deliver Short trading is not legal in many stock markets, but is le l and widely used in other financial market sectors such as fu res and commodities.

Small cap stocks Companies with a small capital base. Generally, these are companies that have been in the market for a while and have an established track record.

Speculative stocks This includes start-up companies. It is usually applied to companies in the mining and Internet sectors because they have few assets and lots of hope.

Spread The distance between the bid and the ask. The term has a different meaning in futures and options trading.

Stochastics, Oscillator An indicator showing overbought or oversold conditions by comparing today's price with a preset 'window' of previous high and low prices.

Stock Another term for shares issued by a company.

Stop loss A trading method used to signal an exit from a trade before losses become too great.

Swing traders Swing traders take positions on both the long and short side, irrespective of the longer term trend. The losing position is closed quickly and the winning position exited in the direction of the price movement.

Technical analysis A form of market analysis that studies demand and supply based on volume and price studies. It is a way of understanding the market based on a belief that price most effectively reflects crowd psychology.

Tested When a price approaches, and then pulls back from, a support or resistance level several times.

Tick The minimum possible price movement up or down in a market.

Tool box A software package that allows the use to set the parameters of all technical analysis studies. Ideally, it also allows the user to develop and test new studies.

Trading system A systematic approach to trading usually based on rules. These can be elaborate computer rules incorporated in a software package, or a simple collection of personal 'do's and don't's' written in a note book. The defining feature is that trading responses are repeated consistently when similar conditions arise. A trading system does not guarantee success.

Transaction size The dollar size of a position; that is, $2,000, $20,000, $200,000. To 'trade size' is to trade large dollar value positions.

Trend The general drift or tendency of price data over a defined time period.

Volatility A measure of price variability in the market. A volatile stock has wide price fluctuations.

Volume The total number of shares, or contracts, traded during a given period.

Whipsaw A price pattern with repeated abrupt reversals in the trend. To be whipsawed is to have a trading system that gets you out on every price dip, and back in on every price rise. This is not good trading as the cost of brokerage fees is significant.

INDEX

Discount Coupon — Trading Workshops

10% off regular seminar fee — single and group rates.

Trading looks easy, but it takes skill. How best to approach your market and survive is a skill that can be learned and improved. Trading success means knowing how to get in by identifying a trade. It means knowing how to manage a trade so you get out with an overall profit.

You can become a better trader by attending a half-day workshop because Daryl Guppy will teach you how to understand the market from a private trader's perspective, how to use those advantages, and how to manage a trade to lock in profits.

Nobody can give you the ultimate trading secret, but Daryl Guppy will show you, using local examples selected by the audience on the day, and highlighting how a private trader identifies and manages a trade. You will enter the market better informed than your competitors.

Daryl Guppy holds regular Trading Workshops. Dates and details are posted on *www.guppytraders.com* ten weeks before each workshop.

How to claim your workshop discount.

When you book your seminar mention that you own *Market Trading Tactics*. Bring this book with you to confirm your discount. It can be autographed if you wish.

Some comments from previous workshop participants.

Thank you very much for an excellent workshop. The atmosphere was really conducive to learning. I appreciated the way you were organized and knew what you were doing. This showed, especially in question time. The workshop taught me so much. (Novice trader)

Went to your seminar tonight, wow, what an experience! You placed before me the final key in my years of study that enabled me to understand and use all that I have learnt over the years. Thank you for a great evening. (Private trader)

The seminar, like your book, was practical and informative. I enjoyed it. And more importantly, I learned from it. For me it brought a lot of the theory into perspective. Let me know when the next one is scheduled. I will mark it in my diary. (Private trader)